M000278392

# INTERNATIONAL ACCLAIM
## FOR ZUZANA PALOVIC AND GABRIELA BEREGHAZYOVA'S
## CZECHOSLOVAKIA: BEHIND THE IRON CURTAIN

*"For those of us who lived under communism, or who escaped from it as my parents and I did, or whose families stayed but had to navigate a pervasive, oppressive, and literally life-threatening system, it is startling to realize how incomplete and often distorted the understanding of the communism era is, especially among younger people. This is true not only in the West, but also in many of the post-communist countries. For this reason, this new book by Zuzana Palovic and Gabriela Bereghazyova about communist Czechoslovakia is especially welcome. Its goal is not primarily to recount history, though there is a lot of historical information in it, but to portray what ordinary life under communism was really like. The positive contributions of communism are not hidden, but they are placed in context. We hear people's personal stories, see photographs, encounter the posters and slogans that were everywhere during those years. Knowing that any person you crossed paths with might be working for the secret police and be ready to report you, not speaking about anything consequential with your children because they might repeat it in school and open you to imprisonment or worse, being faced with relentless shortages of the most basic food and household items, realizing that travel to a non-communist country was an idle dream unless you joined the Party and were vetted by it. All these aspects, and many others, of daily life under communism come alive. The story of the era is extremely well told and serves as a vivid corrective to the uninformed ideas that are currently circulating all too widely."*

John Palka, Professor (USA)
Emeritus Professor of Biology,
University of Washington,
Seattle, Author of "My Slovakia, My Family."

*"This is an important publication, especially in times of growing resentments and idealized reflexions of the communist regime - without a comprehensive understanding of the compexity of totalitarianism in Czechoslovakia. It is rare and valuable, that it is presented from the point of view of the young generation."*

**Anton Popovič** (Slovakia)
Student Activist Leader in Velvet Revolution,
Conductor, Composer, Civic Activist

*"In today's 21st century, it is hard to believe those born after 1993 know anything about the harsh realities of true communism, the most extreme form of socialism. As we turn to our cell phones and look up historical information from "Dr. Google," no one can truly feel or understand what a totalitarian government can do.*

*For our ancestors who lived in then "Czechoslovakia," communism and socialism co-existed and provided a highly controlled environment where basic freedoms and individual dignity were denied. There were certainly no cell phones and very few landlines, and they were all censored. There was no cable or satellite television. There was, however, state controlled and monitored television and radio programs. Commercials were replaced by state messages of propaganda. Churches mostly became museums. People who would not join the Community Party were denied good jobs, even with advanced educational degrees.*

*This wonderfully written book provides a poingnant description of life under communism for reader. It discusses the realities of a time in history that can now be remembered from experience by a growing minority of people who lived through it.*

*The book has relevance to persons of all ages and backgrounds. For some, this new learning is added to their knowledge of the time and for those born after 1993, it is filled* with new knowledge to add to their personal understanding and for that of future generations."

**Cecilia Rokusek, Ed.D.** (USA)
President & CEO,
National Czech & Slovak Museum & Library,
Cedar Rapids, Iowa

"This book is the perfect guide to the era of totalitarian socialism of former Czechoslovakia. It is not just for those who experienced if in their own skin, but also for the younger generations. I highly recommend everyone to read it."

**Jana Cepickova** (Czech Republic)
Director of Museum of Communism in Prague

"The Czech and Slovak people have a worthwhile monument in this book to their noble, dove-like spirit. Drawing on the stories of those who experienced the era and inherited its history, the authors recount the long Czechoslovakian struggle to throw off the brutal Soviet Communist tyranny by protest, prayer and countless small acts of decency and defiance. They show how censorship was defied through humor; government mandated atheism through indomitable faith; and vicious criminality through a daring love of freedom. The men who betrayed their country and people are remembered in their ignominy as instructive examples of injustice and narrow-mindedness, showing what can become of us when we are possessed by ideology and lose our sense of humanity. Though pained by the evils of the communist era, the work reflects a buoyant hopefulness for the future and an eternal appreciation for the individuals who stood up for what was right when the risks seemed out of all proportion to any possible reward. The emotional and informative text paints an unfor-gettable image; the aesthetically striking illustrations speak *volumes. The book is a recollection that amounts to a reckoning. One can't help but hope it augurs well for what is to come."*

**Dr Michael Millerman** (Canada)
Canadian Political Philosopher, Author of 'Beginning with Heidegger: Leo Strauss, Richard Rorty, Jacques Derrida, Alexander Dugin and the Philosophical Constitution of the Political' (Forthcoming, 2020)

*"Adults marvel that 30 years have passed since the events of 1989-91 brought down the Soviet empire and its allied regimes, but for the young, it might as well have been the Roman Empire that fell. The past, L. P. Hartley once said, is a foreign country, and it will remain so for those in Central and Eastern Europe who do not learn from the past – young Americans, too, whose current attraction to socialism is largely due to the fact that the United States has yet to enjoy its most vigorous application. For these reasons, this engaging work of history by Gabriela Bereghazyova, PhD, and Zuzana Palovic, PhD, is most welcome. Its countless contemporaneous photos, creative artwork, brief chapters, individual anecdotes, and examples of the era's dark humor will illuminate and entertain younger readers. Czechoslovakia: Behind the Iron Curtain is an achievement, as well as a public service, and its timing is perfect."*

**Kevin J. McNamara** (USA)
Author of 'Dreams of a Great Small Nation:
The Mutinous Army that Threatened a Revolution,
Destroyed an Empire, Founded a Republic,
and Remade the Map of Europe'

PUBLICATIONS ALSO BY ZUZANA PALOVIC
AND GABRIELA BEREGHAZYOVA

**Slovakia: The Legend of the Linden**
www.legendofthelinden.com

**The Great Return**
www.thegreatreturn.eu

**'CZECHOSLOVAKIA: BEHIND THE IRON CURTAIN'** © 2019

COPYRIGHT © ZUZANA PALOVIC & GABRIELA BEREGHAZYOVA © 2019

PUBLISHED BY GLOBAL SLOVAKIA, BRATISLAVA, SLOVAKIA, ALL RIGHTS RESERVED

CO-PUBLISHED BY HYBRID GLOBAL PUBLISHING, 301 E 57TH STREET, 4TH FL, NEW YORK, NY 10022 USA

**CONCEPT:** *ZUZANA PALOVIC & GABRIELA BEREGHAZYOVA*

**TEXT:** *ZUZANA PALOVIC & GABRIELA BEREGHAZYOVA*

**PHOTOGRAPHY:** *DANA KYNDROVA, JAN LORINCZ, LADISLAV BIELIK, JURAJ BARTOS, LUBO STACHO, DAVID FIALA, MARTIN FILIPEK, NATIONAL ARCHIVES OF THE CZECH REPUBLIC, SLOVAK NATIONAL MUSEUM, ZAHORIE CULTURAL CENTER, TASR, ONLINE ARCHIVES, BEREGHAZY AND PALOVIC FAMILY ARCHIVES*

**ILLUSTRATIONS:** *NINA SEFCIK, MATTEO SICA, MASHA DAMBAEVA, KATERINA BLAHAKOVA, PETRA STEFANKOVA, ZUZANA SMATLAKOVA*

**ERA POSTERS:** *MORAVIAN GALLERY IN BRNO, CZECH REPUBLIC*

**BOOK GRAPHIC DESIGN:** *MARIA SKULTETY*

**FRONT AND BACK COVER DESIGN:** *NINA SEFCIK*

**COPY EDITOR:** *NAOMI HUZOVICOVA, ROGER L. AITKEN*

NO PART OF THIS BOOK MAY BE REPRODUCED OR TRANSMITTED IN ANY FORM OR BY ANY MEANS ELECTRONIC OR MECHANICAL, INCLUDING PHOTOCOPYING, RECORDING OR BY ANY INFORMATION STORAGE AND RETRIEVAL SYSTEM, WITHOUT PERMISSION IN WRITING FORM FROM THE PUBLISHER. ZUZANA PALOVIC AND GABRIELA BEREGHAZYOVA HAVE ASSERTED THE RIGHT TO BE IDENTIFIED AS THE AUTHORS OF THIS WORK.

PRINTED IN TURNOV, CZECH REPUBLIC BY UNIPRESS

FIRST EDITION PUBLISHED IN 2019

ISBN 978-1-948181-88-4

LIBRARY OF CONGRESS CATALOGING-IN-PUBLICATION DATA AVAILABLE UPON REQUEST.

**WWW.GLOBALSLOVAKIA.COM**

# CZECHOSLOVAKIA:
## BEHIND THE IRON CURTAIN

*A History of Communism*

*www.communistczechoslovakia.com*

# In a time of universal deceit - telling the truth is a revolutionary act.

*George Orwell*

# Thank You

*This book would not have been created without the many people who generously shared their stories and memories with us over the years. Some were touching, others shocking. It was an honor to receive, document and narrate them for you to read.*

*A big thank you goes to the photographers Dana Kyndrova, Jan Lorincz, Ladislav Bielik, Jan Lorincz, Juraj Bartos, Lubo Stacho and David Fiala.*

*We are especially grateful to Dana Kyndrova, an acclaimed Czech documentary photographer whose iconic work captures daily life in socialist Czechoslovakia. We would also like to send a special thank you to Peter Bielik, son of Ladislav Bielik - the author of the powerful photographs that document the 1968 invasion of Czechoslovakia. Peter so generously donated his family's photographic heirloom to this project. We are equally appreciative to Jan Lorincz for his documentation of the mass Slovak crossing of the Iron Curtain in 1989, which marked the end of the regime, and allowed us to finish the book on a positive note.*

*To pour life into the greyness of the era was no easy feat. But our exceptional team of international artists achieved this objective gracefully. Thank you Nina Sefcik, Matteo Sica, Masha Dambaeva, Katerina Blahakova, Petra Stefankova and Zuzana Smatlakova for donating their time and energy to this project, simply because they believed in its message. We bow down to their talent.*

*In addition, we are thankful to the National Archives of the Czech Republic, the Slovak National Museum and the Moravian Gallery in Brno for supplying authentic photographic and textual material from their rich archives.*

*We are very grateful to the experienced and knowledgeable team, including international experts who donated their time to help us confirm the historical accuracy of the book script.*

*Thank you John Palka (University of Washington), Michal Kopanic (University of Maryland), Filip Plavcik (Post Bellum Slovakia), Marina Zavacka (Slovak Academy of Sciences), Edwar Makhoul (University of Warsaw) and Michal Salini (Charles University Prague).*

*A big thank you goes to Andy Sokol and Sabina Sabados who have been championing 'Czechoslovakia: Behind the Iron Curtain' and Global Slovakia's mission with bottomless enthusiasm.*

*Finally, we would also like to express a very heartfelt gratitude to those who supported us along the way with all the tasks we could not have done ourselves, from building websites to executing administration and from project management to skillful audiovisual representation. Thank you Juan Carlos Rojas, Jakub Jancek, Julie Korenko, Nelmarie Zayas, Filip Martinek and Helios Media for your teamsmanship.*

# Dedication

*This book is dedicated to all the men and women that experienced communism first hand, including my own family, friends and neighbors. Thank you for your courage to bear the weight of this bondage so that today, your descendants can celebrate freedom as our sanctity and birthright.*

*Zuzana Palovic*

*To my loved ones and all Slovaks who had their hearts broken and dreams crushed and also to those whose lives were made better by socialism. May we come together in compassion.*

*Gabriela Bereghazyova*

# contents

# PART THREE

# PART FOUR

# PART FIVE

# Foreword
by
## DR. IVAN HAVEL

Looking at the map of Europe, it is impossible to miss the two countries located in its very centre — the Czech and Slovak Republics. To this day, they are still referred to as Czechoslovakia in many parts of the world. Its geographic location became symbolic of the complex cultural, political and historical situation of a 20th century Europe.

At first, our countries experienced a period of relative democratic freedom prior to WW II. Then we survived the dictatorship of Nazi Germany, only to be faced with a long-era of communist rule within the Soviet Bloc.

Decades of an inflexible centrally planned economy replaced the native entrepreneurial enthusiasm in our region. The influence of Western modernism was pushed out of our culture, art and architecture in favor of simplistic social realism.

Yet the creative spirit and dreams of freedom were sprouting under the surface despite the intellectual oppression that lasted for way too long. Those dreams manifested themselves several times to bring the public together in an unheard-of unison. This happened in the 1960s and then again in November 1989.

Could it be that the difficult past of the countries in central Europe offers some worthwhile lessons to the youth that has never experienced anything like the regime we survived? That is a big question.

More than ever, we are witnessing material interests taking precedence and politicking replacing honest politics. I am sure that an account of the past, not just an objective presentation of historical facts but a collection of personal testimonies of those who experienced the era, is the best solution to the contemporary challenge. This book is a notable example of Czech and Slovak self-reflection.

Self-reflection should be an incessant and dynamic process with a continually shifting focus. Sometimes, it is filled with pride, and at other times with sadness, or with an intention to set upon a new direction. Above all, it should invite and encourage us all to ponder and reflect. In the end, it is the responsibility of each and every one of us, to set the wheel of such self-reflection into motion.

**Dr. Ivan M. HAVEL**
*Professor of Artificial Intelligence*
*Brother of Václav Havel*

# Authors' Intention:
## COMING TO TERMS WITH OUR HISTORY

The 20th century was a restless era for the planet. Two world wars, staggeringly costly in lives and fortunes, were soon followed by the Cold War. A proxy battle for power emerged between two huge political blocks: on the one side the totalitarian regimes that enforced communism, on the other side the freedom-loving nations of the West that embraced democracy. The so-called Iron Curtain divided these two worlds:

> From Stettin in the Baltic to Trieste in the Adriatic, an iron curtain has descended across the Continent. Behind that line lie all the capitals of the ancient states of Central and Eastern Europe. Warsaw, Berlin, Prague, Vienna, Budapest, Belgrade, Bucharest and Sofia, all these famous cities and their populations around them lie in what I must call the Soviet sphere, and all are subject in one form or another, not only to Soviet influence but to a very high and, in many cases, increasing measure of control from Moscow....
>
> (an excerpt from Churchill's Iron Curtain Speech, 5 March 1946)

In the grand chess game of the communists and the capitalists, Czechoslovakia, a once thriving democracy and one of world's most advanced economies, found itself on the communist side of the divide.

That is the historical overview that we all know, but what about the lived reality? The global quest for power did not just happen in the world of political rhetoric and on military battlefields. It was also enacted in the day-to-day lives of millions of people contained behind the wall.

These stories are far less glamourous than the grand Cold War narratives and spy dramas, but all the more powerful, touching and real. Communism, the greatest ideological experiment of the 20th century, seeped into every cell of those who experienced it in their own skin - for better and for worse.

Czechoslovakia was in the grip of communism for 41 years. When the regime came down in 1989, its legacy lingered. The era is still a fresh wound for the people who lived through it.

Even today, 30 years after the Velvet Revolution, people still struggle talking about their totalitarian history and its impact.

The past is not pretty, and many would rather forget it than address it. After all, the modern Czech and Slovak Republics embarked on an unprecedented transformation towards democracy immediately after the fall of the Iron Curtain. These Central European countries have since joined all the important international organizations, including the EU and NATO.

Yet, the imprints of the former ideology are everywhere, from institutions and schools to intimate relationships. Some of the many problems that plague our countries today, from corruption to a relatively passive civil society, are born out of the previous era, and they continue thanks to our reluctance to really break down what communism did to us.

That is painful. Although these countries have changed a great deal since 1989, and much progress has been made, the process of shedding the past could accelerate and be much more profound if it were accompanied by national and personal reflections.

We, the authors of this book, were born behind the Iron Curtain in the twilight years of Czechoslovak communism. We too were touched by its legacies and we too carry the remnants of the era inside us, despite living most of our lives in the post-Cold War world.

We are persuaded that if our region is to move forward, we must come to terms with our history. There is much to learn from past trials and errors, not just for Czechs, Slovaks, and the former Eastern Bloc nations, but the world at large.

The story of Czechoslovakia is a potent reminder of just how important it is to be wary of rigid belief systems, extreme solutions and policies where the end justifies the means. The voices of Czechoslovakia awaken us to the appreciation of freedom and alert us to the dangers of any regime that fancies itself to be almighty.

Whether you are a survivor of communism or a benefactor of it, an observer born on the free side of the Iron Curtain or a member of the generation born after the collapse of communism, we hope that this book will serve as a beacon and a call to your own self-exploration.

We strongly believe the door to this history must be opened, because if there is ever to be healing, there must be remembering.

**Zuzana PALOVIC and
Gabriela BEREGHAZYOVA**

# Authors' Disclaimer:
## WHERE IS THE DATA FROM?

*Czechoslovakia: Behind the Iron Curtain* presents an intimate portrait of Czechoslovakia's communist era by taking you on a journey into the private lives of those who lived behind the Iron Curtain. The information gathered, codified and communicated here was accumulated during several years of research, reading, personal experience and reflection.

It comes from conversations with grandmothers, fathers, aunts and neighbors, taxi drivers, artists, administrators, business owners, generals, professors, foreign ambassadors, emigrants, leaders of the dissident movement, and Czechoslovakia's former political elite, including communist ministers and prime ministers.

This book is based on recollections of those who experienced communism in Czechoslovakia first hand, those who suffered, but also those who benefited from it. Their memories of critical events, but also of little details taken from mundane life, are woven into a narrative that never loses sight of a wider geopolitical context. The unique Czechoslovak perspective is always honored throughout.

Well aware of the complexity and sensitivity of the topic at hand, the authors took great care to reach beyond Slovakia for information. They spent six months living in Prague to research the Czech experience with socialism and to collect primary source material from national museums and archives, as well as to conduct interviews.

The international research also included trips to Moscow, Russia, in order to develop an understanding of the country and the people that first applied communism and spread it globally. These findings were triangulated with qualitative data from discussions with the former dissident, emigrant and diplomatic communities in Washington DC, London and Berlin, producing a truly wholistic perspective on socialist Czechoslovakia.

Please note that the authors took creative liberties with the collected interview material to set them into a cohesive storyline, one that paints a bigger picture of what life was really like in communist Czechoslovakia.

# A **BRIEF** TIMELINE
## OF COMMUNISM IN CZECHOSLOVAKIA

**1918**

The monarchy of Austria-Hungary is dissolved and the Republic of Czechoslovakia is proclaimed.

**1938**

The Munich Conference results in the cession of Sudetenland to Germany, which is the precursor to the dissolution of the Czechoslovak Republic.

**1939**

Nazi Germany invades the Czech Lands, which became a German province. Slovakia is proclaimed an independent state and Czechoslovakia ceases to exist.

**1945**

Soviet troops liberate the country and Czechoslovakia is renewed.

**1946**

The Czechoslovak Communist Party is voted into power.

**21st - 25th February**

The communist coup is successful, and the Communist Party takes over power in the country.

**1948 - 1953**

The Party purges society of all who disagree with the regime.

**January 1968**

Alexander Dubcek becomes the Secretary General of the Communist Party and embarks on a program of liberalizing reforms known as the *Prague Spring*.

**21st August 1968**

The Soviet-led Warsaw Pact troops invade Czechoslovakia.

**1968 - 1989**

The Normalisation Period brings restoration of order and re- instates Soviet totalitarianism.

**25th March**

The Candlelight demonstration in Bratislava is the first mass public protest against unfreedom in Czechoslovakia.

**17th November 1989**

Students take to the streets to protest against human and civil rights violations. The Velvet Revolution is underway.

**24th November 1989**

The Presidium of the Communist Party resigns.

**29th November 1989**

The provision in the Czechoslovak Constitution referring to the 'leading role' of the Communist Party is deleted. This officially ends communism in Czechoslovakia

**29th December 1989**

Vaclav Havel is elected President, completing the Velvet Revolution.

**1st January 1993**

Czechoslovakia completes the 'Velvet Divorce' which results in the formation of two independent countries, the Czech and Slovak Republics.

**\*An extended timeline can be found in the back of the book.**

# COMMUNISM:
## more than just a political ideology

## LET THE RULING CLASSES TREMBLE AT A COMMUNIST REVOLUTION. THE PROLETARIANS HAVE NOTHING TO LOSE BUT THEIR CHAINS. THEY HAVE A WORLD TO WIN. WORKING MEN OF ALL COUNTRIES, UNITE!"

KARL MARX and FREDERIC ENGELS
Communist Manifesto
1848

When communism first made an appearance, nobody could have guessed it would change the world upside down.

The ideology was nothing short of revolutionary. It promised equality. Not just political equality that gave people the right to vote, but real economic equality. In a Europe caught in the grip of WWI and drained by centuries of grave inequality between the ruling imperial clans and the working-class masses, the ideology was as refreshing as the first spring sun.

Even today, few would doubt the aspiration to build a society where no one was better or worse than anyone else. Who would question the goodness of a world where the dirty, dangerous or just boring yet critical jobs, were treated with no less respect than those of lawyers, judges and doctors?

It was the execution of that virtuous and innocent enough ideal that was the problem. It could not have ended well when a concept tailored for the most advanced Western European nations was pioneered in the land of extreme inequality – tsarist Russia.

In 1917, the decaying tsarist regime, a remnant of the feudal past, was rotting from within. The majority of Russians lived in dire conditions and civil strikes and demonstrations were rising. Communism seemed like an answered prayer, hope amid the chaos. At long last, someone was listening to the pleas of the people.

However, the first communist leaders interpreted Marx's and Engel's ideology in their own way. Some truly bought into it, with all their heart and mind, and championed its virtue till death did them part. Others weaponized it, as a means to rule.

Entwined with political power and implemented in cold blood, the new take on equality become a lethal tool to advance personal agendas. Somewhere along the way, a fairer world for all became corrupted and usurped by reckless men. Dictators took a drastic approach to implement the ideals of communism. Unfortunately, this is how the ideology spread into the world.

Equality became synonymous with sameness, and uncompromising collectivism swept everything and everyone that stood in its away. The swinging of iron fists and other petty sacrifices, including the cost of millions of human lives, were a means to justify a noble end. You can't make an omelet without breaking eggs first.

> *Communism was an ideology that in its applied form was and still is referred to as socialism in Eastern Europe. Communism was the utopian vision and the end goal, socialism was the road to it.*

*What the Soviet Bloc experienced was a development towards Communism. The countries of the former Eastern Bloc never reached Communism. What they practiced was state socialism. And, to this day, Czechs are very strict and particular about using the term 'communism' to describe their experience behind the Iron Curtain.*

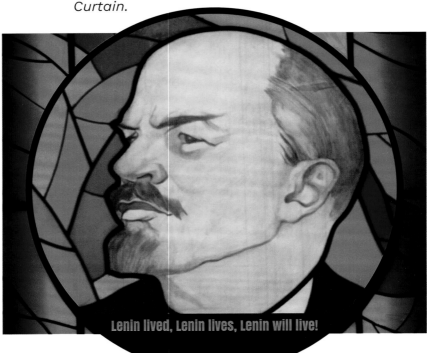

Lenin lived, Lenin lives, Lenin will live!

The good of the collective, the nation, the country always came before the good of the one individual. In communism, the 'we' always came before the 'me', gaving a green light to much abuse.

In this kind of an egalitarian society, everyone was expected to act the same, think the same, and speak the same. Theoretically speaking, it was believed that if everyone had the same, looked the same and thought the same, nobody would feel left out, underprivileged or discriminated. In practice, this philosophy translated into total control of the individual by the state. But, somehow the idea of communism resonated with many peoples and nations.

Almost overnight, communism was turned into a superior new world order.

In the name of equality, the communist elites began to manage, police and later rule large chunks of the globe. These men became akin to God, and their decisions were turned into a universal law, untouchable commandments to never ever be challenged.

A single universal blueprint of the ideal socialist citizen was crafted, and it was to be followed religiously by everyone. People born into this system were expected to accept their fate and blindly follow the prescribed order, without ever asking 'why'.

To wipe out inequality, communism stripped people of their agency and turned them into mere puppets of the regime. Supposedly, it was necessary to make everyone the same. It was also a way of robbing people of their power and therefore reducing the risk overthrowing those that ruled over them.

Like any dictatorship in any era, totalitarian communism ruled by fear, cultivated mediocrity and aspired to penetrate deep into the physical, mental but also spiritual lives of individuals.

This attitude was formally justified by arguing that individuality and individualism were the seeds of all evil. Individual self-interest was the greed that drove capitalism to its unruly destruction. The communists were creating a new world order, one where the collective ruled, not the lone single unit.

What remained unspoken was the fact that individual agency compromised the total power of the Party. Being different signaled the ability to think for oneself, as well as the courage to express that difference.

Freedom of expression was the most eminent threat to the communist power structure, which is why freedom of speech had to be squashed to prevent insubordination. Those who dared to disagree in any way, big or small, were punished. The gulags were full of such free-minded rebels.

The economy was planned centrally. Everything from growing crops to producing toilet paper was controlled by the state and monitored according to five-year plans.

Privately owned properties and businesses were banned. They were far too bourgeois. All enterprises from one-man operations to big industries were collectivized (nationalized).

The social hierarchy was drastically changed. In theory, workers were promoted to the top rank of status, while artists and intellectuals were demoted to the bottom strata of society.

Everyone had an obligation to work. Deviants were labelled as social parasites and imprisoned for re-education, while physical labor was valued above all else.

Everyone had a right to leisure time, education and healthcare. These were free and accessible to all citizens.

The collective good came first - always. Conformism was encouraged and rewarded, while individualism was shamed and actively suppressed. When it came to the party elites, it was the same story. The state did not want cadets that had initiative, nor enthusiasm. What they needed were workers that were capable of following orders.

Did communism do any good at all? The evils of the regime are undeniable, but the ideology fulfilled a very important purpose. It was a thunderous wake up call.

It was an answer to a world where money and power spoke louder than anything else. It arose out of an era where a handful of aristocratic elites thrived at the cost of the proletariat - the workers and the peasants. It also addressed the dire living conditions of millions of people across the world.

Because communism was first trialed in Russia, where the divide between the rich and poor was most glaring, it focused on meeting the most acute and basic material needs of the masses. The leadership aspired to make sure that everyone had food to eat and a warm shelter to call home.

The communist regimes set up centrally planned systems that would allow them to achieve this redistribution of wealth. This is how the communists improved the living standards of millions of people. In communist societies, everyone had access to decent health care, education and stable employment.

The focus on meeting everyone's material needs in an egalitarian fashion had some serious drawbacks. Not much attention was paid to the mental and emotional development of human beings. Furthermore, to make sure that everyone got just what they needed, the Party decided that the economy had to be centrally controlled by them. In short, all assets were collectivized and private enterprise was abolished.

Ultimately, communism was much more than a political theory.

It aspired to control the lives of its citizens from cradle to the grave. The Party managed every moment of people's private, professional and public existence, and successfully did so for decades.

It was a belief system taken many steps too far.

# THE TAILOR
## WHO BETRAYED THE REPUBLIC

*The story of Vasil Bilak is a testimony to the era that made career prospects a reality to aspire to, career prospects that had been out of the reach of ordinary people for centuries.*

*Vasil was born into a poor peasant family, in an even poorer region of eastern Slovakia. Struggling with hardships for much of his childhood, Vasil lost his father, and in turn was raised by an ill-tempered stepfather. Upon completing his vocational training, the young Vasil began his professional life as a tailor.*

*For Vasil, the communist ideals were a solution to the dire poverty he had seen all his life, and so it was no surprise he joined the Party ranks as a young lad. Once communism took power in Czechoslovakia, his career skyrocketed.*

*Bilak went from Deputy Speaker of the Slovak Parliament and Minister, to a Secretary, and eventually, became the General Secretary of the Communist Party of Slovakia.*

*Before the communist coup, it would have been impossible for a tailor, apparently not even a very talented one, to rise to such a prestigious position. That would have been reserved for the crème de la crème of society and then later for the tiny educated class, and Vasil would have had to have been satisfied with making coats and trousers for the rest of his life.*

*Yet, Bilak's story does not end there. His loyalty to the regime and the ideology knew no limits. The man who built himself up from zero to hero, thanks to the opportunities that socialism created for men like him, was to become the first hero of the Soviets, and an anti-hero to the Czechoslovaks.*

*It was Vasil Bilak who delivered the infamous invitation letter to the Soviet Union, which paved the way for the Warsaw Pact invasion of Czechoslovakia in the summer of 1968. Although he denied it for the rest of his life, experts claim that it is beyond a shadow of a doubt, that one of the signatures on the letter indeed belonged to the tailor from the east of Slovakia.*

# DRAWING of the Iron Curtain

At its height, communism ruled half of the planet. Unlike democracy that was built over centuries and expanded into the world slowly, communism rose to dominance much faster. How was it possible that the ideology spread so far and so quickly?

The catalyst was the greatest and most devastating conflict in our history. The Second World War tilted the scale of the global order and aligned the stars for the communists.

As Hitler's ambitions to create a global Nazi Empire moved from words to action, and a war to preserve human decency raged from the Pacific to the Himalayas, the desperate situation forged an unlikely alliance. The East and the West had a common enemy – the Nazis. However much they disliked each other, they were forced to join forces if they wanted to win the war against evil.

Even before the biggest armed conflict in human history came to an end, the Allied powers against Hitler met in Yalta, Crimea, to seal a deal. In February 1945, they split a continent in half. One side would be liberated by the West, and the other side by Stalin's Soviet Union, officially known as the Union of Soviet Socialist Republics (USSR).

The meeting of global superpowers was not just about freeing people from the terror of the Nazi totalitarian regime, it was also about dividing the future spheres of influence. Czechoslovakia, that miracle in the heart of Europe, was unlucky. The country was tossed to the eastern side of the liberation line. It fell right into Stalin's lap.

Some were worried about unintended consequences of an alliance born out of dire necessity. What would happen once the conflict was over? Could Stalin be trusted?

Winston Churchill was the first one to ring the alarm bell. Only one year after the end of the war, he cautioned an unsuspecting Europe of an imminent danger. In an iconic speech delivered in the spring of 1946 in Fulton, Missouri, Churchill coined the phrase the 'Iron Curtain' to describe a metaphorical divide that had already befallen the old continent.

> *From Stettin in the Baltic to Trieste in the Adriatic, an iron curtain has descended across the Continent. Behind that line lie all the capitals of the ancient states of Central and Eastern Europe. Warsaw, Berlin, Prague, Vienna, Budapest, Belgrade, Bucharest and Sofia, all these famous cities and their populations around them lie in what I must call the Soviet sphere, and all are subject in one form or another, not only to Soviet influence but to a very high and, in many cases, increasing measure of control from Moscow... The communist parties, which were very small in all these Eastern States of Europe, have been raised to pre-eminence and power far beyond their numbers and are seeking everywhere to obtain totalitarian control... Whatever conclusions may be drawn from these facts – and facts they are – this is certainly not the liberated Europe we fought to build up.*
>
> *(an excerpt from Churchill's Iron Curtain Speech, 5 March 1946)*

Churchill's concern proved to be spot on and it would not take long for the Iron Curtain to become much more than a metaphor of a retired politician.

The war may have been over, but the Europeans were distraught. They lived amongst the ruins of their towns and cities. Once the relief of renewed peace evaporated, they had to face the consequences of what had happened.

The wounds were deep, the economic situation was far from good. The future seemed hopeless. The allure of an ideology that promised a good life to all sounded like an opportunity for a new beginning.

The East and the West had very different ideas of what the post-war world should look like, and they were equally dedicated to making their vision happen. The battle for restoration and healing also came with the perk of spreading one's influence.

Democracy and communism became fierce rivals in the war for global control.

In the tense atmosphere of these post-war years, the US made a bold move by designing an ambitious foreign aid policy. The Marshall Plan was a platform through which a colossal amount of economic support was offered to a war-torn Europe.

The American government approved US$12 billion (the equivalent of US$100 billion in today's money) to be allocated to the restoration of the agricultural, infrastructural and industrial backbone of Europe. It was not the only objective of the Americans.

The attractive conditions of the US aid package were supposed to discourage Europeans from flirting too closely with communism. It was a clever defense strategy to protect the democratic values on the continent. But, the Soviets were not naïve to the tactic.

Stalin viewed the American initiative as an unwelcome western advance into 'his' territory. According to the Soviets, the Marshall Plan was a cunning political strategy preying on a weak Europe desperate for cash flow. As far as Moscow was concerned, the Americans were breaking the rules of the game. They were trying to enter Europe through the back door.

As the Western European nations were signing up for the deal in glee, the Kremlin was worried. The promise of capital proved a threat to their grand Soviet expansion. One by one, the countries liberated by the USSR, the Central and Eastern

European nations known as part of the Eastern Bloc, were pressured to reject the American offer.

But it was not enough.

A more extreme measure would have to be taken against the pesky Americans. A 'no contact' rule between East and West would put an end to the spread of western influence in their territory. The divide started to materialize immediately after the war.

*It was in Berlin where the political, military and ideological lines manifested into the most famous physical structure of the Cold War. Brick by brick, the iconic wall soon emerged in front of the surprised Berliners.*

*The structure was completed in 1963 despite very vocal international protests. It divided the western part of the city from its eastern neighborhood, which fell into the hands of the USSR as a part of the deal struck in Yalta in 1945.*

*The building of the Berlin wall was the final strike; the absurdity of the reality could no longer be denied. The Cold War was truly a war unlike any other. It might have been less bloody, at least in Europe, but the people suffered nevertheless.*

The Soviets officially justified the move under the doctrine of protection against ideological contamination. The West and its consumption for consumption's sake culture were incompatible with communism. Western habits and behaviors were not to distract the builders of communism.

There was also another reason. A decade into communism, the Soviets were struggling to stop the continual wave of people fleeing the communist East in search of opportunities and freedom in the West. Immediately after the 1948 establishment of communism in Czechoslovakia, citizens started to desert their republic.

Instead of being relieved that those who disagreed with the regime were leaving, the Soviets were embarrassed. The exodus did not reflect well on them, or their ideology. Why would so many people be leaving a communist wonderland if, as the communist leaders claimed, their way of organizing society was far better than any capitalist democracy?

These defections also had a serious economic impact. Some of the most talented and educated individuals, including doctors, engineers, architects and scientists, were fleeing East Germany in swathes. It was an epidemic brain drain. The shortage of skilled human capital was soon felt in society. Something had to be done. Building a wall seemed like the perfect and permanent solution.

Strung around the Soviet Bloc, the Iron Curtain was a set of barbed wire fences. The barricades were multi-layered and two meters high at critical points. The complex defence system was lined by minefields and over 30,000 soldiers. Soldiers monitored the dividing line, armed with AK-47s.

The outer layer of the structure would often have an electrical current running through it. Death by electrocution or mine explosive was to serve as the final deterrent to stop any desperate Easterners from making it west.

What made the Iron Curtain different from the many other walls that exist and have existed on this planet was the fact it was built to keep citizens in, rather than an enemy out.

Although Czechoslovakia was never part of the Soviet Union, it was a member of the Eastern bloc.

What appeared as sovereignty and independence on paper could not have been further from the truth. For over 40 years, Czechoslovakia bore all the weight of Moscow's influence, control and ultimately, suppression as a Soviet satellite state.

# SHATTERED HOPES AND DREAMS

*Jakub was a young man with global ambitions. Already a world-class athlete in kayaking, he was invited to train at the national training center in Prague to prepare for the up-coming 1956 Melbourne Olympics. With a promising future ahead, all seemed as it should be. The idyll was soon to end.*

*Jakub's best friend also had international ambitions. When the time was right, he wanted to cross over to the free world. Over the course of a few months, when he, ironically enough, worked as a truck driver bringing construction material to build the Iron Curtain, he conjured up a master plan. His work place happened to be underneath Devin Castle. Free Austria was just across the Danube, a stone's throw away.*

*Early one morning, he and his colleague decided to go for it, to drive their truck over several meters of river water and set themselves free.*

*Once the two young men made it to the other side, relief swept over them.*

*At the cusp of victory, a cruel blow from the regime came completely unexpectedly. Czechoslovak border guards illegally followed the truck into foreign territory. That was a gross violation of national sovereignty and the rules of non-inter-ference between countries. The drama did not end there. The patrol guards shot at the two-young men. Jakub's friend was shot in the leg, which had to be amputated.*

*Shocked at the news, Jakub rushed to the hospital to check on his friend. He, a rising sports star, felt deep compassion for his buddy who might never walk again. That simple and human act of kindness made Jakub look very suspicious to the authorities. The system did not take kindly to those who tried to flee, nor their 'friends'.*

*Birds of a feather flock together. No matter how many times Jakub explained that he had no idea what his friend was up to and had no desire to run away from Czechoslovakia himself, the secret police did not believe him.*

*That single visit, which was something that any decent human being would do if it were their friend, tarnished Jakub's clean political record. With the stroke of a pen, his Olympic dream vanished. He had to pack his bags, leave the prestigious Olympic training facility and make his way to a coal mine.*

*Eva's story follows a similar pattern. Born to a middle-class family, she was identified as a child musical prodigy. Tracked into a special program for talented youth, Eva spent her entire primary and secondary education diligently preparing herself to be accepted at the prestigious Faculty of Musical Arts in Bratislava.*

*She won many awards and was literally counting down the days until her dream school transfer. Then a sudden turn of events set her timeline into oblivion.*

*Her estranged Uncle Jozef, whom the family had not had contact with for years, had committed an unthinkable act of treason. He defected from communist Czechoslovakia and was rumored to be living somewhere in the United States of America.*

*The Party turned to his family to administer 'justice'. The state did not care that Eva, a young, beautiful, talented young woman, had her entire life ahead. She and her parents found themselves on the 'blacklist', and just like that, her future, ambitions and dreams were stolen from her. It was out of question to continue her musical education. Eva never again picked up a violin.*

# PART
# ONE

# CZECHO SLOVAKIA: THE BEGINNING OF THE EXPERIMENT

THE EXISTENCE OF THE WORLD SOCIALIST SYSTEM AND THE WEAKENING OF IMPERIALISM OFFER THE PEOPLES OF THE NEWLY-FREE COUNTRIES THE PROSPECT OF A NATIONAL RENAISSANCE, OF ENDING AGE-LONG BACKWARDNESS AND POVERTY, AND ACHIEVING ECONOMIC INDEPENDENCE.

*PROGRAMME OF THE COMMUNIST PARTY OF THE SOVIET UNION*

# BLOOD-SOAKED ROAD to communism

Having laid out the big picture, let us now travel into the heart of Europe during the critical moments of the Second World War. This is when the seeds of communist influence were planted for good. We promise that slipping into Czechoslovak shoes and walking a mile in them, during the darkest hour of European history, will be well worth the understanding gained from it.

In 1938, Czechoslovakia became the first victim of Hitler's vision for the Third Reich. Its strategic location and advanced industrial infrastructure were not only tempting but also critical to German war aspirations. Czechoslovakia was one of the world's largest weapon manufacturers at the time. It is no wonder Hitler wanted the country so badly. Red flags were flaring frantically over Europe, but the world was not ready to listen.

Germany was blatantly breaching the articles of the peace treaty it signed after WWI, but the democratic West was not doing much about it. Nobody wanted to engage in another war so shortly after the first global armed conflict in history. To Czechoslovakia, this was as perplexing as it was infuriating. Could the European nations not see what was happening? Did they really fall prey to the fake display of international pleasantries?

The situation escalated in the autumn of 1938. All was ready for the infamous meeting of European powers in Munich, Germany. France and Britain, the upholders of the concord in Europe, were prepared to do anything to avert another war.

It was here that the fate of an unsuspecting country was decided.

The Munich Agreement between Germany, Italy, France and Great Britain ordered Czechoslovakia to hand over Sudetenland to Hitler. This moment was written into Czechoslovak history in black ink as the 'Munich Betrayal'. Czechoslovak representatives were not even invited to the talks.

When push came to shove, Czechoslovakia was standing all alone. The young republic was shocked, broken, silent and abandoned.

> It is a great irony that the only two figures who openly stood up for Czechoslovakia were Winston Churchill and Joseph Stalin. The Soviet Union was the only country to explicitly declare its support, although it did fall short of the delivery in the end.
>
> Churchill also advocated for an uncompromising response to Germany, and the defense of Czechoslovakia. He knew that its fall meant the end of peace in Europe, when he stated: "Many people at the time of the crisis thought they were only giving away the interests of Czechoslovakia, but with every month that passes you will see that they were also giving away the interests of Britain, and the interests of peace and justice".
>
> These eerie words, spoken only a few days after the conference, turned out to be accurate to a T.

In the aftermath of Munich, Czechoslovakia lost one third of its territory and one third of its population, not to mention its dignity and confidence. Emasculated and humiliated in the eyes of the world, it would not put up any more resistance against Germany.

The fact that Czechoslovaks were right about Hitler all along would soon become very clear to everyone. But it was a small consolation for Czechoslovakia, a token plaster over the wound inflicted by their Munich sacrifice. Nobody knew that in ten years, this moment would go on to play into Soviet hands.

In the spring of 1939, German troops marched into Czecho-slovakia annexing the Czech lands. And Slovakia? The country was given an impossible choice and a cutthroat ultimatum. If Slovakia cooperated with Germany, it would be granted its independence, on paper. If it were to refuse the generous Nazi offer, the country would cease to exist. Slovak leadership only had a few hours to decide their fate. In the end, they unfortunately chose to collaborate.

*The Slovak State was a very dark chapter in Slovak history. Political imprisonments without any court procedure whatsoever, the seizure of private assets, false accusations and deportations were standard practices. Two-thirds of Slovakia's Jewish population, around 70,000 people, died in Nazi concentration camps. Slovakia was the only country in Europe that paid Germany for their deportation. Experts say that the human rights violations that occurred during this era broke the people and prepared the ground for the atrocities of communism to come. The people had gotten used to hurting each other.*

As the war went on, destruction, devastation, illness and hunger fortified the Slovak resolve to eventually turn against Hitler in an act of armed insurrection.

The Slovak National Uprising was the second greatest revolt against Hitler in Europe.

It was supported by the US, the USSR and France.

The international and collaborative nature of the uprising was conveniently glossed over by communist historians in the years to come.

The insurgency was squashed by the Germans in the autumn of 1944, but the tides of the war were already turning. Thanks to the uprising, Slovaks managed to repair their re-putation of being Nazi collaborators and proved to the world they were not one with Hitler.

By the spring of 1945, The Third Reich was on its last legs. The Allies were closing in on Germany from east and west. Hitler had lost a string of critical battles. He was running out of material, men and willingness of the population to fight on. Yet, he was not a man who would give up, not even in the face of a total defeat. Slovakia was in for one last violent German fit.

In April 1945, the Red Army was only a stone's throw away from Berlin. Hitler knew that he would have to retreat from Slovakia, but he was not prepared to give up just like that. A decision was made to barricade the city, and to stop the approaching Soviet Army.

Bratislava's main bridge, public transportation, water, gas and electricity were shut down as the city awaited its destiny in pitch black. In the still of the night, Nazi specialists stood by, prepared to detonate key buildings, including the national radio and factories.

But their tactics were all in vain, as it took the Red Army less than a day to push the German army out of the city on April 4th. Over 700 Soviet soldiers, 470 German soldiers and 120 civilians died in the liberation process.

Next came Prague where the scenario repeated itself. The last breath of Nazi fury and artillery bombardment finally gave way, as the Soviets marched in. The final liberation of Prague came at a cost of only 10 Red Army men.

*The Soviet Union suffered losses larger than any other power involved in the war. More than 27 million Soviets perished and 60,000 of them are buried in Slovak soil. Slovakia showed its deep gratitude for the sacrifice that the Soviet Union made by building an impressive memorial atop a strategic location in Bratislava.*

*Slavin was inaugurated in 1960, on the 15th anniversary of the great liberation. It also served as a reminder to the Czechs and Slovaks to whom they owed their lives. Built in the true spirit of the era, the memorial was adorned with vivid reliefs that depicted emotive scenes of war. The dates and names of the Slovak towns and cities liberated by the Red army were engraved on its walls.*
*The impressive structure is topped with the sculpture of a Soviet soldier's boot crushing the Nazi swastika.*

At long last, the war was over. From Bratislava to Prague, the people rejoiced, and Czechoslovakia was once again renewed.

In the West, it was the Americans and British who were seen, portrayed and celebrated as the great heroes of the war. In the East, it was the Soviets. But it was not all flag waving and cheek-kissing joyfulness. Drunkenness, rowdy behavior and looting accompanied the liberators like a sad grey trail through the traumatized land. Watches stripped off the wrists of locals were the most prized souvenir. In the years to come, the misbehavior of the Soviet army, including the rape of many local woman, would be hushed up. It was as if it never happened.

Once the euphoria of post-war celebration faded, a grim new reality set in. Surrounded by ruins, stricken with poverty, grieving for the loss of their homes and loved ones among a landscape littered with dead bodies, tanks and abandoned artillery, the Czechoslovaks were recovering from the shock of what had just happened. Few appreciated the consequences of being indebted to the Soviet liberators.

Yet, there is more to the story than meets the eye. The Czechoslovak desire for a radical change was buried even deeper under the rubble of the war. To find out why the population was so eager to give communism a try, we need to venture into the time that preceded WWII and even WWI.

Prior to 1918, these lands were a part of the Empire of Austria-Hungary. Slovakia was a poor rural province of Hungary, while the Czech lands, one of the most advanced regions of the empire, were allied with Austria.

In Austria-Hungary, a few old aristocratic clans held power. They lorded it over the rest, and did so for centuries.
The Czechs and Slovaks, who were neither of Austrian or Hungarian blood, were disadvantaged. They were merely a petty and unimportant class, occasionally causing some minor annoyance by demanding rights to their own culture, language and later power to govern themselves.

Their Slavic culture and customs were not respected by the rulers, and any upward social mobility demanded assimilation into Hungarian or Austrian norms, including language, dress and behavior. Moving up the economic ladder was no easier.

If you were born into a privileged family, your life was materially wonderful. If you were not, you faced a lifetime of being kept small, looked down upon and reminded of your lesser status in society. Yet, the Czech and Slovak-minded intelligentsia grew against all odds, and the arrival of WWI gave them an opportunity to assert themselves at last.

It was a miracle when Czechoslovakia was founded.

However, the short period of interwar democracy did not last long enough to erase the memory of past injustices. In one way or another, the former elites were hanging on to the remnants of their influence. To the great dismay of the masses, capital remained in the hands of the very few.

Then came the disastrous WWII.

For the Europeans, the unpreceded horrors of the war gave birth to the determination to never repeat history again. Czechoslovaks, among many others, found themselves searching for alternative governments and solutions. They could hardly graciously glance over the fact that the democratic West did not protect them when they desperately needed their support.

The people could not forget that their appeals were ignored as the West had gullibly accepted Hitler's proposition before the eruption of the war.

The Munich Betrayal did not reflect well on the pre-war Czechoslovak leadership either. The public lost trust in their ability to protect their country. When these men returned home, from their exile government in London, they were faced with some serious competition. The Communist Party, the leadership of which had spent the war years in Moscow, was ready to take over power.

# SLOBODA PRICHÁDZA Z VÝCHODU

**FREEDOM COMES FROM THE EAST !**

| Štáty | Doba bojov | | Zväzky (jednotky) ktoré vstúpili prvé do krajiny | Straty nepriateľa |
|---|---|---|---|---|
| | začiatok koniec | počet dní | | |
| Nemecko | 31. 1. 1945 8. 5. 1945 | 98 | 2. gardová tanková armáda a 5. úderná armáda 1. bieloruského frontu | V berlínskej operácii zničených 80 divízií zajatých 480 000 ľudí |
| ostrov Bornholm (Dánsko) | 9. 5. 1945 11. 5. 1945 | 3 | Výsadok Červeného baltského loďstva a 18. streleckej divízie 2. bieloruského frontu | Zajatých 12 000 osôb |
| Čína | 9. 8. 1945 29. 8. 1945 | 21 | Úderné uskupenie Zabajkalského, 2. a 1. ďalekovýchodného frontu | Rozdrvených 10 armád |
| Kórea | 12. 8. 1945 2. 9. 1945 | 22 | 386. strelecká divízia 25. armády a výsadky tichooceánskeho vojnového námorníctva | Nepriateľ stratil asi 700 000 vojakov, z nich 594 000 bolo zajatých. (Obsadený južný Sachalín a Kurilské ostrovy) |

„DŇA 29. SEPTEMBRA 1938 SA ZIŠLA V MNICHOVE KONFERENCIA ŠÉFOV VLÁD FRANCÚZSKA, TALIANSKA, NEMECKA A VEĽKEJ BRITÁNIE. DALADIER, MUSSOLINI, HITLER, CHAMBERLAIN ZA NEPRÍTOMNOSTI ZÁSTUPCOV ČESKOSLOVENSKA NADIKTOVALI ODTRHNUTIE ROZSIAHLYCH POHRANIČNÝCH ÚZEMÍ ČESKOSLOVENSKÉHO ŠTÁTU A ICH PRIPOJENIE K NEMECKU.

PREHĽAD DEJÍN KSČ

## BURŽOÁZIA ZRADILA

15. MARCA 1939
„FAŠISTICKÍ VLÁDCOVIA NEMECKA USKUTOČNILI NOVÝ AKT BRUTÁLNEJ SVOJVÔLE A NÁSILIA; VOJENSKY PREPADLI A OBSADILI ČESKOSLOVENSKO. ČESKÉ KRAJINY PRIPOJILI K NEMECKU A VYHLÁSILI ICH ZA „NEMECKÝ PROTEKTORÁT". SLOVENSKO VZALI „POD OCHRANU", ČO JE LEN INÁ FORMA ZABRATIA TEJTO KRAJINY."
KLEMENT GOTTWALD

### Samostatný slovenský štát vyhlášen.

NIET SPORU O TOM, ŽE KORENE UDALOSTÍ Z 15. A 16. MARCA 1939 SA MUSIA HĽADAŤ V MNÍCHOVSKEJ DOHODE Z 29. SEPTEMBRA 1938

Kronika marcových dní

13. marca 1939  pozval Hitler do Berlína zosadených slovenských „ministrov" Tisa a Ďurčanského, kde im dal príkaz na okamžité odtrhnutie Slovenska od republiky

14. marca 1939  pod nátlakom Berlína zvoláva prezident Hácha do Bratislavy slovenský „snem", ktorý sa – obklopený SS a SA z Nemecka – „uznáša" na „samostatnosti" Slovenska.

V noci zo 14. na 15. marca – podpisujú Hácha a Chvalkovský v Berlíne akt, v ktorom sa „dobrovoľne" vzdávajú suverenity českých krajín a „vkladajú" osud českého ľudu do rúk Nemecka.

sa začína okupácia Podkarpatska Maďarskom

# THE MUNICH BETRAYAL:
# THE BOURGEOISIE BETRAYED US!

Stalin's sweet promise of safety, security and stability was what the Czechoslovak survivors of Hitler wanted to hear.

Many turned to communists to lead the country to a better future. Czechoslovakia had the greatest following and the biggest Communist Party outside the USSR, with a solid membership base of 1 million shortly after the war. The vision that the communist leadership presented to the people recovering from the brutal wounds of the war was both new and refreshing. This ideology was radically different and unlike anything the people had heard before.

To add insult to injury, news spread after WWII, that the Nazi war effort was backed by financiers, corporations and bankers. It proved that the capitalists were willing to fund mass murder, if it guaranteed a profit. Even the rational Czechoslovak middle classes were disappointed.

This is why the Communist Manifesto, a foundation document of the entire movement and the promise of a more just world, one where all people were equal, sounded so appealing. Of course, Soviet Russia was the first state to apply it, and the fact that the system came from fellow Slavs made it more appealing to the Czechoslovaks. The Communist Party was already strong before WWII, but it grew even more influential after the war.

The gates of Czechoslovakia were wide open.

*It was not just Czechoslovakia that decided to follow the shining beacon of the new ideology. Communism was spreading quickly across Europe and into Latin America, Africa and Asia. But, the expansion of the USSR into Central and Eastern Europe was also practical. After the war the Soviets badly needed resources. The Red Army had given its all in its effort to defeat Hitler, including Russia's people and capital. Stalin was looking to secure new raw materials to keep its industrial production in motion. The territories in the west became critical economic, social and infrastructural assets. In Czechoslovakia, these included the developed steel and artillery industry, as well as its metal mining sector.*

# The RED DAWN

Stalin's sharp political instinct guided him to start the preparation for the takeover of Czechoslovakia even before the war ended.

Klement Gottwald, the Secretary General of the Communist Party of Czechoslovakia, fled to Moscow when the Party was banned in 1938. A fervent opponent of the Nazis, Gottwald actively engaged with the London Czechoslovak government in exile to form a united front against fascism.

In Moscow, Gottwald was groomed to become Stalin's right-hand man and an ace up his sleeve. In fact, as history proved, Gottwald was the man who would lay Czechoslovakia at Stalin's feet when the time was ripe.

*The Communist Party of Czechoslovakia (established in 1921) had a strong following long before the war broke out. It was spearheaded by the industrially advanced Czech lands. The working class employed at the many factories across the region felt exploited by the industrialists. This dissatisfaction dated back to the former Empire. The Great Depression in the United States, which also affected Czechoslovakia, only radicalized the people further. Barely earning a livable wage, communism was a fresh idea that promised a decent life to those working hard to make a living.*

When Stalin liberated Czechoslovakia, he delivered on his part of the deal. Now it was Gottwald's turn.

Only one year after the war, Czechoslovakia started to play a dangerous game.

1946 brought the first free elections in renewed Czechoslovakia and the Communist Party set out to work. The success was astounding. The Party received an impressive 31% of the public vote. The opposition was so fragmented, this number equaled victory for the communists. They had to cooperate with other parties to form a government, but they were the loudest and strongest voice in it.

From that moment on, events unfolded very quickly. The communists began to attack the democratic strctures of the state and the past politicians that had enshrined them.

*It was the Czechs whose votes catapulted the Party into power. The Slovaks, a Catholic and deeply religious nation, were much more wary of an ideology that did not recognize the authority of the Pope. Moreover, Slovaks had a less then favorable experience with the passing of the Soviet Army. About 7,000 people, some war criminals but most of them innocent individuals, were sent to gulags after the war by them.*

*Slovaks were also suspicious of the concept of collective ownership. Many of them were petty farmers who were emotionally and historically deeply attached to the little plots of land their families had harvested for generations. To this day, people in Slovakia say that communism came from the 'West' and not from the 'East'.*

The odds were stacked against Czechoslovakia. Even nature seemed to have conspired with the Kremlin. The devastating war was followed by yet another tragedy – a couple of harsh winters succeeded by an unusually hot and dry summer in 1947. A severe food crisis was looming on the horizon. Some say that the hunger of 1947 was worse than anything the Czechoslovaks experienced during the war years.

History is full of sad stories of regimes and empires that failed to feed their people. From the Easter Islands to the French Revolution, starvation has been a precursor to great revolutions and the mysterious disappearances of advanced cultures. Czechoslovakia in the 20th century was no different.

During that fateful year, as the situation escalated from bad to worse, Czechoslovakia initially embraced the Marshall Plan for the reconstruction of Europe in 1947, but it was forced to reverse its decision shortly after. Of course, the U-turn came on the direct order of Joseph Stalin. Moscow was clear and deadly serious. If Czechoslovakia was to accept the American dollars, the USSR would consider it an act of betrayal.

Czechoslovakia was trapped.

It was indebted to the Soviets for its liberation and written off by the Americans - who, upon the rejection of the Marshall Plan, refused to supply Czechoslovakia with grain. The USSR was only too willing to step in. They helped feed the hungry stomachs of the people, who feared they were on the doorstep of what was promising to be another harsh winter. Shortly after the grain deal was sealed with the Kremlin, an advisor to the Czechoslovak president wrote:

> *We asked for 200,000 or 300,000 tons of wheat. And these idiots started the usual blackmail ... At this point, Gottwald got in touch with Stalin, who immediately promised us the required wheat ... These idiots in Washington have driven us straight into the Stalinist camp ... The fact that not America but Russia has saved us from starvation will have a tremendous effect inside Czechoslovakia – even among the people whose sympathies are with the West rather than with Moscow.*

> *(Hubert Ripka, December 1947)*

Prophetic words. Once the decision to align with the East was made and the grain was accepted, there was no turning back.

It all came to a head in February 1948. A group of 12 ministers submitted their resignations to President Benes. They did so in an act of protest against the unethical practices of the Communist Party. The Party controlled the very key, Ministry of Interior, and was using it to track down democratic resistance.

The resignations were a part of a political ploy to outmaneuver the Communist Party. The hope was that this symbolic gesture and move would trigger an early election. President Benes was expected to turn the resignations down, but it did not work out according to plan. In the end, the president signed it and Klement Gottwald, the leader of the Communists, was over the moon when he learned the news. Stalin's protégé could at last begin the systematic takeover of the country, a plan that had long been in operation already. Why did the president sign that document?

The Communist Party did not hide its ambition to rule in Czechoslovakia as a single party government. Although the Party thought that it would have to wait until the next election to win the vote of the people, it also had a plan B in place.

Behind the scenes, the Party was prepared to use force to secure its victory. The Ministry of Interior started distributing weapons to civilians to build a militia and the proletariat proved eager to use them. If it came to it, they were ready to fight and die for the communist vision.

The ailing president was aware of just how dangerous the situation was with so many armed people in the provinces. Under pressure, and to prevent a civil war from erupting within, he accepted the unfortunate resignations, to the great surprise of those involved and even Gottwald himself. The very man the democrats tried to bump off was now holding total power in his hands.

The moment to shine had arrived, and Klement Gottwald did not hesitate to take it. This was the opportunity that he and Moscow had been waiting for. Swiftly, the Communist Party assembled a new government, seized control of the parliament and shut down all free media in Czechoslovakia to gain complete control over the situation.

> Some say that the entire regime was built on the premise of envy. The centuries of the rich oppressing the poor gave way to hatred and disdain. As soon as an opportunity arose, the latter took it to avenge themselves. That is why the working classes, formerly the bottom of society, were blindly loyal to communism and its Czechoslovak forefather, Klement Gottwald. Well versed in the art of spinning populist narratives and himself a proud member of the working class, he knew exactly what to tell people to push their buttons. They willingly and happily surrendered their power to become obedient servants of the regime. For the first time in history, it was advantageous to be from the working class.

Initially, these moves were justified as a necessity in the name of protecting peace and stability. A free election was promised, once everything calmed down. However, that free election never happened.

Almost immediately, a special order was sent out to all border patrols. It read *"Do not let anyone out of the country without a special exit permit".* Action plan 'Czechoslovak isolation' was under way, to seal Czechoslovakia in the Soviet capsule for the next four decades.

WORKERS
AND
PEASANTS
UNITE!

The well-orchestrated coup was successful. February 25th 1948 entered history books as 'Victorious February'. Just like that, communism won in the heart of Europe without a single shot fired.

Did the Czechoslovaks bring the totalitarian dictatorship upon themselves? The Soviets had swayed many other Europeans, for the French, the Italians and the Greeks all voted for the Communist Party in large numbers. The difference was that in Czechoslovakia, the Kremlin influence campaigns were not counteracted by US ones. The heart of Europe lacked such preventative attention.

> *Pain is the indicator of a need to heal and it only appears when there is no immediate threat to our physical existence. The natural coping mechanism of the human anatomy makes it so. This is why the psychological wounds of the war only began to reveal themselves not during, but after the conflict. However, the trauma was too great for many. There was no mass counselling, rather, the public was encouraged to sever its ties with the past and focus instead on the future. That, paired with the promises of collective progress, sounded like a soothing lullaby. The alchemy of the new ideology worked like magic. The spell was cast.*

Everyone wanted to move on after the war. In Czechoslovakia, the way forward was a tossup between two arrangements. Czechoslovaks could pick up where they left off when the war started and allow the elites to continue to rule the day. Or, they could try something new. The alternative was the teachings of Marx and Lenin as implemented by Stalin in the name of a brighter, fairer and more inclusive world.

The communist solution made perfect sense in the context of war-tried Europe, when people prioritized peace, safety, and security.

Although Czechoslovaks were not without fault, they did not sign up for 41 years of Soviet control. The people from the heart of Europe had witnessed several governments and regimes come and go in the 20th century. Most believed that the events of 1948 were temporary, just a storm in a tea cup. Unfortunately, reality was different. From that moment forward, Czechoslovakia was firmly committed to its full transition into communism.

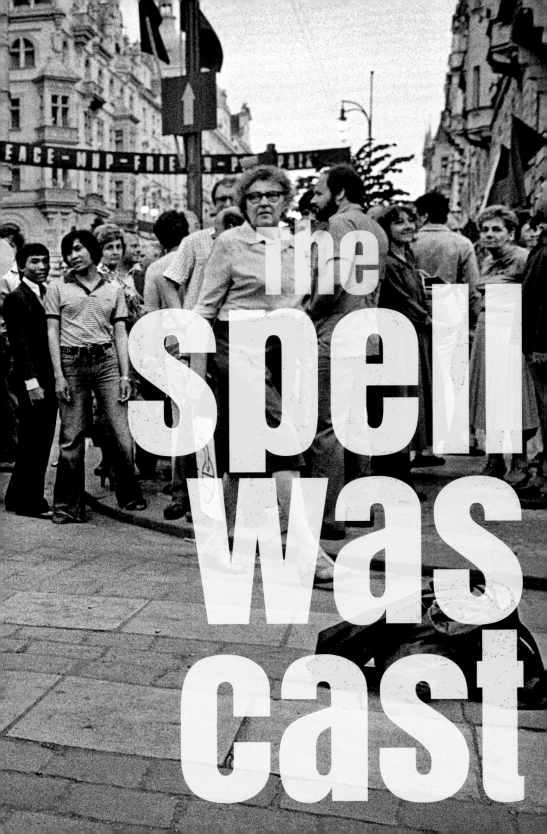

The only minister who did not identify with communism and stayed in his position after the coup was none other than Jan Masaryk. The son of the legendary Tomas Garrigue Masaryk was the Minister of Foreign Affairs and a public celebrity.

Jan was concerned about Czechoslovakia warming up to Moscow and disturbed by the country's withdrawal from the Marshall Plan. Upon his return from negotiations in Moscow, he is believed to have told a close friend, "I went to Moscow as a Czechoslovak minister, I came back as Stalin's vassal".

Jan Masaryk went as far as to publicly declare his disapproval of the coup.

Masaryk's dead body, dressed only in pajamas, was found below his bathroom window in March 1948, a couple of weeks after the coup.

The case has never been satisfactorily clear. Initially, the regime claimed that it was a suicide. Subsequent investigations suggested it was either an accident or a murder.

In any case, Masaryk Junior was a liability to the communists. He was an icon of the golden era of Czechoslovakia, a son of the beloved founder of the Republic, and therefore impossible to execute as a traitor. Did the Party opt for another way?

Czechoslovakia was bracing itself for dark, dark times. In the next chapter, we will look at the ins and outs of turning a population of 15 million to communism. But for now, let us just say that the advent of communism was no wishy-washy stroll through a utopian ideological orchard. It was rough and ruthless.

The dictatorship of the proletariat was the first and critical evolutionary stage of communism. No one said it would be pretty.

Civilian deportations to Soviet gulags, sprouting Czechoslovak forced labor camps, death sentences and the systematic removal of all those perceived as dangerous to the absolute dictate of the one-Party state became a tragic everyday reality. No one was safe.

All actions were ideologically justified as the eradication of any threat to change that was deemed necessary to paving the new way forward, for the greater good of all.

> *The party understood that it needed soft and hard power to achieve its objective. This is why the People's Militia was formed, and the Communists secretly armed the workers and the peasants of the country. The strength of the party was dependent on how much the proletariat supported them. To arm the peasants was to also validate the peasants and of course to empower them. Yet, 'the working class fist' became a repressive apparatus whose sole purpose was to enforce the will of the Party.*

Make no mistake. These were brutal years of oppression at all levels of being – public and private, physical and psychological, personal and collective. This is the era when people were watched and reported upon by their neighbors. Opponents of the regime were tortured, and priests were executed. The heavy grey hand of the Kremlin fell upon Czechoslovakia mercilessly.

The archives reveal that in 1948 alone, 248 political prisoners were sentenced to death and executed. By 1949, over 130,000 anti-state persons had already been registered at the Ministry of Interior. 4,500 Czechs and Slovaks were tortured to death in Czechoslovak prisons and labor camps. 7,500 were taken to gulags. 205,000 people were imprisoned, often on false charges and for fabricated political crimes. And more than 600 teachers lost their jobs and thousands of students had to leave their universities immediately after the coup.

As much as the communists tried, there was something even their most clever and influential operations and greatest threats could not alter: the quintessentially Czechoslovak passive resistance to the authorities. These people had been through two devastating wars and were exposed to every rhetoric and ideology Europeans had come up with in the last couple of centuries.

They learned that regimes, leaders and dictators come and go. Change is the only constant in life, and Czechoslovaks developed a unique coping mechanism because of it. They may have nodded their heads in public, but in the privacy of their own homes, they thought and behaved differently. They did their best to preserve at least some sense of individuality and sanity.

Czechoslovaks are renowned for having mastered the art of passive resistance. Witnesses recall one rainy May 9th when the Eastern Bloc celebrated the victory of the Soviet Union over fascism. All households were required to express their public gratitude to Moscow by decorating their street-facing windows with Czechoslovak and Soviet flags. It rained and rained on that particular day and people took their Czechoslovak flags in. The Soviet ones were dutifully left in windows until they lost all color in the rain.

# GOTTWALD:
## THE ACE UP STALIN'S SLEEVE

*Klement Gottwald was born to a humble background. He was committed to the values of Marxism-Leninism long before WWII broke out, paying regular visits to the USSR to learn from the 'best'. In 1929, he boasted in the Czechoslovak parliament that he was going to Moscow to break the necks of the enemies of communism.*

*Once the war started to rage, Gottwald fled the German occupation of Czechoslovakia to Moscow, where he was taken under the protective wing of Stalin himself. He was an ideal candidate, and Gottwald aspired as much for the victory of the working classes as he did for the physical destruction of his opponents.*

*Czechoslovakia was bitterly betrayed by the Allies in Munich and it was no wonder many, including Klement Gottwald, were suspicious of the West and their true intentions. Even the exiled Czechoslovak pro-democratic government in London felt a bit iffy about relying solely on the West to renew harmony and justice in their homeland.*

*Stalin was a shrewd politician, with a keen eye to the future. For six years, Stalin groomed Gottwald, a man eager to stroke his own ego and inflate his power. Little did he realize then that he had made his bed in a snake's nest.*

*The victory of the USSR against Hitler and the rise of their puppet into power sealed the birth of a new alliance. Little by little and step by step, Stalin secured his monopoly over the heart of Europe.*

*In time, Gottwald became the ruthless executioner of Stalin's agenda for Central Europe.*

*In 1946 Gottwald became the Prime Minister of Czechoslovakia, and in 1948 the President of the republic, but the success was not all it seemed.*

Gottwald lived in a state of perpetual fear for much of his rule. Rumor has it that he went insane from the paranoia and soon perceived even his closest allies as his greatest threat. To clear his way and to protect himself from his enemies, he had 14 influential communist politicians, including members of his very inner circle, arrested and jailed on fabricated charges. In a public show trial, 11 of them were sentenced to death on 8 June 1948.

KEEP IN REVOLUTIONARY STEP!

## The DEATH OF STALIN and a SHY LIBERALIZATION

March 1953 brought the unthinkable to the entire Soviet Bloc. Joseph Stalin, the father of global communism, the leader and the protector of the people, and the man whom many could not imagine dying, died.

The enfant terrible of the East would no longer wave his iron fist in a fearsome threat. The man who was behind the rise of the Red Empire, but also the cause of relentless suffering, psychological torture, murder and mass genocide, was gone. As the USSR wept, the rest of the Eastern Bloc oscillated between grief, fear and relief.

Stalin was gone but there would be one last and final salute to the generalissimo. The grandiosity of Stalin's funeral knew no limits. No expense was spared. An extravagant pageant was put on to entertain and distract the people from the looming power vacuum. The man who had always been there, to take care of everything from Hitler to American imperialism, was no more. What now? Who could lead the empire forward?

As the Soviet leadership pondered the question of the century, a procession of flowers, gifts and devotees flooded into Moscow. Artists recited their patriotic poems while pioneers cried crocodile tears in his honor. Lofty speeches, military parades and a long march accompanying Stalin to his final resting place were arranged.

Rumor has it that in the hysteria of heighted emotion, hundreds of people were trampled to death by the large crowd around Stalin's casket. Czechoslovakia too was suitably upset. Communist mourning rituals included synchronized solemn gatherings in towns and cities, where more flowery pro-communism speeches and poems were recited.

A minute of silence was held across the republic and newspapers published obituary after obituary for the hero of the war and savior of the world. A framed photograph of Stalin decorated with a black ribbon was displayed in homes and shopping windows. This was a mandatory expression of Czechoslovakia's heartfelt condolences to the Soviet Union's loss.

*Czechoslovakia was mourning so sincerely that even its own national leader died, a few days after the Red Czar himself. The joke circulated that President Gottwald was so devoted to his idol, who scared the wits out of him, that he followed him even into death. Gottwald died upon his return from Moscow, having attended the grand funeral in the name of Czechoslovakia. The end of Gottwald's life was emblematic of the era. Some say the heart of the hopeless drunk, who towards the end of his career struggled to stand up straight, gave way because he could no longer bear what he had unleashed on his people. Perhaps he realized that the ends did not justify the means taken in the brutal Czechoslovak transition to communism that he had so masterfully spearheaded?*

Just as Stalin's passing blew a cold air of insecurity into many a heart, it brought respite to others. When Stalin was laid to rest next to the preserved body of Lenin, a wave of relief reached Czechoslovakia. The death of the dictator brought a much-needed shift in energy, to a very a fear stricken and stagnating Eastern Europe. The breakaway from his Iron Grip, eventually gave rise to a more relaxed form of communism.

The beginnings were unassuming. First a heartless man who fancied himself to be one of the workers and peasants took power. He was seconded by a political grey mouse as the First Secretary of the Party. What a team they were.

When Gottwald passed away, the power in the country was divided between two Antonins. Antonin Novotny became First Secretary and Antonin Zapotocky stepped into Gottwald's shoes as President. It was not exactly a lottery jackpot to have those two men guiding the nation forward. Both had blood on their hands. Yet, it was the beginning of a careful timid liberalization.

A former head communist revolutionary trade unions and prime minister from 1948 to 1953, Zapotocky was a man who notoriously could not match his words with his actions.

He boasted a proud working-class background and liked to be referred to as the workers' father. He loved nothing more than being loved by the people. Yet, when the workers protested against his policies, Zapotocky showed no mercy or understanding for his kind.

Much of Zapotocky's era fell into oblivion except for one infamous policy.

The post-war restoration of order, and the building of communism, took a very tangible form with the building of factories, roads and many mushrooming housing estates.

This infrastructure was expensive. Czechoslovakia was in serious debt and faced a shortage of all goods. In fact, Czechoslovaks had a lot of surplus cash stashed away under mattresses and in bank accounts, but nothing to spend it on. Moscow and Prague alike were seriously concerned about civil unrest.

Then an ingenious solution sparked in someone's head. With the help of the Kremlin, Czechoslovakia's government concocted a secret scheme that is bitterly remembered today as 'The Great Swindle'. This involved replacing all Czechoslovak money with a newly printed and minted currency.

In the process, the Czechoslovak crown was grossly devalued.

What was worse, the Party lied about the reform until the last moment. Two days before its implementation, Antonin Zapotocky made a speech promising the people that the talk about monetary reform was but a rumor. He did so to prevent a bank run and a potential civil rebellion. But, the truth was that by that point, the new money had already been printed in the USSR and was already on its way to Czechoslovakia.

What an unpleasant surprise it was when Czechoslovaks woke up on June 1st 1953 only to find out that they had been ripped off by the Party that was meant to be protecting them. From one day to the next, the communists had taken their entire life savings away, with one signed sheet of paper.

Slovaks brought in 11 billion crowns and only received 422 million back. The rest was kept by the state. Overnight, the Czechoslovaks lost 80% of their cash value. They would never forget Zapotocky for unashamedly deceiving them.

Many a heart was broken by the blatant fiscal betrayal. True, most people only had humble savings, but still this was the money that had been diligently put aside to make a dream happen — a house, a cottage or a new fridge.

Some recall receiving unusually large sums from parents who did not trust the Party talk in the days leading up to the reform. They were told to spend it 'wisely' on 'something worthwhile'. Others remember their mothers going on a fashion shopping spree to buy themselves a new pair of shoes to sooth the pain of being robbed. There were also those who were angry and disenchanted enough to break their usual grey silence.

The monetary reform sparked a revolt in Plzen. The uproar was observed by a little boy who decided to skip school to see what was going to happen. He saw angry people gathering in the square shouting 'We won't be robbed!' and throwing coins at the town hall gate. By the time the crowd had grown to several thousand unhappy Czechs, news spread that the army was called in to smother the resistance.

It was too late to escape; the streets were blocked off and the police began documenting those present. They would all have to pay the price for disturbing the public order. Luckily, the little boy appeared innocent enough and the police let him go; he had already learned that it was best not to protest.

K VÁNOCŮM PATŘÍ KAPP

# ANTONIN ZAPOTOCKY:
## THE MAN WHO STOLE CHRISTMAS

*Antonin Zapotocky was a product of a brutal era that did not care much for the people's emotions. A survivor of German concentration camps, Mr Zapotocky had a long and tainted track record of a true dictator. But Czechoslovaks will forever remember him also as the man who tried to re-brand Christmas.*

*Baby Jesus, the ultimate Czechoslovak Christmas character, the bearer of gifts and an emblem of hope, fell into red suspicion. According to the communists, he was simply far too powerful (and religious) of a symbol to be tolerated.*

*Cold-hearted Zapotocky had enough of the fairy-tale nonsense. In a 1952 Christmas speech addressed to the children of Czechoslovakia, he smashed apart the legendary figure with stern ideological logic.*

*Jesus, a child born in a stable and sleeping on a bed of hay, was an archaic symbol of the old and unfair world. Worse than that, he was a part of a clever capitalist plot to spread consumerism. Baby Jesus was a tool utilized by the elite to subliminally remind the working class that they belonged in the stables.*

*But the Christmas ritual could not be done away with and so a lesser evil approach was applied.*

*Baby Jesus grew a beard and was replaced by the image of Father Frost, an import from Soviet Russia. Cloaked in a pretty fur coat and hat, the new gift bearer followed the red star of communism to reward the many good boy and girls of communism - a much more appropriate story, than the naked bourgeois baby.*

*This is how they attempted to infuse ideology into Czechoslovakia's most sacred ritual. The covert message was: communism was the new religion, the Party was the new God and its leaders were the new Jesus.*

When Antonin Zapotocky parted with this world in 1957, it was the other Antonin's turn to take over the Czechoslovak reigns. Novotny's rule was as bland as his personality. The sneaky, stone-faced man was a true product of the old era, minus the fire of a fervent believer. On the contrary, a political insider once described him as *"a frigid political hoodlum with the approximate charm of a petulant cobra".*

Novotny was too cold and dry to win over the hearts of Czechoslovaks who called him the 'Frozen Face' behind his back, but what he lacked in magnetism, he made up for with his tirelessness and unwavering loyalty to the Kremlin. He learnt from his predecessor that toeing the Soviet line was rewarded.

Unwittingly, Novotny contributed to growing freedom in Czechoslovakia. It was not due, however, to any deliberate action to loosen the controls of the regime. Even though Novotny was fanatically devoted to central planning and obsessed with controlling everything, he lacked the un-compromising ruthlessness of Gottwald and Stalin. Slowly but surely, Novotny began losing control.

By the mid-1960s, Czechoslovakia began to resemble some sort of an extraordinary liberal communism, until matters escalated in 1968. Under Novotny's not-so-watchful eye, the media gained more gravitas and freedom. It was thanks to their pressure that Novotny was forced to resign from his position.

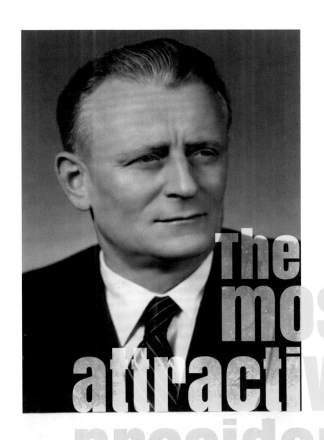

# The most attractive president in the world

He might not have been charismatic, but Antonin was handsome. In the 1960s, Novotny was voted the most attractive president in the world. But, his end was sadly symbolic of his namby-pamby rule, when Antonin died in 1975, many were surprised that he was still alive.

# The PRAGUE SPRING of 1968:
## Thawing of the DEEP FREEZE

## "IN THE SERVICE OF THE PEOPLE WE FOLLOWED SUCH A POLICY THAT SOCIALISM WOULD NOT LOSE ITS HUMAN FACE."

ALEXANDER DUBCEK

Like a herd of wild bison, a wind of change swept Czechoslovakia off her feet. A wave of de-Stalinization began across the Eastern Bloc. When the harsh reprisals of Stalin's era gave way to political relaxation, Czechoslovaks decided to jump on the trend as well.

It started with a change of leader. The tolerated Novotny was replaced by the beloved Alexander Dubcek.

Czechoslovaks believed that this warm-hearted man could lead them to a better tomorrow. He was also the miracle they had been waiting for. Dubcek was not just another politician blurting out communist formulas. He was a humanist and he had a vision which did not included murder.

Dubcek was the father of the idea of 'communism with a human face' who made the impossible probable. He aspired to replace the stiff ideology with a better or more progressive version. Once in power, he set off to change Czechoslovakia from the ground up, with an ambitious set of reforms.

Under his enthusiastic leadership, the bold policies of the state began to reflect the demands of the people, who wanted greater freedom of expression, freedom of religion, freedom of assembly and freedom of movement. The reigns of the Czechoslovak regime began loosening, much to the worry of the Kremlin.

ALEXANDER DUBCEK

During this time, the people began to travel abroad more, voice their opinions and even express their criticism of the state and ideology. They were doing all the things that were previously a big no-no. Czechoslovaks took advantage of the new opportunities, and the country began to experience a renaissance. Across the republic, the pent-up tension started to subside.

The availability of goods improved, persecutions dropped and enthusiasm and the will to live life to the fullest returned to people's hearts. Czechoslovaks began to feel safe to be themselves again, and the silent grey cities and town began to awaken from their slumber.

The reforms very quickly snowballed into a full-blown (near) revolution known as the Prague Spring. Evidentially, the brutal 1950s catalyzed a paradigm shift in the 1960s. After the deep freeze, came a warming. The political thawing in Czechoslovakia, and elsewhere in the Eastern Bloc, was at first tolerated by the Soviets.

However, as the loosening of the grip started to translate into the destabilization of the Eastern Bloc, just like the East Germans and Hungarians had already tried, Moscow grew more and more impatient.

*Czechoslovaks were not the only ones who were unhappy with the way things were. Part of the reason why Soviet leaders were so rattled by the events in Czechoslovakia was that their house of cards was built on flimsy foundations.*

*Things were shaky since the 1953 uprising in East Germany, and the 1956 revolts in Hungary and Poland. Behind both insurgencies were poor economic conditions. While the rest of Europe was experiencing an increase in living standards, the situation on the other side of the Wall was less rosy.*

*The Germans were the first to protest, but it only took two days before the activity was crushed. The Hungarian attempted revolution lasted for weeks. The situation was deemed very serious when Hungary even declared a withdrawal from the Warsaw Pact. The price to pay was hefty. Hundreds of Soviet tanks and thousands of soldiers rolled into the country claiming a death toll of 2,500. 20,000 were wounded and 5,000 were sent to Soviet gulags.*

Tensions hit a boiling point when Dubcek asked for greater economic equality between the USSR and Czechoslovakia, more sovereignty, and the withdrawal of Soviet advisors from Czechoslovak territory.

However, the boldest request of all came with his request for greater freedom of press. Unwittingly, he sparked a war in the Kremlin, the power center that set the fate for the entire Eastern Bloc. In a battle of the Titans, the 'pro-reform' and the 'pro-Stalinist' factions clashed in the cradle of communism over what to do about Czechoslovakia.

As the situation in the heart of Europe was escalating, even the Kremlin reformists began to sweat and tremble. It was too much change and too fast. The opening of Czechoslovakia, the continental gateway to both the East and West, posed an imminent threat to the Soviet monopoly in Eastern Europe, as well as their reach into the West.

Losing the industrially advanced Czechoslovakia could lead to the collapse of the entire Eastern Bloc. What was to stop Poland, Hungary, Romania and the Baltic States from doing the same? What was to stop the imperialists from sweeping in? Dubcek's campaign for greater national sovereignty compromised the Soviet's absolute control. Nothing ruffled their feathers more than having their appearance of strength disrupted.

From then on, events unfolded quickly, taking the unprepared Dubcek and his administration by storm. Although Alexander had advocated for the liberalization of the regime, he did not support its overthrowing it. But, it was too late. The smaller and greater allowances appeared to have whet the Czechoslovaks' appetite for ever more freedom.

The Soviets first counteracted the transition by deploying soft diplomatic tactics. In the process, Dubcek was courted, befriended and sweet-talked to halt the reforms. When this proved futile, Moscow began to amp up their game. Czechoslovakia received clear threats. The heated phone calls between Prague and Moscow were an ominous sign that frustration was growing.

Dubcek did what he could to appease Brezhnev. He promised that the Czechoslovak Republic would remain devoted to the cause of communism and was not by any means planning to break away from the Soviet Bloc. There was no intention to disrespect the special friendship.

All claims fell on deaf ears, as Dubcek ventured beyond the fragile boundaries of the Soviet's patience by granting his people the freedom of press. It was simply a step too far.

Some say that Dubcek pushed too hard, too fast and too soon. Instead of being strategic, he naively believed that he could preserve communism while lifting censorship. He had no idea what he had unleashed. Czechoslovakia provoked the beast and as a consequence all hope for change was buried for decades. Others are persuaded that Dubcek was not nearly tough enough. Whatever the truth, Czechoslovakia was about to pay dearly for its dream and flirtation with freedom.

To stop the Czechoslovak reforms, Moscow decided to take matters into its own hands.

In the night of August 20th to 21st 1968, a Warsaw-Pact army consisting of soldiers from five countries and led by the Soviet Army crossed the national borders of Czechoslovakia. Over half a million soldiers marched down the tranquil and unsus- pecting streets of Slovak and Czech cities. A total of 6,300 tanks and 800 planes poured into the country to execute the orders of the Kremlin.

Houses shook as the tanks tumbled through towns and the air was filled with the whirring sound of airplanes landing.

*The suppression of the Prague Spring was a sticky matter. The image of the USSR was tarnished following the interventions in Germany, Poland and Hungary. Not only did they look like baddies in the eyes of the world, but the aggressive Soviet foreign policies damaged relations with their allies.*

*Another military invasion would be bad press, but the Soviets found a cunning solution by engaging the armies of the Warsaw Pact to do their dirty work for them. The entire operation was portrayed as an international response to aide, and not a hostile foreign invasion.*

*Soldier by soldier and tank by tank, five Warsaw Pact member states rolled into Czechoslovakia for a 'friendly visit'. It was even stated that the exasperated Czechoslovak leadership had invited them. Apparently, a note that read 'we need your help' was sent to Moscow. This is how the 21st of August 1968 was branded as an act of assistance to an ally.*

# The BETRAYAL of 1968:
## The SOVIET OCCUPATION of czechoslovakia

'Operation Danube' was underway and Czechoslovakia stood no chance of defending itself. The country and her people were caught by surprise, and very quickly realized that fighting tanks with bare hands was simply impossible. Alexander Dubcek also made an explicit stand and ordered all domestic troops to lay down their arms. He wanted to prevent blood from being spilled in his homeland.

As the tanks rolled through towns and cities, causing extensive damage, a clear message was communicated to the people of Czechoslovakia, the entire Soviet realm and the world beyond the Iron Curtain: communism was here to stay. Any aspirations for reform would be crushed.

But it was not a moment of a heroic grandeur. When the Soviet soldiers arrived in Czechoslovakia, most did not even know where they were. They were instructed to head to Germany and fight for the communist cause. When they found themselves in the calm flow of normal Czechoslovak life, without a single armed insurgent in sight, they too were confused. It was a distant cry from the war call they had heeded.

Instead, the soldiers saw normal people going to work and running their morning errands. Some locals even set out to persuade the confused invaders to go home. There was no armed revolution in Czechoslovakia to crush. In the eyes of the civilians, this was all a big misunderstanding. They did not plan to revolt against Moscow, they just wanted a little more freedom – within communism.

The reaction to the invasion was explosive. The people were outraged by the violation of their sovereignty. Their country was not to be occupied. When a woman ran out into the streets of Kosice to welcome the invaders as if they were the 'liberators', the people were shocked.

How could she side with the enemy? The aggravated mob chased the woman down the streets of the Eastern Slovak capital, tearing away at her clothes. She was a traitor and traitors were to be hung. Fortunately, the woman escaped through a narrow alley, but the sight of her running naked and screaming left a scar on the locals.

Another poignantly sad story only recently emerged from the archive of a small village in western Slovakia. As the tanks rolled into his region, a man set out to the streets to welcome them with a bouquet of flowers in his hands. One of them ran him over.

*After the invasion of 1968, hope died in Czechoslovakia. What happened was too disturbing to put into words. In the days following the invasion of half a million soldiers a silence befell the country. Some said it was post-traumatic shock, others said it was the arrival of a spiraling and deep depression.*

*Czechoslovak hospital rooms were also filled with expectant mothers miscarrying their children. Fearing for war and with the sound of tanks still reverberating in their bones, the mothers lost faith in the future. Their unborn babies were the silent victims of the callous political maneuver.*

# 1968

Long queues sprawled out into the streets for hundreds of meters, as the Czechoslovaks took grocery shops by storm to prepare for whatever lay ahead. When neighborhood stores ran out of stock, friends and families travelled to nearby towns and villages in the hope of finding salt, sugar and flour still on shelves.

The invasion of Czechoslovakia was dirty business. To clean it as much as possible, the propaganda machine provided an alternative truth to whitewash the population. The Party bluntly stated: 'The military intervention was requested by the Party and the government officials of the Czechoslovak Socialist Republic'.

Propaganda posters with the Kremlin's interpretation of what was happening in the heart of Europe were dropped from planes and handed out by the invading soldiers to civilians. Every morning at 7AM, in the days following the invasion, helicopters dropped copies of newspapers to be circulated en masse on the streets and squares of the republic.

Every morning, the smoke of little fires fed by the paper delivery rose up into the Czechoslovak occupied skies, in a silent act of protest.

# PHOTOGRAPH OF THE CENTURY

*Several photos were taken as the tanks poured into the streets of Bratislava. One of them captured the emotional response of a people betrayed. It would go on to become one of the most famous photographs of the 20th century. It immortalized a touching and deeply sobering act of human defiance, in the face of stone-cold military arrogance.*

*The photo is of an anguished man standing face to face with the barrel of a tank, ripping open his work overalls exposing a brave and naked heart.*

*The story behind the photo is as heart-breaking as the pitiless invasion itself. It reflects the story of an excited country high on the hope of a Prague Spring, a hope that was unsuspectedly and brutally violated.*

*The author of the famed photograph was Ladislav Bielik, a local sports photographer. Just like his country, his life was blooming at the time of the reforms. Having just married the woman of his life, the two love birds were excited to embark on a bright shared future. Czechoslovakia too had begun to change for the better.*

*Mr and Mrs Bielik spent the long Slovak summer dipping in and out of Bratislava's many lakes, walking hand in hand as they explored the hidden trails of her Carpathian woodlands and daydreamed about all they would do with their new-found freedoms. Life was looking up.*

*But, unbeknownst to them, fate had a different destiny in store for them and for Czechoslovakia as well. In the blink of an eye, or in the turn of a day, everything the people and their leader Dubcek had fought for was flipped on its head.*

*On that fateful late August morning, Ladislav witnessed Czechoslovakia sinking into despair.*

*As the shock of the invasion charged through Ladislav's body, he knew he could not waver. Putting his skillset to use, he ran onto the streets of his hometown and began to feverishly take* photos. He vowed to himself that, no matter the risk, he would document this black moment so that everybody would know what happened.

This was no easy feat, considering the thousands upon thousands of troops patrolling the streets, seizing cameras and arresting photographers. The Soviets knew that if any such evidence made it to Western hands, the consequences for the Kremlin would be unsavory. Nothing was to leak out, which is why newspapers and printers were the first targets to be seized by the invaders.

Fortunately, luck was on Ladislav's side. The soldiers were having a hard time finding the headquarters of the newspaper he worked at. Desperate to follow their orders, the soldiers started asking the locals for directions in Russian. The Slovaks employed a clever deflection tactic, however. They earnestly gave the occupiers false information.

This gained Ladislav 120 critical minutes. The young photographer managed to publish his photos in an emergency newspaper edition. Quick witted, Ladislav went even further. He published additional prints and gave the photographs to the people on the streets, specifically targeting foreign tourists. He knew that they were more likely to smuggle the evidence out of the country and show the world what really happened on August 21st.

News of the invasion quickly spread across the front pages of newspapers across the world. In the hurried confusion, it was assumed that the photo was taken in Prague. Czechoslovakia could not communicate with the West and so the mistake was never corrected. Ladislav, a true hero, was never recognized for his effort in his lifetime. Claiming authorship over the photograph would have put his life and that of his family in danger.

Yet, Ladislav's effort was not in vain. His photographs stopped the Soviet propaganda machine from twisting history. The iconic image was so powerful that it stirred the hearts of even the most phlegmatic of Westerners. In turn, both Austria

*and Yugoslavia temporarily opened their borders, turning a blind eye to their own immigration controls in order to offer the fleeing Czechoslovaks an escape corridor.*

*Ladislav lived the remainder of his life in an occupied Czechoslovakia, and never even told his family about the photographs he took on that disremembered day. As for Emil Gallo, the bare-chested man standing before the tank, he died three years after the invasion.*

The invasion was universally condemned by the international community, but that is where their actions stopped. The leaders of the free world stood by and watched on. In the throes of pathos, they did little more than discuss the inappropriateness of the Soviet aggression among themselves. West Germany, the geopolitically most vulnerable country skirting the Western border of the Soviet world, failed to issue as much as a gesture of support for the violated country.

Czechoslovakia received no military help from anyone.

NATO retracted its troops by a full 50 km from the Iron Curtain when news of the invasion reached them. It was beyond symbolic. Silently, the act communicated to Moscow that the West was not interested in war with the Soviet Union. The double betrayal of Czechoslovakia was too painful to admit for the average citizen. The reaction, or more specifically non-action from the West, became something of a taboo topic, much like the Soviet invasion itself.

*It was bad enough that the Soviets violated the country, but the inactivity of the West was very hard to stomach. Why was it such a painful blow for the Czechoslovak people?*

*Just 30 years earlier, Czechoslovakia was invaded by another country. Back then it was Nazi Germany that was rolling out its global ambition. Three decades later, the same pattern was repeated, except this time, the assailant was Soviet Russia.*

*Both 1968 and 1938 marked two of the greatest betrayals of Czechoslovakia in the 20th century. The only difference was that Hitler had actually persuaded the European community to allow him to annex part of the country, while the Soviets justified their actions by mobilizing their allied armies.*

*In both cases, the free West did nothing to stop the violation of national sovereignty. The liberal democracies of the West allowed Hitler and later Brezhnev to have their way with the country. When they needed it the most, the vulnerable and unarmed Czechoslovaks were abandoned by the world. To this day, people in the region feel the West turned their back on them.*

Speculations about that fateful August day abound. The fact that half a million soldiers were deployed to invade a country of 15 million raises suspicion. The mission could have been easily executed by 50,000.

Rumour has it that the Soviets had much greater ambitions. It is said that there were three top secret envelopes containing strategies for three alternative timelines. They were 'Operation Danube', 'Operation Danube Canal' and 'Operation Danube Globus'.

Only one was realised, the rest were destroyed after the invasion. Experts speculate that 'Operation Danube Canal' targeted Yugoslavia, another country that refused to sing along to the Moscow dictate. 'Danube Globus' was an even bolder plan. It considered the possibility of a NATO retaliation to the Soviet penetration into the heart of Europe.

Could it be that the Warsaw Pact leaders were ready to do much more than they did? It would certainly explain the exceedingly large army and military assets that were mobilized in the Czechoslovak operation.

We may never know the truth, as all evidence of the infamous envelopes seems to have vanished from archival records. Yet, every now and then, the hunt for the intention behind the Czechoslovak invasion reveals new classified material. It trickles out of the vaults of foreign embassies and Slovak state institutions, reigniting the conspiracy fire.

What is beyond doubt is that the invasion was turned into an invisible occupation of Czechoslovakia. Soviet military bases were set up around the country, discreetly hidden from public sight. These soldiers did not walk around in their uniforms and they did not make their presence explicit to the public. But, it would take until 1991 for all the Soviet bases in Czechoslovakia to be officially shut down and for the 70,000 occupying soldiers to depart.

After 1968, most Czechoslovaks were unaware that Soviet troops remained on Czechoslovak soil.

*In the Kremlin, the non-action of NATO following the Czechoslovak incident spurred some serious discussion about further geopolitical advance by the East.*

*Some 10-years later, the military operation 'Seven Days to the River Rhine' was developed. It was a top-secret Warsaw Pact plan that some argue was the Soviet blueprint for a Third World War. Its ambition was to infiltrate Western Europe by claiming Austria, Belgium, the Netherlands and Denmark, through the chess*

*maneuver of a nuclear face off. The seven-*
*day nuclear warfare operation would bring*
*the frontiers of the communist empire to*
*the River Rhine, deep within the territory*
*of West Germany.*

You might wonder what the average Soviet citizen thought of the invasion. The majority did not really have a reason to question the mainstream narrative provided to them on Soviet television. The incident in the heart of Europe was portrayed as a friendly act of restoring order in Czechoslovakia. The Warsaw Pact brotherhood was invited by the Czecho-slovak leadership, who feared a counter-revolution was stirring in their homeland.

What is more, such conflicts, with smaller and larger countries, were taking place all over the USSR. What occurred in Czecho-slovakia was just a blip on a much larger Soviet monopoly. The people in Soviet Russia were also dependent on the state for work, shelter and food. They had little to gain and a lot to lose from challenging Moscow's geopolitical acts.

# A HUMAN TORCH

*Jan Palach was born in 1948 to a confectioner renowned far and wide for his delicacies. The change of the regime brutally interfered with the life of his family. The sweet shop was closed in 1951 and it did not take long for the regime to shut down their manufactory. With nowhere else to go, his father secured a lowly manual job at a local bakery.*

*Jan, on the other hand, longed to study philosophy. To make it possible, his mother, despite all the hardship suffered at the hand of the Party, joined its ranks. It was the only way for her son to go after his dream and her strategic move paid off.*

*The regime had little need of philosophers, let alone those with a questionable background, but Jan was admitted to study political economy at university. Moreover, he got the rare chance to experience the exotic abroad. Although Jan travelled east to the USSR several times, something was not quite right. Something was missing. All the excitement of travel could not hide the fact that his freedom was limited within the Soviet Bloc.*

*The political thawing of 1968 renewed Jan's hopes and aspirations. With the visionary Dubcek at the steering wheel of the Republic, life was looking up.*

*A day before the Soviet-led invasion that destroyed the budding 'socialism with a human face' movement, Jan returned from his last trip to the USSR. What he saw back home shook him to the core. If he detested something, it was violence; the violent takeover of Czechoslovakia was something that he could not accept.*

*Jan was among a group of students who took advantage of the partially opened borders after the invasion and travelled to France. Unlike many others, Jan returned, but he had changed. For the first time in his life, Jan had seen what freedom looked like and felt like.*

*Back home, reality became unbearable. The loss of hope was too much for the young man to swallow and his uncompromising stance towards the USSR only darkened as the months moved on. He wanted the censorship to be lifted. He wanted the propaganda to be stopped.*

*With no way out, Jan Palach decided to take drastic action. In an act of political desperation, he set himself on fire on Wenceslas Square in Prague, on the 16th of January 1969. His hope was not that people would worship him as a hero. It was a call to arms and a tool of awakening.*

*Jan's last words written in a letter he left in his brief case at the square read:*

> *Given the fact that our nations are on the verge of desperation and resignation, we have decided to express our protest and stir the sleeping conscience of the nation.*

# After 1968:
## Back to 'NORMAL'

The autumn of 1968 marked the beginning of the return to 'normal' in Czechoslovakia. It was surprise and relief to many, including high officials on both sides of the Eastern Bloc wall. As much as the blooming Prague Spring had brought hope to freedom fighters in Czechoslovakia and all over the globe, the reforms also challenged the geopolitical order of the world. The change in status quo made some players feel very uncomfortable.

A delicately maintained power balance between East-West was the only thing that prevented the Cold War from erupting into a global pandemic. Neither the East nor the West was eager to break this fragile implicit arrangement by meddling too much with the affairs of their opponent. The rise of a reforming heart of Europe had blurred the divide between democracy and communism and was a step into the risky unknown for both polarities.

The Prague Spring challenged the heartless practice of communism, just as it confronted democracy as the West knew it. Czechoslovakia, situated on the buffer zone of the Cold War, began to organically harmonize ideologies that most believed to be incompatible. It was inconceivable to some Westerners that communism and freedom could flirt with and possibly even merge into one. If history proved something time and time again, it is the great reluctance of humans and systems to change.

After the invasion, time started running backwards.

All the progress that the country had painstakingly achieved was undone. The new hardline leadership bulldozed over all the hopes and freedoms of the Prague Spring. The backslide was extraordinarily brutal, yet not ferocious, passionate or openly violent. It was not executed by soldiers, but by bureaucrats. 'Normalization' took the form of a solemn administrative savagery carried out with exemplary dullness.

The government did not shut down the borders immediately after the invasion. It was not a counterintuitive reaction, but a pragmatic move. The Party elites understood that they had to let the resistance bleed out of the country in order for things to calm down. In those emotionally charged times, public outrage could easily spill over into social unrest. To prevent any further headaches, the door to the West was left a little ajar.

According to estimates, around 100,000 Czechoslovaks left the country. Among them were some of the most iconic figures of Czechoslovak culture, including writer Milan Kundera and film director Milos Forman. Both went on to become global superstars and pioneers in their fields.

Protests and revolutions had rocked Eastern Germany, Poland and Hungary before arriving in Czechoslovakia. Bullets were fired, and much blood was shed during 1956 in Hungary in particular, but the administrative ruthlessness and severity of revoking all reforms in Czechoslovakia was unmatched by anything else seen in the Soviet Bloc.

Unlike other uprisings in the region, the Prague Spring was not led by manual workers seeking better working conditions. The campaign was powered by some of the country's brightest intellectuals and most influential artists. Some of the reform leaders were communists and even government officials, with much insight into highly sensitive classified matters.

Together, these people were pioneering a new vision. They were educated, well-spoken, persuasive in their arguments and, above all, respected by society. These women and men of the revolution were real influencers. They stood in stark contrast to the cold and dispassionate leadership that people were used to.

Moscow was correct to foresee that the collective consciousness was heading towards a major tipping point on the frontier of the Red Empire. The Prague Spring and its ideals had developed at a breathtaking speed.

It only took a few short years of 'warming' in the 1960s, to bring Czechoslovakia to a turning point. The Soviets feared that an attack on the very principles of the ideology was a real possibility. Was this level-headed, earnest and articulate Czechoslovak intelligentsia the force that could bring the entire communist system down?

The first priority was to reinstate firm leadership loyal to the Kremlin. Out went Dubcek and his inner circle, then all the other supporters of the Czechoslovak freedom experiment. To make them really feel the weight of their 'mistakes', the regime opted for a slow and dull process that lasted for months and even years. It also served another purpose – that of disremembering their existence and their bravery.

*The dignity of the reform movement and its faces were systematically eroded, through a tragically dispassionate mouse and cat game. The idols of the Prague Spring were denied not only martyrdom, but also respect and significance. The new government acted as if nothing had happened. There was no drama, and there was no excitement.*

*The denial of an emotional charge in the aftermath of the chaos confused the public. Complacency soon set in. Had the Prague Spring even happened? Hope was futile, when there were no more heroes to believe in or fight for. As the people watched their collective dream dissolve, there was nevertheless a quiet appreciation for the civilized manner of handling the situation.*

Czechoslovakia experienced an abrupt return to Soviet-style communism; gone was 'socialism with a human face' and back were the old and familiar propaganda slogans of the 1950s. Unashamedly, the post-invasion narratives cynically claimed that "the USSR was a pillar of global peace and progress", or that, "the Soviet army was a protector of peace".

A new government was sworn into power in a discreet control handover. Another Slovak, Gustav Husak, took the reins of the republic into his hands.

# WHAT BECAME OF
# ALEXANDER DUBCEK?

*Dubcek's downfall was far from spectacular, mirroring the dull, dispassionate, but consistent normalization process. He stepped down as First Secretary of the Party in the spring of 1969, and for a short period of time was the Ambassador to Turkey.*

*Some say Dubcek was sent abroad so as to ease his emigration. If he were to defect to the West, the Party could denounce him as a traitor and he would also be out of site for them. This never happened and an uncomfortable Dubcek remained a thorn in their eye. He was expelled from the Party, and then passed around like a hot potato, before settling in a job in forest management.*

*Dubcek did not take part in dissident activities, but instead he shielded himself from the state and the public that used to worship him. He spent his retirement pottering around in his garden. When 1989 came, the fall of the Iron Curtain resurrected Dubcek back to fame.*

*His return to the spotlight was only natural. He was the much beloved icon of the legendary Prague Spring and the people always remembered him that way.*

*Who knows what he felt, when he stood next to Vaclav Havel on the balcony above Wenceslas Square, greeting hundreds of thousands with outstretched arms nearly 20 years after his demise. Pride? Joy? Vindication?*

*Alexander did re-enter politics and went on to become the speaker of parliament. But his life came early to an infamous end by a fateful and much disputed car crash.*

*Dubcek was not the only one to pass in this way. There were several car crashes that occurred immediately before and after the revolution that swept the Eastern Bloc. The victims were high officials of the regime, or its covert operatives. Could these have been assassinations? Did Dubcek know too much?*

Gustav Husak was nothing like his predecessor.

The apathetically feared ruler was but a puppet of Moscow, a stern and obedient follower and the worst of party hardliners. The Soviets felt they could not trust the frisky Czechs to bring back order, because they were the force and engine behind the Prague Spring. Instead, the Soviets reached into the ranks of Slovaks despite Dubcek being himself Slovak.

The choice was strategic, for Slovakia had benefitted much more than the Czech lands under communism. With time, the Catholic Slovaks, once resistant to communism for denying their religion, had grown more benevolent toward the Kremlin. For Moscow, Slovakia became a promising new ally.

The change of the leader was but the beginning. At the heart of everything in Czechoslovakia was the Communist Party, and that had to be cleansed of all dangerous individuals with big ideas.

The entire Party membership base was screened for 'unreliable individuals'. Committees were held, from top to bottom across the republic, to map, and extract the selected profiles.

Their unlucky holders were scrutinized ever more closely and punished accordingly. That usually meant the loss of a society status, demotion, revocation of all privileges, travel and holiday permits.

With committees popping up, left, right and center, fear of losing a good life spread like wildfire. Friends and colleagues proved willing to disclose, even fabricate claims, in the hope of saving their own jobs and the future of their children.

The invasion was but a step towards wiping Czechoslovakia clean of hope and faith. The objective of the Kremlin was to shut down all aspects of the independent Czechoslovak social and cultural life, the lifeblood of the country and the birthplace of freedom and exploration.

Writers, journalists and artists associated with the former ideals and leadership were banned. Politically inconvenient intellectuals were demoted and contact with them came at a personal risk. University professors, scientists, historians, doctors, engineers and teachers were dismissed from their jobs. Their departures were justified on the grounds of protecting society from their insidious liberal influence.

The brutal ways of the past, including physical oppression, staged show trials and punishment by death, were done away with, in favor of a more sophisticated form of control. Shame, blackmail and withholding of opportunities became the new means for social control. Unexpected layoffs, career demotions, and the denial of access to education and career growth, in addition to housing and travel restrictions, became the new norm. This was an era of indirect terror.

The state's most immediate tactic was to jeopardize access to one's livelihood. If that proved ineffective, they went after the family bloodline, by denying education opportunities for their children. Not wanting to compromise their children's future, most parents became complacent. They proved willing to forgo their ideals for the sake of the next generation.

Strict censorship was back. All media was brought back under direct control of the state. Live TV transmissions were banned as a measure to prevent any accidental slips from the official narrative.

This allowed a handful of bureaucrats to take control of the entire national media thus the country. Their tentacles reached far and wide. Several years of swift and systematic action installed a grey cloud of silence above Czechoslovakia. A famine of spirit had begun. Husak and his cohorts were successful in executing a strategy spun in Moscow.

Why did Czechoslovaks allow this to happen?

Just as much as there was a reformist movement, there was also a large enough population that feared change. The invasion and restoration to normalcy brought back safety, stability and a simplicity of life.

The heart of Europe would remain in the tight embrace of Soviet control for another two decades.

*Slovaks were rewarded for cooperating with the Soviets. Slovaks had been governed by the Kingdom of Hungary for a thousand years and then when Czechoslovakia was founded, they simply did not have enough experience and human capital to be equal partners to the Czechs. Many still did not feel equal to the Czechs after WWII. On October 27th 1968, the Czecho-Slovak Federation was approved by parliament and a dual-state republic was born. It could have been an act of great gratification for Slovaks, but the deal was made on paper only. In reality, not much changed and Slovakia continued to be run centrally from Prague.*

GUSTAV HUSAK

*The loner who spent his life desperately searching and failing to find company became the face of post-1968 terror. He never let anyone get close to him. Perhaps it was a reaction to his own hardships and a painful history of personal losses.*

*Gustav's mother died when he was a baby. During WWII he was frequently imprisoned for his communist and therefore anti-Nazi opinions, yet he was always released when he demonstrated a willingness to cooperate. He actively participated in leading the Slovak National Uprising of 1944 against the Nazis.*

The end of the war only brought a short-lived respite. This time, Husak was pursued by his own. He became a victim of the Stalinist purges in the 1950s, labeled "a bourgeois nationalist", and imprisoned again, this time for life. Moreover, his close friend died in the communist frenzy. Gustav's marriage did not survive the pressures of his politically charged life.

When Czechoslovakia relaxed after Stalin's death, Gustav's conviction was overturned, and his party membership restored. Nine years in prison devastated him and his marriage, but the experience did nothing to erode his devotion to communism. To Husak, the imprisonment was but a big misunderstanding and his divorce a gross mishap.

Strengthened by fire, Husak proved to be a shrewd political animal, able to adapt and survive through anything. He skillfully navigated the dangerous waters of the Prague Spring, moving from Dubcek's supporter to his critic. With the support of Moscow, Gustav rose from the ashes to become the First Secretary of the Party and later the President of Czechoslovakia. He also married again only to experience yet another loss when his second wife died in an air crash only two years after their wedding.

Despite his political resurrection, the glitz and glory of the high life and his annual two-week long vacation at the Crimea Sea with Breznev, his life was sad and empty. To add insult to injury, the people he 'ruled over' saw in Husak a powerless puppet, not a hero prepared to sacrifice his life to protect them.

In his desperate need for validation, Gustav developed a savior complex and cut off himself from anyone who challenged his role as the father of the community. Sometimes he quite literally had those people removed and locked in prisons, out of his sight. Without a friend and without a woman, it was easy to emotionally distance himself from his decisions.

Husak's fall from grace was spectacular. The benign dictator, who ruled without challenge or competition for nearly two decades, was forced in 1989 to resign by the will of the people. When he died in 1991, he was not even granted his last wish, to rest beside his mother.

Alone in life, Husak proved to be also alone in death.

Once the situation in Czechoslovakia was stabilized, life quickly returned to 'normal' and the country was back in Moscow's favor. Yet, the frustration of the people continued to fester just under the surface. Husak knew the dangers of this and set out on a charm offensive, the communist way.

To lighten up the mood and appease the people, the government flooded the Czechoslovak market with new goods. They hoped that these electronic luxuries, such as radios, color televisions and fridges, would keep civil unrest at bay by distracting people from what was going on around them.

The economic micro boom of the 1970s was short lived. People wanted more than just consumption. They craved real freedom. Public restlessness was simmering, protruding to the surface every now and again, in acts of public vandalism and alcoholism.

Widescale alcohol consumption became a big problem. Even the Party was concerned and posters carrying slogans such as 'Alcohol Shall Not Compromise Fulfilment of 5-year plans' were plastered on pin boards across the republic to put people off drinking or, at the very least, to prevent them drinking at work.

One of the reasons behind the excessive wallowing in beer and spirits was the lack of opportunities available and the suppressed self-determination of the individual. With no opportunity to take hold of their lives, many people allowed their own bitterness and resentment to get the better of them. One of the ways to numb their growing frustration - and pain - was by drinking it away.

> *Although depression was rife, it was not diagnosed or officially acknowledged. There was hardly any mental health education available, nor was there any supportive infrastructure of psychologists. The only way the state coped with these individuals and their conditions was by locking them in asylums, so as not to be a nuisance to the builders of socialism.*

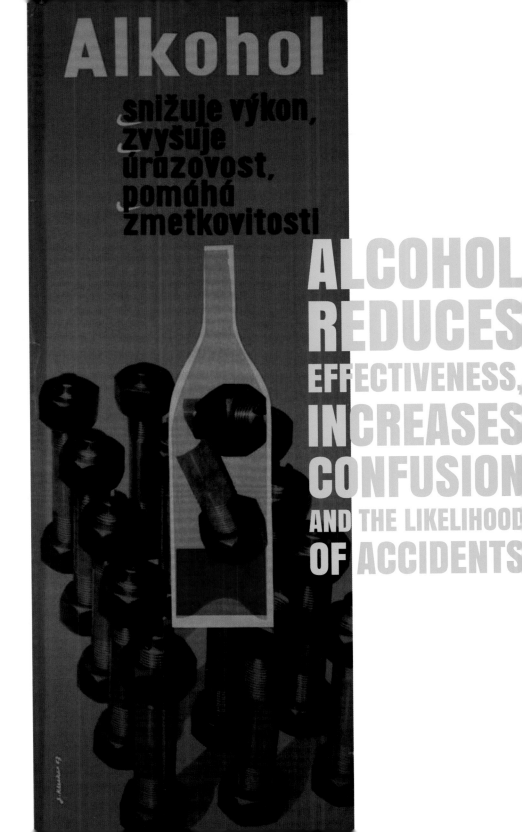

# PART
# TWO

# THE NEW RED ORDER:

## how to make a PERFECT SOCIETY overnight

Anyone who thinks that the communist regimes of Central Europe are exclusively the work of criminals is overlooking a basic truth: the criminal regimes were made not by criminals but by enthusiasts convinced they had discovered the only road to paradise. They defended that road so valiantly that they were forced to execute many people. Later it became clear that there was no paradise, that the enthusiasts were therefore murderers.

*MILAN KUNDERA*

The master plan of turning the world communist was not written in a black book. There was no procedure manual, safely stored in a vault behind one hundred doors and two hundred locks. The master plan was a living strategy that existed in a handful of minds, that were ambitious, determined and ruthless enough to execute its mission.

Great ambitions require great sacrifices.

The transition to communism required nothing short of a revolution - in thinking, behaving and governing. Such a change would not occur overnight, but the communists were up for the challenge.

The Kremlin also understood that its model could only be implemented internationally via a local leader. Harnessing devoted and home-grown leadership was a far less costly methodology than imposing communism by force, from the outside-in. Some things are the same no matter where you are. Whether you are from the East or from the West, those in power are clever in seeking out ways to maintain their supremacy.

The Czechoslovak-Soviet bond was first groomed during WWII. Gottwald's communist center of resistance in Moscow is a case in point. However, relations were further strengthened during regular summer holidays in Crimea, and skiing outings in northern Slovakia. There Soviet and Czechoslovak communist leaders regularly met, got jolly, exchanged ideas and received advice.

Of course, it was quite a one-directional flow.

To make sure Czechoslovaks got it 'right', Moscow dispatched a cohort of advisors to facilitate the transition after the 1948 coup. They came to transform key institutions and industries, including the police, military, courts, ministries and industrial backbone of the republic. Although their presence was discreet, they were influential, knowledgeable and respected.

Together, the Soviet advisors and the Czechoslovak communists set out to turn the whole country communist as fast as possible. A series of thorough social, cultural and political reforms followed, but not before removing everyone and anyone who could challenge the New Red Order.

To the outside world, it might have seemed that Czechoslovakia was deeply converted to the iron grip of communism. In reality, the transition was far from certain. The self-assured confidence and poise of the Czechoslovak leadership was but an illusion. The façade was used to mask their profound insecurity from the masses.

Being so close to the West, the Czechoslovak leaders knew that not all 15 million Czechoslovaks identified with the gospel of the Kremlin. Before the war, unlike many other Central and Eastern European countries, Czechoslovakia was a democracy and one of the most advanced economies in the world. Although the new leaders believed in the Red promise, they were also paranoid about, well, everything.

Deep down, the regime fretted over any challenge to its dogma. They were also acutely aware that their rise to ultimate power was not all kosher and the people still remembered an alternative way of life, governing and running a society.

> *Totalitarianism is a system that not only refuses to accept a diversity of opinion, but also a balance in power. In totalitarian states, decision-makers are not held accountable for their actions and decisions by any independent body – there is no independent judiciary, no freedom of press and absolutely no political alternatives or parties. Such leaders can quickly become dangerous, as their power can grow exponentially while remaining very much unchecked.*

If the communists lacked something, it was an ability to integrate a diversity of opinion. They were so insecure that they opted to rule the world, not from conviction, but from fear. And we all know that nothing good can come out of fear, which is why converting Czechoslovakia to communism was no smooth, graceful or glorious ride. It was a thorny road marked by blood, tears and brainwashing.

# NOSTALGIA FOR THE PAST

*Even today, the older generation especially can be nostalgic about the past, partly because they were not exposed to any negative information about the regime for much of their lives. Despite the many flaws of the regime, they feel that life before 1989 was more moral. Money wasn't the highest authority and aspiration, nor a signpost of self-worth. People found value in other things.*

*The socialist vision united people to work together. It was not just a motto, but a higher purpose for many. The international component of communism also ignited the public. If you speak to the older generation of Russians or Ukrainians, they will say that xenophobia did not exist under communism. Everyone in the Soviet Union was treated as equal.*

*The people of the USSR united behind the notion of supra-national identity. They did not refer to themselves as Russians, Ukrainians, Kazakhs - but as Soviets. This belief did not, however, spill over into the other countries of the Soviet Bloc, who preferred to see themselves as communists.*

*Whatever the case, there was a strong sense of international cooperation and moral integrity. For generations, children were socialized into acts of service, including labour brigades, such as forest cleaning, harvest picking or volunteering at local hospitals.*

*Censorship protected the population of the communist brotherhood from violence and pornography on television. There were no news of murders or corruption. Media content propagated Soviet values and morals – work, community and family  - and encouraged people to live in harmony with their government.*

*Perhaps the shortage of goods played a role too. With commodities perennially unavailable, the people had to work together to make due. The lack of access to resources honed a certain survival skillset, one involving mutual help and assistance.*

*Indeed, others would call this blissful ignorance, unhealthy dependency and elicited politeness. Every coin has two sides.*

# FIRST You Need an ENEMY

The easiest way to justify a radical regime change is by creating an evil enemy, threatening the very lives of people. There is no hero without a villain and the Communist Party wanted to be seen as the hero of the people more than anything. It was not difficult to carve out the perfect villain out of capitalism, especially after colonialism began to be questioned.

On the eastern side of the Iron Curtain, the enemy narrative revolved around the debouched blood-sucking Western imperialists. They were the governments that conquered more indigenous nations in order to extract their resources and oppress their populations. The Western exploiters became the convenient common enemy of communist comrades across the world.

Having a threatening heartless foe at the very gates of one's country, or rather persuading enough people to believe in it, created an atmosphere of instability and fear. Luckily, the Communist Party of Czechoslovakia, assisted by the USSR, had the solution. They had the medicine to sooth the public the fear that they themselves had manufactured.

The narrative was appealingly dramatic. The socialist brotherhood, led by the USSR, found itself encircled by capitalists. Surrounded by bourgeois states exploiting the working classes, the propaganda engine created a state of danger and high urgency as it bravely exposed the cunning policies of the West. The imperialists were looking to subvert peace and incite another global war.

Having a real enemy channeled the attention of the people away from their eroding human rights, and the uncomfortable way the communists actually seized power in their country. If the threat was perceived as real, then the Czechoslovaks would acquiesce more easily. The Party would be seen as their protector, not the usurper and destroyer of democracy.

The entire ideology and its implementation could only be justified by pointing out the evils of capitalism.

It was as simple as pointing a finger and saying 'look at them, look how awful they are' to drive attention away from their own flaws. The diversion was surprisingly very effective.

In practice, no opportunity was missed to besmirch the West and to glorify the East.

While the international success of the Eastern Bloc in science, agriculture, industry, education, culture, sports and politics were exalted, the West was portrayed as sinister, distorted and backward. In no way was it a match to the progressive and righteous Eastern Bloc. Even if the West somehow miraculously managed to be better at something, this would either be twisted or not talked about at all.

> *Reality could not be further from the propaganda truth. Czechoslovaks were fleeing the country in the thousands. Each time any forbidden reminders of the West managed to sneak past the strict border controls, they were held close to sacred. Such was the adoration for democracy and capitalism.*

Sometimes the propaganda machine made up rather silly stories, other times it exploited tragedies and misfortune, as proof of the inferiority of capitalism. Any downturn in Western societies, an economic crisis or a natural disaster, were weaponized to persuade Czechoslovaks that they really were better off behind the Iron Curtain.

The communist matrix knew no limits when it came to discouraging people from searching for alternatives. The people's faith in communism was to be blind. That is the only way the system could be maintained.

The blatant propaganda exposed the deep neurosis of Czechoslovak leadership. Far from being the self-assured rulers of the world ordained by the will of the Kremlin, the regime thrived and relied on making others look bad.

It did not compare itself to the best and then rise to meet that standard, but rather compared itself to the lesser. When the lesser was not available, it was created.

> *In the Soviet sphere, cosmopolitan was a word with a tarnished meaning. Those who demonstrated cosmopolitan inclinations were not to be trusted. They were worldly and open minded, which meant they were ideologically corrupt and morally weak. Cosmopolitan persons embodied a lifestyle that was alien to the values of communism, which is why these individuals were perceived as Western wannabes, or even worse, class traitors to their fellow proletariat.*

The fragile ego of the Party didn't admit any form a criticism, let alone the possibility of making a mistake. Taking responsibility for one's own actions, or failures for that matter, was not normal in the regime. It was best to deny that anything went wrong. Or better yet, blame another for it.

Recycling the narrative of the 'bad, bad West' and its imminent threat upon Czechoslovakia was easier for the Party than doing the hard work of keeping themselves in power by making people happy. The unsustainable strategy produced many ridiculous situations to joke about, retrospectively.

Czechoslovak authorities took propaganda with deadly seriousness. Perhaps it was less severe over on the other side of the divide but make no mistake – the West played its part dutifully too. The Cold War was fought with words, not only weapons, and both actors spat fire, hurled insults and painted each other in darkest of shades of black. As a result, stereotypes of Eastern Europe, ranging from the lose morals of Eastern European women to not having roads to drive on, are still circulated in Western societies today.

# A STORY
## OF THE IMPERIALIST BEETLE

*The anti-capitalist campaign escalated into a fully-fledged information war by the 1950s, when operation 'Potato Beetle' was activated. At the time, rural Czechoslovakia was affected by an infestation of small, brightly coloured insects that feed on the leaves of potato plants.*

*The pest epidemic had a devastating effect on the economy and national food supply. Fearful of a public rebellion, the spin doctors of the Party mobilized an epic narrative in 1952. According to them, the Americans were frustrated by the progress and successes of the Eastern Bloc. The US Military sent planes to fly over the republic under the cover of night and dropped the pest over the crops.*

*The story resonated with the people. The humble potato had been the food staple of nation, dating back to the 18th century. Versatile, filling and very easy to grow, the potato was the beacon that sustained the rural way of life in the region.*

*Through wars, natural disasters and famine, the reliable potato has always been there to feed the people. The Slovaks in particular had developed an emotional attachment to this food staple. When their primary food source was threatened, the communists jumped in on the opportunity.*

*The potato crisis was used as a prop to demonstrate what the amoral West was capable of. Supposedly, they would not stop at anything in their effort to win the Cold War race, even if that meant starving the Czechoslovak population.*

*The potato beetle situation was further declared an imperialist attack by the leadership in Moscow. The Americans proved ready to start a biological war against the East, and the Communist Bloc had to protect itself. Regional 'Committees for the fight against the American Beetle' were set up. A policy brief mobilizing the population read:*

> *It is the patriotic duty of all citizens to participate in the national search in order for the American beetle, a product of American imperialism, to be destroyed in our lands and to be stopped from spreading further to our eastern allies.*

It was a clever ploy. It was also a desperate attempt to avoid responsibility for a looming nationwide famine. Needless to say, the campaign hit the nail on the head and the public was outraged.

# THEN You Make ALLIES

Having a powerful enemy makes it necessary to make powerful friends to support you in the good fight.

With their rise to power, the Soviets quickly discovered just how skewed the international playing field was. Global politics was a man's world, ruled by an old boys' club, and these gentlemen's agreements were maintained by informal meetings and tacit agreements.

If they wanted to be taken seriously, the Soviets would have to create their own parallel structures, substantiated by their own league of allies. Apparently, proving global prowess meant more than securing their influence in Eastern Europe.

The international conduct of the Eastern Bloc mirrored the communists' views on the value of human relationships. They were sticky, messy and unreliable. Nevertheless, closeness facilitated supervision.

The closer the economic and political ties between the Red allies, the easier it was for Moscow to exercise control over them. The befriended socialist states were to be scrupulously monitored. However, to simultaneously cultivate a sense of brotherhood, the operation was disguised under the catchy propaganda mantra: 'together always with the USSR'.

The Warsaw Pact, founded in 1955, was a direct response to the North Atlantic Treaty Organization. It was a pact of friendship, cooperation and mutual assistance across countries in the Soviet sphere of influence. Its goals, akin to those of NATO, were to maintain peace and security, but in the communist world. The organization promised to function like a council, where all the members would participate on an equal basis, in a collective decision-making process under the slogan 'Long live the USSR - the warranty of world peace!'.

In reality, the Warsaw Pact was an extension of the Soviet Ministry of Defense. Its purpose was to integrate the militaries of its 'territories' into a larger transnational apparatus, controlled by yours truly: Moscow.

UPŘEDU, ZPÁTKY NI KROK

TAKE A STEP **FORWARD** TO THE LEFT, AND NOT A SINGLE STEP BACK!

The Pact's largest military engagement was not an act of defense against an invading army, but rather gross violations against their own member nations. The invasion of Czechoslovakia in 1968 was yet another example of this pattern.

The Eastern Bloc had its own OECD (formerly Organization for European Economic Cooperation) too. Established in 1949, The Council for Mutual Economic Assistance was an economic union set up by Stalin himself. This byproduct of the Marshall Plan became known to all the citizens of the Eastern Bloc as RVHP (COMECON in English).

COMECON's member states were brought together more on the basis of ideology than economic interests. Together, the Soviets and their allies, which stretched nearly half the world, crafted five-year master plans to dutifully follow.

Czechoslovaks, as well as their comrades to the east of the Iron Curtain, all played along. Together, they made up phantom statistics to meet their unrealistic productivity quotas. Failure to fulfil a 5-year plan was not an option.

The gap between what was promised and what was reality inspired many a joke. RVHP, the Czechoslovak abbreviation for COMECON, was humorously flipped and stood for *'Radujme se, veselme se, hovno mame, podelme se'* (translated as *'Let's rejoice, let's be merry, we have shit, so let's share it'*).

150

Membership was not so much a privilege as it was a duty. Czechoslovakia, like others, had little choice but to join all these clubs mandatorily. International summits were mostly an exercise in pleasantries and applause, rather than about building international ties and economic partnerships.

The only exception, of course, was the Soviet Union to which none of the usual rules applied...

*In 1950s, exotic Vietnam joined COMECON. It was a part of Moscow's strategy to keep the West at bay in Asia, while also expanding the communist empire into the unknown. The alliance had a very-tangible impact in Czechoslovakia that was in dire need of labor. Vietnamese helped to plug the gap.*

*North Vietnamese students were brought in on a short-term basis to address critical manpower shortages and to learn new skills from an industrially more advanced Czechoslovakia. They were then expected to return to Vietnam and re-seed their new knowledge back home. But, some 26,000 Vietnamese stayed on and with them came a new culture that shook up the stale ethnic waters of Czechoslovakia.*

*Today, the Vietnamese presence can still be seen, felt and savored in both the Czech Republic and Slovakia. They bring vibrance to the region in Vietnamese shops, restaurants and delicatessens, but also business and politics.*

There are several ways of becoming a global superpower and spreading one's influence over the planet. International organisations are one modality, while development aid is another.

No matter if you are in the East or West, living in the ancient past or present day, international development agendas have never been a purely philanthropic endeavor or PR campaign. On the contrary, international aid is a useful tool for strengthening the power of donor nations in developing countries.

The Soviets could not rest on their laurels, if they wanted to keep up in the race for global dominance with the West. Dressed up as development aid, Moscow tested the geopolitical waters everywhere from Cuba to Nicaragua and from Iraq to Vietnam.

The USSR and its buddies swept into countries neglected or ideally rejected by their ideological rival. Resource-rich nations were a priority (some things never change), but as far as the communists were concerned, there was no country too small or insignificant.

During the latter half of the 20th century, Africa became a prime target for such influence operations. Proxy wars erupted across the continent, as militias armed by both sides of the divide battled it out on a ground, in a grand ideological chess match.

> Back in the day, Vladimir Lenin sent a call to Czechoslovakia, asking members of the Communist Party to relocate to the USSR to help build the socialist vision as well as earn some decent money.
>
> Hundreds of Czechoslovaks arrived in some of the most remote republics of the USSR (including the family of Alexander Dubcek), to apply their know-how and develop the country's manufacturing sector. Sadly, some of those people were later purged, killed or imprisoned. Others returned home.

*In the run up to WWII, the remaining Czechoslovaks living in the USSR were given 48 hours to leave the country or become fully-fledged Soviets and enroll in the army. Among those who returned from Kirgizstan was the family of Alexander Dubcek.*

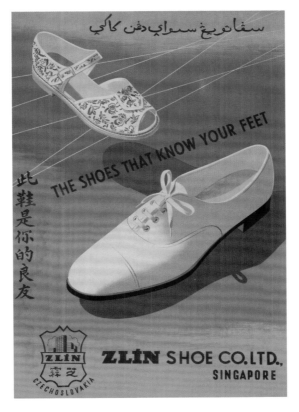

As one of the most advanced economies of the Eastern Bloc, Czechoslovakia was entrusted with a privileged role. The internationally recognized Czechoslovak brand, from industry to science and from culture to athletics, provided the validation Moscow was looking for. Czechoslovakia was to become the go-between, an extended arm of Moscow in Africa, the treasure trove of raw resources. And the mission? To convert the Third World to the gospel of communism.

# CZECHOSLOVAK TRACES IN LIBYA

*ON THE BASIS OF AN INTERNATIONAL TREATY BETWEEN THE CZECHOSLOVAK SOCIALIST REPUBLIC AND THE SOCIALIST PEOPLE'S LIBYAN ARAB JAMAHIRIYA, AT THE END OF OCTOBER AND THE BEGINNING OF NOVEMBER 1977, 625 CZECHOSLOVAK MILITARY EXPERTS ARRIVED IN TRIPOLI. THEY WERE MEANT TO ASSIST THE LIBYAN ARMED FORCES IMPROVE THEIR TRAINING AND TO IMPROVE THE BATTLE READINESS OF THE AIR FORCE, ARMOURED FORCES, AND ARTILLERY.*

PAVEL ZACEK
*Director of the Institute
for the Study of Totalitarian Regimes*

Muammar Kaddafi rose to power in 1969, having failed to meet a compromise with the West, which had turned its back to Libya. Tensions rose to an alarming high after an embargo was imposed on the country. As a result, Libya could no longer export its oil to key markets. This opened the gate for the USSR to enter the immense playing field of North Africa.

Libya was desperate. It was also in dire need of help with its economy, education and health development. Not to mention that Kaddafi was hard pressed finding a new trade ally. With all its handicaps, Libya offered the Soviets a major advantage. The country was an abundant oil reserve, a gold mine for the East.

The best and brightest Czechs and Slovaks were selected to execute Operation Libya. Some enrolled out of conviction, others to escape the dreary reality of a stagnating Czechoslovakia. Like young people anywhere, they were eager to see the world. They wanted to learn, meet new people and apply their skills in exciting projects.

Czechoslovak advisors, technicians and military instructors were landing in Libya and elsewhere to help build factories, water dams, education systems and military strategy, as well *as to advise on how to implement the tenets of the ideology into reality.*

*Going abroad was not only a rare opportunity to live and work internationally; it was the only chance to make some real money. International envoys could earn twenty-times the national Czechoslovak salary. In a single year abroad, one could earn what would take 20 years in Czechoslovakia.*

*People were not the only asset that the Czechoslovak government deployed. With Czechoslovaks also came ammunition and military tech, as the country was a large weapons manufacturer.*

# IMPOSE an Information Blackout

Autocracies throughout eras and countries know that knowledge is power. Therefore, the control of information is indispensable to maintaining absolute power over the masses. The totalitarian government of Czechoslovakia was no exception.

Under the guise of 'protecting' the people from dangerous and misguided information, the state became the only source of it. All media was heavily monitored and the stories it circulated were carefully crafted to cater to the regime and its vision. TV, newspapers, magazines, films and books were under close scrutiny.

A ban on all content from the West was imposed. This did not affect just politically charged contemporary news, but also four hundred-year-old classics, including Shakespeare and the works of some great ancient philosophers. Needless to say, any Western goods including music, films, jeans, nice smelling soaps and colorful sweets were banned from entering the country. Such was the insanity of the era.

Censorship was justified as necessary if the people were to be protected from foreign ideological contamination and live in peace. In reality, it was about control and brainwashing. Living behind the Iron Curtain meant being exposed to blatant mind control every day and every minute. At school, work, home, the store or even a party, banners and posters, slogans and statements followed one at each and every step. Even on holiday.

While information coming from the outside was kept to a minimum, the Party ceaselessly bombarded people with its own truths. The doctrine of communism was most effectively mobilized on radio and on TV, where it could slip into people's minds under the guise of entertainment. Most programs were dedicated to the support and glorification of the regime, and its infinite greatness.

# A HAMMER FOR THE WORKER,

# A SICKLE FOR THE PEASANT

Even the smallest of victories was celebrated with a theatrical campaign, to make people believe their lives were getting better. Meeting and exceeding five year-plans, from building a new factory or a block of flats, were adorned with much ideological rave and artificial enthusiasm. Ideally, they included smiley children, in their pioneer uniforms, ready to fight for socialism.

The combination of withholding information, outright lying and omnipresent disinformation campaigns contributed to a loss of orientation. Living in Czechoslovakia was like being locked in a dark room with no ray of light allowed in to help one make sense of oneself or the surrounding world.

> *Disinformation is not to be confused with misinformation. Misinformation refers to passing on inaccurate information, usually unintentionally, as a result of mis-understanding something. Disinformation, on the other hand, is the deliberate spreading of false information, with an intention to deceive the other. This is what the Party was doing day in and day out.*

Czechoslovaks were waking up with propaganda and going to bed with propaganda. Many stopped reading newspapers all together. The excitement of reading about the newest tractor model, introduced at a god-forsaken farm on the fringes of the republic, wore off quickly. Others continued buying them, but for the sport pages only. The most socially astute used the newspapers to keep up-to-date on which opinions were politically correct, and which should be avoided.

# Out with the old: The GREAT PURGE

It did not take long until it occured to the Party that it was necessary to 'clean' the country from the within.

The republic was teaming with inconvenient individuals with even less convenient views, intimidating influence and sympathies for the West in politics, society, culture and religious groups. These men and women were a source of perennial threat to the wobbly foundations of the new regime.

However, even the communists in the darkest of times had some sense of decorum. As much as they wished, they could not just dispatch whoever displeased them to the other side. They needed to base their claims in some evidence. Arrests would have to be followed by judicial rulings if they were to gain public approval and maintain some pretense of fairness.

Very soon it occurred to the forefathers of Czechoslovak communism that the solution to their nerve-wracking insecurity was to follow the Soviet model of gathering information on everyone. If the state knew everyone's secrets, it would also have plenty of compromising material to get rid of anyone, anytime.

The grounds were laid for a grand and gory performance. But let us take you behind the scenes and into the dark apparatus of the state, before we continue.

The infamous STB (which stood for 'State Security') was the Czechoslovak equivalent of the Soviet KGB. The STB was the eyes and ears of the Communist Party, and its web stretched far and wide. The agency was the backbone of a paranoid regime that stood or fell depending on its ability to control everyone.

To do that, they simply needed to know as much as they could about as many people as possible, preferably everyone.

Pressured to track, interrogate and remove subversives, the STB was not choosy with its methods when it came to making people speak. Physical and psychological torture were justified as necessary defense of the communist ideals.

The dark art of the STB was not their own. They were blended with the techniques first introduced to the region by the Nazis.

soviet 'interrogation' techniques

### 'The Fridge'
referred to staying in a cell with a temperature of 0°C or colder for the whole night. The prisoner was forced to undress and sleep on the concrete floor.

### 'The Cage'
was placed in the middle of the cell and the prisoner was locked inside. He or she would only receive 1/3 of the normal food ratio, and that only after three days of starvation.

### 'The Saw'
soundtrack would be played from speakers in the cell. It produced an insufferable noise for human ears and caused prisoners to hallucinate.

### 'The Isolation Cell'
was a solitary confinement chamber that cut prisoners off from the world. It was not uncommon for people to enter a state of delirium, where they would lose all sense of place, purpose and self.

### 'The Electric Shock'
was an all-time favorite. It was sometimes done overtly, other times covertly when an unsuspecting prisoner received an electric shock when he or she touched the light switch in their cell.

All those who refused to give in at the very beginning and say what the STB wanted to hear, even if it was a lie, would pay a price for their courage. This included being exposed to an arsenal of special interrogation techniques. You name it, the communists used it.

Interrogators played mind games with the accused. The role play of good cop vs bad cop was followed by screaming and beatings. Many innocents were beaten black and blue, their bones, noses and teeth smashed with bare hands, police batons and electrical cords. Their brains were also picked and prodded, through psychological torture techniques as well as drugs.

Prisoners were forced to stand, kneel or sit in uncomfortable positions or walk in circles for days without sleep or rest. If nothing else worked, their families were threatened. That was the ultimate move. A great many Czechoslovaks proved willing to do and say anything to protect their loved ones.

It did not matter that these techniques routinely produced false confessions. As long as there was something palpable, in black and white ink to hide behind, that was enough.

The list of targets was ominously long.

# <sup>step</sup>ONE:
# THE POLITICAL OPPOSITION

First came the members of the political opposition, especially those who were held in high public regard. In a state used to democracy, it took some cruelty to uproot its memory and eliminate the rival ideology. Shrewd politicians aided by specially trained advisors set out to humiliate democrats, so that the Czechoslovak bigwigs and their comrades in the Kremlin could sleep better at night.

Prosecuting prominent politicians killed several birds with one stone. It got rid of inconvenient ideological and politically savvy competition. It also created the semblance of a dangerous enemy lurking from within. The presence of national traitors also justified brutal reprisals.

Czechoslovak show trials were the largest in the whole of Eastern Europe and started as early as 1948. These political spectacles knew no mercy and scared people into submission. Better to stand with the Party than endure torture.

They showcased the lowest of the low, the traitors of the regime, and were often consumed as entertainment by the masses. The courtrooms became a theater for the regime to parade its power and play God. The Party decided who died and who lived.

A show trial took some meticulous planning. The quotas setting the exact number of people who were to be executed or else sentenced to life in prison were produced in Moscow. Czechoslovakia was to deliver on the objective.

This was not about justice. The aim of the show trials was not to uncover truth, but to consolidate power quickly. Confessions were written for the defendants, who were expected to merely memorize them and sign on the dotted line before the camera. If they were unwilling, psychological and physical torture was applied to break their will.

The theatrical plays of brutality and ignorance were used to send a clear signal to the public: do not mess with the Party.

Caught up in the whirlwind of emotions, swept by a wave of hatred, anger, loathing and mostly fear, Czechoslovakia entered a mass hypnosis. Perhaps, it was easier to believe in the system, then to live in a reality where the state hounded and killed innocent civilians.

Ordinary people often chose to believe that danger really did lurk around the corner, and that the Communist Party was the only thing that could protect the hard-working and righteous Czechoslovaks from it.

These same people were encouraged and even inspired to write letters to the state, asking for the execution of those revolting enemies. Such was the insanity of the post-war era.

# DIGNITY IN THE FACE OF FANATICISM

*I HAVE CHANGED MY MIND MANY TIMES, REARRANGED MANY VALUES, BUT, WHAT WAS LEFT AS AN ESSENTIAL VALUE, WITHOUT WHICH I CANNOT IMAGINE MY LIFE, IS THE FREEDOM OF MY CONSCIENCE.*

MILADA HORAKOVA

*Milada Horakova was a prominent Czech politician in interwar Czechoslovakia. A woman of valor, she was a key figure in the resistance against the Nazis. She survived brutal German interrogation and a concentration camp, only to fall into the hands of communists shortly after the war.*

*Milada was an inconvenient political subject, with even less convenient ideals. Her pro-democratic beliefs, strong persona, network of contacts, including influential foreign figures, were all surpassed by her public popularity. She was a force of nature on the scene.*

*She was too cosmopolitan to be trusted and too strong to be broken.*

*Milada's name was high on the black list, yet she refused to leave her motherland. She stayed on in Czechoslovakia because she believed in her country. And she would pay the ultimate price for it.*

*For three years before her arrest, Milada was closely watched by the STB. The problem was that the surveillance efforts proved fruitless. The communists could not find any evidence to raise legal charges. Frustrated, the investigators decided to coerce witnesses into signing pre-written false confessions.*

*At long last, Milada was arrested on trumped up charges of espionage and treason. The public trial against Mrs. Horakova was one of the saddest moments in Czechoslovak history. It was orchestrated by Moscow advisers to publicly break Milada's spirit, make her renounce her values and betray the people she stood for.*

*Drugs, the withholding of food, inhumane cell conditions, interrupted sleep, drowning, beating, brainwashing and solitary confinement did not make her 'speak'. Milada refused to play the game. A conclusion was made by the party: she was a liability that had to be done away with.*

*No cruelty was spared as the effective propaganda machine was set into motion. Every day, teachers drilled the story of a loathsome Milada into the malleable heads of school children. In a perverse example of public entertainment, local Party officials organized community get-togethers to listen to radio broadcasts of the trial.*

*All throughout the republic, there was a convenient silence about Milada's fight against the Nazis, her survival through the concentration camps, and her return to her homeland with a political vision. Anything was said to get the public on the dark side.*

*Milada was convicted and sentenced to death. The execution was rushed as an international campaign was mobilized to admonish her and all that she stood for. The matter was getting out of hand. A petition of protest was signed by Albert Einstein, Winston Churchill and Eleanor Roosevelt, among other influencers, and delivered to Prague. But nothing would stop the men in grey.*

*Milada Horakova was hung on June 27, 1950, and became the only Czechoslovak woman and mother to be sentenced to death. Her death also sent a clear message to Czechoslovaks: the revenge of the Party knows no mercy.*

*These were dark times, when truth and courage were hard to come by.*

*The punishment did not end with Milada's execution. Her only daughter Jana was denied access to education. She was denied studying medicine five times because she refused to publicly denounce her mother. Milada's daughter eventually left Czechoslovakia and settled in the US. A letter that her mother wrote to her from prison, awaiting the verdict, took 40 years to be given to Jana by the state authorities.*

zvídati státní tajemství,

b) Dr.Milada Horáková, Dr.Josef Nestával, Dr.Jiří Hejda, František Přeučil, Antonie Kleinerová, Dr.Oldřich Pecl a Záviš Kalandra dopouštěli se vyzvědačství delší dobu, ve značném rozsahu a způsobem zvláště nebezpečným a vyzvídali státní tajemství zvláště důležitá,

c) Dr.Jiřímu Hejdovi byla povinnost uchovávati státní tajemství výslovně uložena. ——

T í m   s p á c h a l i

I) všichni zločin velezrady podle § 1.odst.2 (odst.1 lit.a,c/) zák.č.231/48 Sb. a podle § 1 odst.2 lit. b/ téhož zákona,

František Zemínová, František Přeučil a Jan Buchal mimo to též podle § 1 odst.3, lit.c/ téhož zákona,

II) všichni zločin vyzvědačství podle § 5 odst.1, odst. 2, lit.c/ zák.č.231/48 Sb.,

Dr.Milada Horáková, Dr.Josef Nestával, Dr.Jiří Hejda, František Přeučil, Antonie Kleinerová, Dr.Oldřich Pecl a Záviš Kalandra též podle § 5 odst.2, lit.d, e/ cit.zák.,

Dr.Jiří Hejda mimo to též podle § 5 odst.2, lit.b/ téhož zákona, a

o d s u z u j í   s e

za to všichni podle § 1 odst.3 zák.č.231/48 Sb. se zřetelem na ustanovení § 34 tr.z.:

1) JUDr Milada Horáková k trestu   s m r t i ,

2) Jan Buchal k trestu   s m r t i ,

3) JUDr Oldřich Pecl k trestu   s m r t i ,

4) Záviš Kalandra k trestu   s m r t i ,

5) JUDr Josef Nestával s použitím ustanovení § 113 odst.1 zák.č.319/48 Sb. k trestu těžkého žaláře na   d o ž i v o t í ,

6) JUDr Jiří Hejda s použitím ustanovení § 113 zák.č. 319/48 Sb. k trestu těžkého žaláře na   d o ž i - v o t í ,

DR MILADA HORAKOVA AND HER COLLABORATORS HAVE ENGAGED IN ESPIONAGE FOR A PROLONGED PERIOD OF TIME, TO A GREAT EXTENT AND IN THE MOST DANGEROUS OF MANNERS TO SPY ON IMPORTANT SECRETS OF THE STATE.

BY DOING SO, THEY HAVE ALL COMMITTED:

I) CRIME OF HIGH TREASON

II) CRIME OF ESPIONAGE

AND ARE HEREBY SENTENCED FOR THESE CRIMES:

1. DR MILADA HORAKOVA TO DEATH PENALTY

2. JAN BOUCHAL TO DEATH PENALTY

3. DR OLDRICH PECL TO DEATH PENALTY

4. ZAVIS KALANDRA TO DEATH PENALTY

5. DR JOSEF NESTAVAL TO LIFE IMPRISONMENT

6. JIRI HEJDA TO LIFE IMPRISONMENT

# step TWO:
## THE RELIGIOUS QUESTION

Communism was deeply suspicious of religion, what Karl Marx had referred to as the 'opium of the masses'. The materialist ideology did not mesh well with surrendering to a power higher than that of the Party. Czechoslovak communists feared the spiritual realm and its influence. The authorities from the Vatican were just another competitor to eliminate.

The fear was not unfounded. Especially in Slovakia, the Catholic Church reached the most remote corners of the country. Slovak priests had been guiding the thinking of millions of Slovaks for centuries. The Vatican was also a Western institution, connected to Western power structures. Indeed, the 'religion question' gave the Party much to worry about.

Ultimately, they would be proven right. It would be the Catholics who would first rock the boat of the mass consciousness in the 1980s in Slovakia - but let us not jump ahead.

How to stop people from going to church?

The communists were clever. They knew it was too risky to make religion illegal. Taking such a radical action towards such a highly sensitive issue would do more harm than good. The last thing that the leadership needed was an emotional backlash against the government. Why openly provoke the deeply religious Slovaks, when much more sinister solutions were at hand?

To get people on their side, the Communist Party set out to discredit the Christian leadership of the country in an indirect attack on the religion. Surely, the people would then turn to the Communist Party as the new ultimate authority, and source of spiritual hope.

The priests, the frontline of religious influence, needed to be pushed out. The Party mobilized its propaganda machine to circulate disinformation. False claims were made, accusing clergy members of conspiring against the regime and betraying the working class by spying for the West. Show trials and vicious prison sentences ensued.

Those that remained needed the consent of the state, if they wanted to continue to give sermons and serve the religious community. That meant one thing - they had to align themselves with Party interests and narratives.

Monks and nuns were regularly rounded-up and sent to forced labour camps as well. All male and female monasteries and religious orders were abolished during this period. Independent religious publications were banned.

> *Forced labor camps were first introduced to Europe on a mass scale by the Nazis. They used these establishments to lock up anti-fascists and force them to work as slaves, until they could no longer perform.*
>
> *A similar system of slavery was implemented in Bolshevik Russia. These were reserved for prisoners of war, and later perfected when communism took off the ground for real.*
>
> *The model of Soviet labor camps was then transplanted into Czechoslovakia. Six camps were built in Slovakia, while many more opened in the Czech part of the republic. These prisons housed over 15,000 political prisoners the so-called enemies of the state.*

Christians in Slovakia were more persecuted than in any other communist country, even more than in the USSR. 1950 was a black year for religion in Slovakia. 1,500 Catholic priests were imprisoned and the Greek Catholic Church, the roots of which dated back to Byzantium, was abolished altogether. The government seized all church property.

> *Some explain the ferocity towards the Catholic Church in Slovakia by what happened during WWII. While the Czech*

*and Polish clergy was prosecuted by the Nazis, the pro-Nazi Slovak State was headed by a Catholic priest. Moreover, a third of parliament had been priests.*

*Catholicism became a state-enforced doctrine. It was easy to label all Christian churches as an enemy of the people after after the war. Many Slovak communists had been themselves Catholics, striving to prove their worth to the new regime by sanctioning a zealous anti-religion policy.*

Next came negative incentives to make people think twice before attending any religious service. These affected particularly those who had something to lose by remaining connected to a religion, mostly professionals, such as teachers and clerks. If they were seen going to church, wearing religious icons and symbols, or caught carrying a picture of a saint in their wallet, they could be professionally ostracized. That meant, losing their job. Or they could be denied a highly-coveted holiday permit.

And yet, people stubbornly clung to their belief system, particularly manual workers, who didn't have much to lose 'socially'. These people continued attending Mass, much to the dismay of the Party.

If religion could not be wiped from the public consciousness, perhaps it could be slowly eroded and eventually forgotten. The modernization of the country proved a useful decoy. Major new roads had to be built to meet public demand and 'facilitate ease of traffic'. Why not build them right next to churches?

And so they did. Places of worship were already centuries upon centuries old, and the party hoped that the new infrastructural developments would destabilize their foundations to the point of collapse. Simply taking down such important landmarks would have been a step too far. A passive aggressive move was far more appropriate.

In Bratislava, the most iconic religious landmark of the city, the jewel of Gothic architecture and the signpost to its royal history, took a big hit. St Martin's Cathedral, once a coronation cathedral of eleven kings and eight queens of Hungary, found itself exposed to one of the main traffic veins of the city. The Jewish synagogue that used to stand next to the cathedral was demolished, just like so many others across the country.

*Communism did not care much for the matter of ethnic diversity or identity. All people were to find their place within the Czechoslovak communist persona. This approach hurt many, such as the Rusyns of Eastern Slovakia, who were among those who suffered most. Their unique identity was very much tied to their religion. Most of them were Greek Catholics. First, their Church was wiped out and many of the priests, who formed the intellectual backbone of the community, were sent to prison. To add insult to injury, seven Rusyn villages were covered forever by water when a new water dam was built. The traditional architecture and family homes of generations disappeared overnight, further chipping away at the Rusyn identity.*

# AN ERA THAT PRODUCED MARTYRS

*Zdenka Schelingova was a nun who worked in a hospital in Bratislava. She was actively engaged in helping political prisoners from the clerical ranks escape the republic via the hospital. However, the cruelty of the era caught up with her.*

*Zdenka eventually fell into a trap, set up by agents of STB, when she attempted to help a group of priests and seminarians escape in 1952. She was arrested, tortured and spent months leading to her trial living in a cold and windowless cell. She was sentenced to 12 years in prison for treason, but not before she was tortured by her investigators.*

*The nun was drowned, tied and beaten, in order to release information about the Underground Church. Sent from prison to prison, and subject to regular beatings, her breast was torn from continually being kicked. It was amputated without anesthesia.*

*Zdenka was released from prison due to her poor health. The state did not want her in prison on the government's account. That would make her a martyr. Instead, the nun was released, but could no longer return to her convent. A friend provided her shelter for the last weeks of her life. Zdenka died in a hospital in the summer of 1955 and was beatified by John Paul II in 2003.*

# step THREE:
## THE INTELLIGENTSIA

Czechoslovak intellectuals were far too inconvenient to be tolerated. Doctors, surgeons, accountants, notaries and lawyers, not to mention artists, actors, writers and poets, were high on the Party agenda of people to watch. They were considered dangerous because they demonstrated advanced mental capacities, the ability to express themselves and, most worryingly, the skill to influence and lead the masses.

# DO NOT:

**czechoslovak prison rules**

✖ talk to a guard without invitation or request

✖ sleep or doze off in a bed outside of designated hours

✖ damage the cell furniture

✖ stand close to a window

✖ sit on the blanket or straw mattress

✖ communicate with other prisoners or make eye contact with them

✖ sing or make any sounds

✖ refuse to eat

✖ sleep with head, hands or forearms covered

The non-conforming intelligentsia was hunted down. Some found themselves in prisons, others in uranium mines or other health-destroying work places. These were renowned for their substandard working conditions, where no sane person would seek employment at will.

This is how the country ended up with an impressively over-qualified manual labor force. The broiler rooms of Czechoslovakia were full of professors, mathematicians and writers. The best art directors, playwrights and doctors in the republic were driving trams, drilling in the mines, loading trucks and cleaning toilets.

The party had only one objective - push out all dissent. It was much less concerned with the loss of human resources.

With the most competent people removed, the communists were left with a serious shortage of skills. But, they didn't even bat an eyelash, and instead used the opportunity to fill the empty slots with 'their people'. These were politically reliable individuals who demonstrated unquestionable loyalty to the regime. It only had one drawback. Those people came from the fields and factories, and often lacked the necessary education and skills.

A culture of incompetency and mediocrity flourished as a clean personal record and devotion to the Party were more important than real competencies. Inept yet powerful, it was no surprise they failed spectacularly in getting their jobs done. This had a devastating effect on the national economy.

*Truth be told, most intellectuals resisted taking on leading positions, even if they weren't hunted down by the communists. That would mean shaking Party hands and kissing Party cheeks. How could they live with that? It was a question of conscience.*

*This is why many opted for a quieter life, far away from the unrelenting eye of the state. Manual jobs were also a blessing in disguise. They occupied very little brain capacity, allowing people to pour their thinking into secret creative endeavors. Writing became one of the most popular outlets for venting frustrations. A great many books, novels, plays and poetry collections were born out of this predicament.*

# MAKE THEM FEAR
## THEIR OWN SHADOW

It has never been easy for a handful of individuals to control an entire population. Time and time again, absolute rule required a fragmented population. This was achieved by sowing fear and distrust. The tried and tested method used and abused by dictators worldwide took a particularly nasty turn in Czechoslovakia. Just like that, the Central European showcase of democracy turned into a surveillance state.

The Czechoslovak leadership prioritized eroding trust between people. A population that did not trust one another would not be able to unite and bring the single Party rule down. If the Party wanted to stay in power, they had to stop the masses from rebelling against them. *Divide et impera.*

> *Communism produced the largest surveillance states in history. In East Germany, the ratio of agents and informers to civilian was 6:1. Now that's terrifying. In Czechoslovakia, according to the archival records released after the fall of the regime, some 30,000 civilians were recruited to work as clandestine informers for the state.*

Making people fear each other was not even so hard. Two destructive world wars that happened within 20 years left a deep scar on each and every family in the republic.

Communism built on this trauma. The initial brute period of 1948-1953, when the state literally killed people and put them in prison with the objective to scare the population into obedience, eventually gave way to more sophisticated measures of control.

Prisons, forced labor camps and death sentences were replaced by more refined strategies of administrative terror.

These policies prevented Czechoslovaks from confiding in each other, gathering together in larger groups, and expressing their opinions.

Speaking against the Party was akin to conspiring against the state. Questioning the actions of Moscow or, God forbid, the ideology, was an obvious redline. The communists understood that words are precursors to action, and should be nipped in the very bud. They practiced thought-control.

Do not think for a moment that you were safe in Czechoslovakia as a 'normal person'. Even if you did not carry the ideals of freedom close to your heart, had no entrepreneurial drive, nor religious inclinations, you were still watched. This regime trusted no one.

> *Citizen surveillance and street checks were a normal part of everyday life. Guilty until proven innocent was the state mantra. It was assumed that everyone was up to something illicit, or would be, if let uncontrolled.*

The smallest of unintentional signs of resistance could be easily interpreted as a crime against the state. A politically incorrect joke could have you demoted instantly. Meeting with a politically unreliable individual could cost you and your family jobs or even place of residence.

People thought twice before they said anything out loud. In the black and white world of communism, words were taken out of context. This meant that everything and anything could be interpreted as slander against the Party or even worse, Moscow itself.

No shadow was innocent. The Party had to have access to all the nooks and crannies of individual and public life. When left unmonitored, counter-revolutionary activities could be brewing anywhere, especially in people's private homes.

To maintain total control was synonymous with restricting privacy to the bare minimum. This meant penetrating the private world of the individual. A narrative was crafted to explain, justify and normalize such violation. Of course.

"You don't need privacy, if you have nothing to hide" became the mantra of the era.

Privacy became synonymous with danger in the public imagination and the people willingly gave up theirs to prove their goodness and innocence. But still, it was not enough. The government needed to know for sure that all was under control.

Relentless monitoring became a critical component of how civil society was subverted. The bugging of phones and homes was a standard Party practice. The STB did not even bother to hide their tracks. They wanted the population to know that they were being watched. The very possibility of this happening sent shivers down the spine of millions of people.

The Party went even further. It encouraged ordinary people to snitch on one another in order to widen their reach and deepen their penetration into the intimate lives of men, women and children. This would both guarantee access to the most private of information and alienate people from one another.

It did not take long for an extensive surveillance network staffed by ordinary people to be established. If they would not do it voluntarily, there were plenty of techniques to make them. The regime routinely forced law-abiding citizens to act as informants under threat of doing harm to their loved ones. Even worse, children were conditioned through the educational system to scoop and report on their parents and grandparents.

Others betrayed their friends, family and neighbors in exchange for privileges and comforts. The culture of spying and reporting offered endless opportunities. Motives ranged from professional advancement to seeking vengeance over a broken heart or getting a better grade on a university exam.

> *Every day was permeated with little and greater instances of injustice. A culture of despotism prevailed – at home, at work, in a grocery store and at the post office. If you were the unfortunate target of such an attack, it was unlikely that anyone would come to your aide no matter how unfair. Instead, people just stepped aside and allowed it to happen. They were too afraid to speak out on behalf of themselves, let alone anyone else. Unfortunately, this is what allowed small human indecencies to accumulate into monstrosities.*

Of course, there were also those who were blindly and entirely devoted to the ideology of communism. They firmly believed that they were doing the right thing by reporting on their neighbors, friends and family. After all, they were helping to build a better world for everyone by pacifying those who tried to damage the greater good of the collective. It is a fine line to toe between maintaining peace and harmony and suppressing freedom.

No realm was off limits. Spies worked their skillsets from public benches to school classrooms, from cadre boardrooms to religious rituals, from Friday night outings to the intimacy of the bedroom.

*Despite egalitarian ideals, communism produced cleavages in society. Lo and behold, the Party and its leaders became the most prominent members of the society. This came with privileges, higher salaries, better housing and more desirable holidays.*

*At the same time, the Party members had access to sensitive information. They could easily expose the regime and its many deficiencies. They also knew about the personal dirty laundry or other party members - whom was in bed with whom or was selling secrets to the West. This made them dangerous and in turn the most closely watched persons in the republic.*

Weaknesses both perceived and real were punished, misfortunes were exploited, and psychological blinds spots were mapped and stowed away in files to be used against citizens. Unexpected lay-offs from a job, the denial of a university education, the rejection of a holiday permit or the tearing up a lifelong dream to have a car or flat, were also dished out at will. The Party did not hesitate to use mind control and material goods to its advantage.

# LET'S BUILD SOCIALISM, REVEAL SABOTEURS AND ENEMIES OF THE REPUBLIC TO STRENGTHEN PEACE!

In turn, the people were kept in a state of perpetual suspense. Anybody could be arrested at any given moment, for any given reason. A prison term would hang over someone's head, even for as little as being caught reading an 'imperialist' Shakespeare play.

The fact that you never spoke or even cared about politics did not matter. Even compliant Czechoslovaks would lose their entire futures, with the stroke of a pen. Sometimes it was a mistake, other times a matter of convenience. And this applied not just to the 'guilty' party, but also their offspring. Once a sin against the ideology was committed, the Party went after the family bloodline.

Opportunities of getting a university degree and a good job were taken away from children, if their parents fell into disfavor with the government. Mothers and fathers would think twice about going against the Party, for they did not want to face a lifetime of guilt, for one act of youthful rebellion.

A life lived under surveillance created constant psychological duress. It may have been more subtle than explicit violence, but it was just as terrorizing. Czechoslovaks grew terrified of sharing their authentic self, and expressing what they really thought and felt about pretty much anything.

You never really knew 'who' you were dealing with. Was the person in front of you a friend or a spy? Perhaps they were a relative of a high ranking senior official in the Party? Could you speak with them openly? Could you joke with them, or not?

If a waiter brought you cold soup, a doctor treated you rudely, or an administrator neglected your application, one had to stay quiet. Better not raise a complaint, because who knows who they were connected to. They could be the only son of a high communist commissar or the niece of the police captain. It was better to be invisible than to risk becoming an unnecessary enemy and target.

*It was impossible to live in such a state of constant suspense, which is why most choose to withdraw into the safety of their inner world. With everyone in their own detached bubble, establishing connections with others was very difficult.*

*The final effect was truly astounding – a sense of unity was lost in society. Detaching from one's community and emotions also made it easier for people to become informers on one another. Without emotion, betrayal was that much easier. This proved to be one of the Party's most efficient control tactics.*

The Czechoslovaks were not naïve. They knew that they were being watched, which is why they always had their performance face when out in public. The culture of surveillance also eroded any remnants of community. Anyone could be a spy – the smiley neighbor, the convivial uncle or the chatty waitress at the dairy bar. All could be ready to report or, worse yet, fabricate evidence to advance their own interests and please the Party.

All in all, the Czechoslovak STB had some 17,000 agents. The records indicate that over 30,000 civilians collaborated with the agency during the 1950s. The Party archives contained thousands upon thousands of individual profiles summarising one's personal life, even intimate details and daily routines.

Although it was physically impossible for these men and women to listen to every phone call, bug every single household or eavesdrop into every conversation, it was enough for Czechoslovaks to believe that every wall had ears: they started self-censoring themselves.

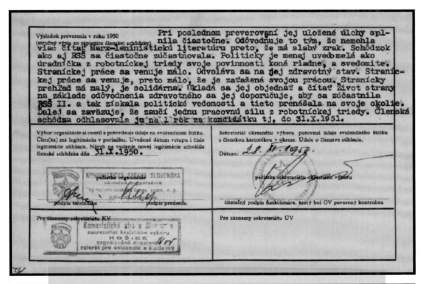

THE LAST SCREENING CONCLUDED THAT THE SUBJECT ONLY PARTIALLY FULFILLED THE TASKS ASSIGNED TO HER. SHE JUSTIFIES NOT READING ALL THE PRESCRIBED MARXIST-LENINIST LITERATURE DUE TO WEAKENED VISION. SHE ATTENDED SOME MEETINGS AND COMPULSORY MARXIST-LENINIST SCHOOLING, BUT HER POLITICAL CONSCIOUSNESS IS LOW. SHE CARRIES OUT HER ADMINISTRATIVE DUTIES AS A WORKING-CLASS CLERK PROPERLY AND DILIGENTLY. YET, SHE DEDICATES LITTLE TIME TO PARTY WORK. SHE CLAIMS THAT SHE CANNOT CARRY OUTHER PARTY DUTIES BECAUSE OF HER HEALTH PROBLEMS. SHE ALSO STATES SHE IS TOO OCCUPIED BY HER REGULAR WORK. HER KNOWLEDGE OF THE COMMUNIST PARTY AND ITS WORKINGS IS LOW BUT SHE IS SYMPATHETIC TO THE PARTY IDEALS. IT IS RECOMMENDED THAT SHE ORDERS AND READS 'THE PARTY LIFE' (A JOURNAL OF THE COMMUNIST PARTY OF CZECHOSLOVAKIA). BECAUSE OF HER HEALTH ISSUES, WE SUGGEST SHE ENROLLS IN THE SECOND GRADE OF THE PARTY EDUCATION PROGRAM TO ACQUIRE POLITICAL KNOWLEDGE AND TO FURTHER CIRCULATE IT IN HER ENVIRONMENT.

SHE COMMITS HERSELF TO TAKING-ON ONE WORKING CLASS APPRENTICE, APPROVED BY THE PARTY COMMISSION AS A MEMBER OF THE CZECHOSLOVAK COMMUNIST PARTY, FOR ONE YEAR.

# LIVING WITH A PACKED SUITCASE

*The greater majority of Czechoslovaks lived in constant fear. A former accountant from Bratislava recalls the suffocating atmosphere of the era. Living with the knowledge that the STB could always twist and turn facts the way it suited them was nerve-wracking, even for obedient rule abiding citizens.*

*The cruelty of the state and the conduct of the police were more than just rumors. It drove one accountant into cutting all meaningful ties with friends and family in order to protect himself. The lack of emotional intimacy was outweighed with some semblance of safety.*

*The man developed a rich internal life and lived within his own little bubble, far away from the unbearable reality outside of it. Nevertheless, he kept a suitcase at hand, for the day the relentlessly secret police would come looking for him too.*

*Even though that dreaded midnight knock never came, the possibility of it destroyed his mind.*

# CONFISCATE
## all assets

### IF YOU PUT THE COMMUNISTS IN CHARGE OF THE SAHARA DESERT, THERE WILL BE A SHORTAGE OF SAND IN FIVE YEARS.

WINSTON CHURCHILL

Karl Marx summed up the core principle of communism into one punchy sentence: "Abolish all private property". Once in power, the Communist Party of Czechoslovakia party put these words swiftly into action.

Private ownership, believed to be the weed suffocating equality and preventing people from prospering, had to be torn out by the roots. The process of cleansing the republic of the evils of capitalism began even before the 1948 coup, when key sectors came under the control of the state, but the nationalization after 1948 was blatant legalized theft by the government.

The few took from the many, for the greater good of all. The banking sector was obliterated immediately. Other industries followed shortly. This brought nearly all employees into the state sector.

Big businesses were targeted first, next in line were small and medium-sized enterprises. The Party was remarkably efficient in executing its flagship policy.

By the early 1950s, Czechoslovakia had nationalized nearly all industries. By 1960, the private sector was wiped out completely. Collectivization, transferring property from private to public hands, was completed.

With a single swoop of the pen, millions of people lost their livelihood. Many had to part with businesses that were a family heirloom, and the source of livelihood for generations.

# TOWARD AN EFFECTIVE AGRICULTURE!

EFEKTÍVNEJŠIE AJ PRI VÝROBE OBJEMOVÝCH KRMOVÍN

Not only were local businesses confiscated, but their owners were expelled from the cities and towns that had been their homes.

Their offense against the state?

It could have been merely a sense of independence and entrepreneurial spirit. There was no room for such self-actualization or agency in the new vision for Czechoslovakia. The Party needed a complacent population, fully dependent on the government that provided them with work, as well as food and shelter, to avoid any bumps on the road to a better tomorrow.

If no one was able to feed themselves and look after their families, if no one could sustain themselves but relied on the state for both necessities and luxuries, then the danger of a revolt would be limited to manageable proportions.

# CRIMINALIZATION OF
# SELF-SUSTENANCE

*The story of one family and their shop selling lamps in the heart of Bratislava speaks volumes about the economic and social injustices of the era. Its hero is a humble man who had survived the devastation of the Second World War and returned to his beloved city and business, ready to resume a normal life. Fate had a different destiny in store for him.*

*The shop owner was classified as 'bourgeois' by the new regime, which meant he was classified as a speculator and exploiter of the working class. In the eyes of the new regime, he had committed the crime of all crimes, daring to run his own business. This had devastating consequences not only for him, but also his family.*

*The confiscation of the family business was just the beginning. The state decided that it was also necessary to confiscate their home. The residence and nest of three generations was taken away and allocated to a more trustworthy citizen, with no ties to a bourgeois lifestyle.*

*This devastated the family, a tight unit that relied on one another for support but also love. They would soon become completely estranged.*

*To escape the family shame, the owner's brother moved to a faraway town where he knew no one and no one knew him. He wanted to study at university and that would not be possible with a tarnished family record. His only chance was to forget and disown his family, to start somewhere else from scratch.*

*The shop owner's wife and daughter also left Bratislava. They had to find a way to make a living. In the end, they found jobs in a small rural town and both worked as local seamstresses for the rest of their lives.*

*As for the once successful small business owner himself, he became but a ghost of his former existence. Unable to secure consistent work because of his damaged reputation, he struggled to support himself. For the remainder of his life, he moved from one town to another, taking whatever manual jobs came his way. At times, he needed to work for free, just so that he could cover his food and lodgings.*

*What happened to the shop? The once cherished, tiny, family-run business, which provided a valuable service of lighting up the homes of the community, sank below rock bottom. It was nationalized and passed on to a local party member who had no knowledge of how to service lamps, let alone where to order them from or how to sell them to the public. In short, the business became a disaster.*

*This is not just one sad story of one petty entrepreneur. By subverting small businesses, the Party subverted communities. Ultimately, the entire population was forced to seek employment from the state. This is how the state owned people's lives, this is now it enforced obedience.*

The process was most dramatic when it came to the collectivization of rural Slovakia. Up until then, the country was still very much an agrarian society, where most people were employed in agriculture. It had been so for centuries. Ever since feudalism was abolished, petty farmers looked after their little plots of land as their source of livelihood.

Out of the blue, all the land and animals, the beating heart of rural life and the backbone of the country's economy, were collectivized. State officials were sent from city headquarters to inspect the countryside personally, in order to count all the chickens, cows and pigs.

The many small and independent farmers who had worked this soil for centuries were forced to hand over their livelihoods to the state. Overnight, their land and their equipment were no longer theirs. It now belonged to all, or rather it all belonged to the Party. The collectivization of the country's agricultural system brutally interfered with the traditional way of life in Slovakia. Age old rituals and values were torn up as farmers were pressured to join collective farms.

V PEVNEJ JEDNOTE KSČ A ĽUDU ZA ĎALSIE ÚSPECHY PRI BUDOVANÍ VYSPELEJ SOCIALISTICKEJ VLASTI

THE COMMUNIST PARTY AND THE PEOPLE BUILD AN ADVANCED SOCIALIST HOMELAND TOGETHER!

Not all were ready to throw in the towel. Well to do farmers had a lot to lose and resisted the government for as long as they could. With their family legacy at stake, they challenged the authorities and sabotaged the government's efforts to seize their assets. The counteraction was as brutal as it was nasty.

The Party mobilized the peasants and farm hands, those who had nothing to lose and everything to gain through the redistribution of power, to their advantage. The righteous anger of the peasants towards those that traditionally had more than them was fueled by carefully targeted smear campaigns.

Landowners were labelled 'kulaks', a derogatory term, and the new dirty word of the era. A kulak was an affluent farmer, or more specifically, a land-owning individual who lived off their land. It did not take long before anyone who stood in the way of the Party became a kulak, rich or not.

**PEACE TO THE PEOPLE
LAND TO THE PEASANTS!**

The communists stated that if a society was to prosper, it had to rid itself of these capitalist exploiters, the blood-suckers of the people. The allure of becoming a collective farm owner was enticing and persuaded many a farm hand to buy into the collectivization effort.

Faced with mounting public pressure to assimilate, farmers simply stood no chance. Sometimes at gunpoint, they were forced into signing applications to 'willingly' enter collective farms.

> *Truth be told, those who had more than everyone else had long frustrated people at the bottom of society. When communism redistributed assets, it saved many*

*a poor family. After the war, there were women left widowed, with no source of income and multiple children to support. There were also men who had lost arms and legs fighting the Nazis, and were not able to find their place in the job market after the war. Collectivization also ushered in new technologies that the Slovak countryside was in desperate need of. Many were thankful for modern technologies that made tough life a little easier.*

All was good when all was planned.

It was only natural for a regime so distrustful of the free hand of the market and obsessed with controlling everything to maintain meticulous supervision over the economy. It was the only way of making sure there was no class exploitation and wealth discrepancies. The economy, the backbone and the feeding hand of any society, came first and foremost. A new invention was ushered in; five-year plans laid out the production plans for all the goods and services made in the republic.

This is how the Party made sure that there was just enough of the same, not too much nor too little. The system was made easier by the fact that everyone was assumed to be the same and have the same purchasing preferences. Diverse needs are much more difficult to plan and meet than the universal and uniform, and so the goods available on the Czechoslovak market were, well, far from varied, colorful or novel.

Plans were not mere objectives, they were definitive, and had to be met by everyone, from farmers to miners, and from car manufacturers to toy makers. Every plan constituted a law; breaking a plan was equal to breaking the law. Every firm and every individual within them had to work and produce according to these administered goals. Those numbers were

# WE WILL TURN 5-YEAR PLANS INTO REALITY!

carefully selected to dazzle not only the Kremlin, but also the West. The well-oiled Czechoslovak machine was powering full steam ahead.

It soon turned out that what looked like a good idea on paper was not so easy to translate into reality. People cannot predict everything, and so every now and then, the normal course of life would interfere with the state's economic ideals.

A factory would burn down, or the weather would be less then benevolent, and that only meant one thing - there was a shortage of something at all times. Furthermore, micromanaging everything slowed down labor productivity. The people may have gathered to work, but they were kept from it by executing pointless tasks and unnecessary procedures.

Far from agile, the East of the planned economy was both heavy and clumsy. The system did not adapt easily to change under any circumstances. As a result, there would be no chocolate, no toy cars or no cherries available. Tough luck. The country eventually got used to the perennial shortages of goods and the empty shop shelves.

There was another issue with the economic plans. They were so enthusiastically ambitious that they were impossible to meet. Yet, in the true paradox of the regime, these artificial quotas were nevertheless strictly monitored and measured. The communists were always keen to track grand progress.

Everyone knew that the stats were all made up, and everyone joined in on the role-play and pretended they were not. This charade played itself out without so much as a raised eyebrow, day by day and year by year. Together, the Socialist Republic of Czechoslovakia was not only meeting but exceeding its impossible targets.

A mere 100% excellence was too lame, on par with the weak measly West. No, the communist republics were doing even better, overcoming their own expectation by 120%!

To control market demand, which was just another devious way of controlling people's lives, the state intentionally stalled and limited the purchasing process. You could only buy what was available, in other words, what the Party considered suitable and appropriate.

This applied to everything from food to underwear style. Major buys could not happen spontaneously or impulsively. Yes, you had to save up to buy a car or a house, but what made the communist economies truly outstanding were the long waiting lists for what the people craved the most – houses, apartments, plots of land and cars.

> *Private ownership was not abolished completely as would be the case in an ideal communist scenario. Even the communists had to make some compromises. People were still allowed to 'own' houses, cottages and cars for their personal use. But they had to prove to be deserving of them first. To get what you really wanted – in due time - required a spotless personal record and limitless patience.*

It is not surprising that in such an environment of unmet needs, the black market and grey economy flourished. Not all could be controlled or eliminated, and where there is demand, humans will find a way of meeting it.

Tradesmen, like carpenters and bricklayers or hairdressers and cosmeticians, traded their craft for bartered goods on weekends, away from the preying eyes of the party. Entrepreneurial souls always knew how to get their hands on what was in short supply and illicitly sell it to those desperate enough to pay a prime price.

It is true that nobody was starving during communism, but nobody flourished or prospered either. The propaganda slogan 'For a Better Tomorrow with Socialist Production' did little to appease people.

# CONSOLIDATE CULTURE

## "I CARRY THE BARS WITHIN ME."

FRANZ KAFKA

It is no big secret that culture is a potent force that shapes the world. It is a source of hope, elation and desire. To truly dominate a society, you need to command control over its cultural expressions. Above all, you need to control those who produce it. Communist governments all around the world were not just building a political system, they were building a new culture, fit for the one and only Red Empire.

Although the idea of building a perfect society, where no one was better or worse than anybody else, was noble, its implementation was far less humane than the vision it promised to create. The communist society, which was based on the pillars of equality and justice for all, was also a place where one had to sacrifice their individuality completely.

There was to be one culture, one way of thinking, one way of speaking and one way of being. For all to be equal, all had to be made the same.

*Real life is more complicated and messy than any utopian doctrine can ever account for or aspire to admit. No two people are alike. We all came to this world as individuals, not as cogs in a faceless machine. We all see, feel and experience the world individually, which means that we also have different desires, talents and tastes. To believe that a single central authority has the right and means to fit everyone into a single blueprint is as naïve as it is cruel to the human being.*

The Communist Party of Czechoslovakia set out to do the impossible and persevered in pushing their unrealistic agenda until the very end. In practice, this meant that all diversity was to be removed, not only when it came to politics but also to culture and self-expression. A universal greyness was to descend upon the once diverse and colorful mosaic of Czechoslovakia.

After the First World War, Czechoslovakia had more Hungarians and Germans than Slovaks as a result of being a part of the former Austria-Hungary. This was a dangerous fact for a young republic seeking to establish itself.

The fracturing of a post-WWII Europe brought an opportunity to deal with this inconvenient problem. Czechoslovakia, among other Central European countries, began ethnic purges. The expulsions of the ethnic Germans were followed by the Hungarian-Slovak population exchanges in a transnational effort to prevent ethnic tensions, and the eruption of another conflict.

Although the wheels had been set in motion even before the communists took power, they sure knew how to harness the social mood to justify the obliteration of difference. This time it took the form of doing away with the bourgeoisie. These individuals stood in the way of the creation of a single and unified culture. They were also in possession of the country's tangible assets.

With the Germans and the Hungarians removed, and the Jewish community devastated after the Second World War, the nobility and bourgeoisie (read Czechoslovak middle class) were the next targets in line. And they lost it all – their titles, their lands, their glamour and their power. Professional demotions and property confiscations administered a severe and final blow to the community that had once ruled and governed the region.

At the same time, the quickly industrializing towns and cities needed workers. It was the perfect opportunity to alter the dynamics and demographics of society, once and for all.

The already weak remaining upper and middle classes were confronted with an influx of workers from the countryside. The incoming mass brought with them a very different kind of culture, that of the worker and the peasant.

The unskilled working mass found itself esteemed with new status. The workers and the peasants were no longer the lowest of the low, a label that no human being deserves, ever. On the contrary they were now the socially privileged proletariat.

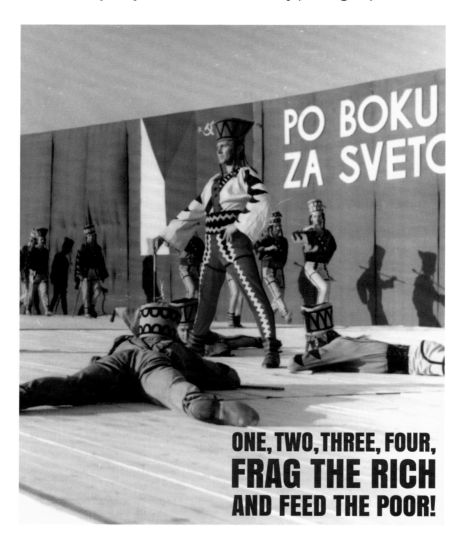

ONE, TWO, THREE, FOUR,
FRAG THE RICH
AND FEED THE POOR!

For centuries, the needs and desires of these people had been pushed aside, but now fate was on their side. The tables of the uncompromising hierarchy had finally turned. The culture of the proletariat was now not only in vogue, it was the only option. In communism, the proletariat became the ruling class, the class that set the compulsory standards and values for everyone else. One of the popular slogans of the era "Every cook should learn to govern the state" says it all.

The grand days of the aristocracy were over, as were the refined tastes of the bourgeoisie. The sophistication and diversity of the past had to be sacrificed in order to create a society that would be a true fit for the new era.

As the workers and peasants laid out the new values, standards and morals, the foundations for making everyone the same on the class spectrum were laid out, and it was just the beginning.

> *The great elimination of wealth came with its one unique pros and cons. On the one hand, the culture, customs and knowledge of several layers of society were sadly forever lost. On the other, the rural population of Slovakia, the former peasants, farm hands and petty farmers, who had suffered a great deal of injustice for centuries, awoke to a promise of a dignified life. Unfortunately, meeting that promise was another matter. Old habits die hard, and the feudal contempt for the peasant lingered on, even during communism.*

Having dealt with the uncomfortable classes, the brownnosers of the imperialist West, the system of elimination moved on to its next culprit: the individual. In communism, individuality was not welcome in any way, shape or form.

A good Czechoslovak was to not have any personal opinions, views, concerns or even style, taste or preference. Instead, they were expected to embody a universal, party approved, fictional standard of the perfect socialist worker.

The principal duty of every Czechoslovak man and woman was to commit to the building of the communist dream in work, body and mind. What did that mean? He or she had to be physically able, mentally subdued and complacent to the values of the regime.

Failure to do so was punished. In Czechoslovakia, being anything else was not a matter of healthy diversity, it was portrayed as wrong. Why?

People who had a mind of their own, from artists to scientists and from bus drivers to chefs, were feared by the regime for being insubordinate. Such individuals were inclined to think and act for themselves and this made them dangerous, especially, to the communist mission to build a society where everyone would be the same.

This ruled out not only the independent souls craving to express their uniqueness, but also all those with any physical or mental imperfections. Those deemed socially undesirable faced some of the greatest injustices. Rather then integrate these members into society, the communists decided to turn a blind eye on their lives and hardships.

> *The state did not cater to the needs of the disabled. Stairs, narrow hallways and tiny elevators made it impossible for wheelchair users to participate in daily life. As a result, people who did not live up to the ideal, healthy worker prototype were forced to reside in asylums so as not to bother society with their imperfections. When out of sight, it was easier to pretend they did not exist.*

Forget about standing out from the crowd in any way.

The impossibility of expressing one's individuality led to a collective schizophrenia. Czechoslovaks would parrot the Party truths in public, but harbor different thoughts in their minds and hearts in private. Double speak made life easier. It allowed the people to maintain the façade of being the perfect workers when necessary. But, it also came at a cost.

> *The shaming and punishing of those who do not conform is not unique to communism. The fear of being left out and the desire to fit in have been sealed into our psyche for a very long time. At the roots of humanity, when survival depended on everyone pulling on the same rope, individuals who were different were chased out of a tribe.*

> *During challenging times, like those of famine or war, but also individual moments of hardship, we have a tendency*

*to revert to the primordial instinct to be one of the pack. We all do have an innate drive to fit in as survival has a greater chance as part of the tribe.*

Some people lost orientation of who they were and what they stood for. Moreover, the mix of suppressed individualism and spoon-fed education proved to be a lethal cocktail. Subject to control tactics since their early education, Czechoslovaks were paralyzed when it came to making a decision, whether it was about holidays, buying a car or moving to a new home. Never allowed to think for themselves, adults had a hard time coping when they had to use their own brains.

Ironically, although communist Czechoslovakia was built on collectivist principles, it was not a cohesive and united society. The Party took great care to implement the divide and rule strategy, to prevent people from coming together and toppling the regime over.

By far, the most effective emotion to fragment a society is fear. People who live in a state of fear express great loyalty to anyone who brings them a semblance of security. The Czechoslovaks were no exception to the rule; they mistook the imposter for the real thing. Genuine safety and security in life was replaced with a mere feeling of relief.

After the war, Czechoslovakia was a broken nation fearing for its own survival. The communists simply added to this insecurity through systematic use of terror. The Party was both a villain and a hero, much to the confusion of the population. People yearned to be saved and to be protected. They were seeking the proverbial knight in shining armor to save them, and they were willing to give away their power of self-determination in exchange.

The Iron Curtain was first and foremost in people's minds. It was a state of powerlessness that kept Czechoslovaks scared of their own shadow. If there was no self-trust, there could be no trust of the other, and therefore no sense of solidarity or ability to work together. This is how the few controlled the many, for close to half a century.

*Emotions are unpredictable, uncontroll-able and capable of bringing down regimes. Anger is dangerous. The Party feared public emotions as the devil fears holy water.*

*To thwart any impulse of bravery or hope, the apparatchiks went out of their way to create an environment hostile to any form of feeling, other than numb indif-ference. No emotion, positive or negative, was safe to feel. Anger was cut at the root and so was happiness. A happy person is very difficult to control.*

*A socialist population was to be sober and serious. Communism was about living a life of service, and with service came suffering. Those who had the au-dacity to smile with their teeth showing, or to laugh in public, were treated with contempt.*

# A BOY WHO REFUSED TO ACCEPT HIS FATE

*Karel was a teenager when communism took over Czecho-slovakia. The tense atmosphere of a regime that knew no jokes was becoming unbearable for a young man with a great many dreams and aspirations. He was not ready to give them up and satisfy himself with a monotonous life from which only death would relieve him.*

*Together with his friend, Karel prepared a plan. It took a year, but finally in October 1949, they were ready to execute their very own 'freedom mission.' Karel left home as usual, early in the morning to go to school. But instead of turning right, as was expected, he set out on a daring and dangerous journey to flee the regime that wanted to clip his wings.*

*In the early morning of the chosen day the two boys crossed the Czech-German border. They were lucky – it was harvest time, and the fields were full of workers. In the maze of wheat, nobody even noticed the two young men.*

*What a relief it was when they crossed the border and were arrested by the German police. They had made it! But also, how heart-breaking it must have been to leave behind their parents and friends, without even saying goodbye.*

*Going from camp to camp, the life of a refugee was not glamorous. Eventually, Karel made it to Austalia. He never became bitter because he lost everything, but accepted that the way of life in the old country did not suit him and that leaving it came at a price. Karel also admired the people who stayed and survived in Czechoslovakia.*

# GIVE
## SHELTER and WORK to EVERYONE

### MANKIND MUST FIRST OF ALL EAT, DRINK, HAVE SHELTER AND CLOTHING, BEFORE IT CAN PURSUE POLITICS, SCIENCE, ART, RELIGION, ETC."

FRIEDRICH ENGELS

Communism was not all about whipping people into obedience. The Party approach to governing used carrots, as well as sticks. The Party sugar-coated the deal and gave people a ground- breaking promise. Every good worker shall have a warm and comfortable home. As simple as it sounds, it was a master stroke. State-guaranteed lodgings were a promise worth more than heavenly gold, in a country picking itself from the ashes of the war.

The Party stuck by its word and with the fulfilment of the promise came a lifestyle revolution.

For centuries, the lives of Slovaks were rooted in the countryside and followed a rural rhythm. Slovak society was still predominantly agrarian at the end of the Second World War, and well behind the standards of living in Western Europe and even elsewhere in the region. Communism brought with it the first systematic industrialization. The modernization of Slovakia addressed large social inequalities and improved living standards for millions of Slovaks.

Food, consumer items and services became more abundant and, more importantly, widely accessible to the masses. No one was to be hungry, homeless or jobless in socialism. This promise also kept the public pacified and obedient. People were loyal to the state, because the government did take care of them.

Even though it was the Czechs that elected the communists into power, once in office, loyalty to the regime was much stronger in the Slovak part of the republic. They were grateful to the Party for making their lives significantly and visibly more secure.

> *All in all, by 1965 over 500,000 Slovaks were employed in industry, in comparison to just over 200,000 in 1948. The widespread access to education to formerly agrarian populations also saw a change in social dynamics. By the 1970s, over one third of the Slovak population had graduated from secondary school.*

The modernization of the countryside spurred migration movements, as people started moving to larger cities to find employment in the booming industrial sector. This catalysed a massive rural to urban relocation. Naturally, the regime had to provide new accommodation to meet the rising demand.

# ŽIVOTNÁ ÚROVEŇ

Ide o to, zaistiť ďalší rozvoj našej vlasti, šťast-
ný a spokojný život pre súčasné i budúce gene-
rácie. To je cieľ, za dosiahnutie ktorého stojí za
to bojovať.

Gustáv Husák

V roce 1980 bolo v SSR
viac ako % všetkých bytov
postavené po r. 1946,
80,9 % všetkých bytov
malo vodovod, 76,4 %
kúpeľňu, 34,4 % plyn zo
siete a 55,2 % ústredné
kúrenie. V rokoch 1961
až 1980 vzrástla vybave-
nosť domácnosti chladnič-
kou z 9,1 % na 85,8 %,
práčkou z 44,2 % na 82,3 %,
televízorom z 11,1 % na
85,2 %, osobným automo-
bilom v rokoch 1970–1980
z 12,3 % na 31,3 % Počet
telefónnych staníc na 100
obyvateľov vzrástol
v rokoch 1948–1982
z 1,19 na 18,02 staníc.
V rokoch 1960–1981
vzrástol počet študentov
na gymnáziách, stredných
odborných a odborných
školách z 90 332 na
175 468 a na vysokých
školách v dennom
štúdiu z 20 494 na 59 256
študentov.

# RISING LIVING STANDARDS –
# A GOAL WORTH FIGHTING FOR!

*Do you remember the strategy of systematically removing 'uncomfortable' Czechoslovaks like democrats, bourgeois, priests and all the rest of the imperialist vermin after the coup of 1948?*

*These people left behind many empty homes and the communist leadership was quick to find a highly pragmatic and convenient use for their flats and houses. The drones of the new labor force were pouring into cities to fill vacancies in the booming industrial sector and needed somewhere to live.*

*The influx of the rural population was so quick and so large that the communist machine could not produce new homes quickly enough. Luckily, they had at their disposition all those confiscated flats. These were quickly redistributed to the incoming petty farmers and their farm hands.*

A construction fever of quintessentially Eastern Bloc housing estates, the signature architecture of the era, began. But that was not enough, the Party also needed an interim solution to the pressing need for apartments. The men in grey came up with a particularly cunning plan that would allow them to do so much more than just address the housing shortage.

Private apartments and houses, particularly those that were still in ownership of 'inconvenient members' of society, were measured. Those that were regarded as too large for single-family use, were classified as dual-family arrangements. Their owners, often families that had lived there for generations, were forced to open their homes to the new builders of the republic, and co-habitate with complete strangers.

The old bourgeois families had no right to protest against such an invasion of their privacy. Laborers and high-ranking Party officials were two of the most highly regarded professions in in Czechoslovakia. It was both an honor and a privilege to live with them.

In practice, it looked more like this. Upon order of the state, a doctor's family would all of a sudden have to make room for that of a coal miner's, arriving to Bratislava from a faraway mountain village. The shock was often followed by humiliation, when privacy and personal boundaries were blurred. Class differences also resulted in unnecessary conflicts and abuse, often at the expense of the original homeowners.

This was an unmissable opportunity to instill the principles of communism into the daily lives and routines of the fresh city dwellers. Many of these workers and peasants had never lived in towns before, let alone large cities. Above all, the policy completely altered the dynamics and demography of urban centers, which is exactly what the Party wanted – to irreversibly replace the city bourgeois with a pure and trustworthy proletariat.

But this was just a quick-fix housing solution. The Party had a much grander vision in mind. Czechoslovakia was to become the embodiment of the ideology's commandments and these were to be set in stone in unmistakable socialist tower bloc estates. One of the largest ones in Central Europe was erected in Bratislava.

An international contest was announced in 1969. Eighty-four architectural proposals from 19 different countries were submitted to the Czechoslovak government. They all presented their visions of urban development, that later became known as the 'Bronx of Bratislava'. A Japanese team suggested for that land south of the Danube be modelled into an assortment of low-rise modern buildings. Others suggested a tasteful new Danubian Venice.

Both projects were visionary, the issue was that urban aesthetics were not high on the list of priorities for the Czechoslovak government. In the end, it all came down to cost and timing. The Party needed to build housing for its proletariat, and it needed to do so quickly. The result of the construction fever, a prime example of the thinking of the times, was the housing district of Petrzalka. Construction commenced in 1973.

*While in the West tower blocks only hous-
ed disadvantaged families, in the Eastern Bloc they became immensely popular.
Variants of Petrzalka sprouted across
Czechoslovakia and the entire Eastern
Bloc. These were palaces for the workers
and it was in Czechoslovakia they sprouted up the largest scale, per capital. Over
a million new tower blocks were built
between 1953 and 1991.*

These tower blocks made of pre-fabricated panels represented communism to the tee. They were a signpost of
equality understood as uniformity. The district's inhabitants
had identical flats, manufactured with such precision that
they were virtually indistinguishable from one another. To a
visitor, the settlement still feels like an endless maze of
dreary sameness.

*Few remember that Petrzalka, the eyesore
of the Bratislava skyline, was once a little
paradise. Before the monotonous rectan-
gular panel blocks of concrete were raised,
Petrzalka was home to greenery and
leisure. Public gardens, idyllic apricot and
cherry orchards, old-fashioned fun-fairs
and river beaches much beloved by the
locals could be found there. A true emblem
of the era, Petrzalka swallowed the joyful
playfulness and carefree atmosphere of
the cute urban haven, and replaced it
with cold monotonous greyness.*

# MAKE
# THEM
# FORGET

## "THE STRUGGLE OF MAN AGAINST POWER IS THE STRUGGLE OF MEMORY AGAINST FORGETTING."

MILAN KUNDERA

The regime did not take kindly to any remnants of the past, imperial or democratic. The past was all about class exploitation, a memory that was not worth remembering, which is why it had to be buried. The intention was not just to alleviate past injustice and pain, but also to trigger a total Czechoslovak 'reset'.

By wiping the collective memory clean, the regime wanted to erase any good and positive associations with what was before. All previous economic, social and ideological development was to be deleted. If there was nothing to remind people of the past, then nothing would challenge the communist narrative of the future.

The strategy was two-fold. First, the Party diligently placed blame for all that was ever wrong in the country on the exploitive ways of the former elites. History was full of such examples. However, they also channeled a great amount of energy into inconspicuous strategies devaluing the role of memory by corrupting self-trust.

If the people did not trust the validity of their own experiences, they could be easier manipulated. Without memories, it was difficult to question what the Party was saying. Without access to empirical evidence, like history books and other source materials that proved otherwise, the people had a hard time differentiating fact from fiction.

To wipe the slate clean and start afresh was enticing but

removing the past all together is dangerous. It is like cutting a tree's roots, and thereby throwing an entire nation off center.

All visual traces of the past were to be removed, especially any reminders of bourgeois and aristocratic lifestyles. Colorful private villas, as well as palaces of the aristocracy, that had been carefully maintained and proudly passed down through generations, were seized.

Some quickly fell into intentional neglect as the state had no desire, or professional capacity, to look after them. Others adopted a new more 'sensible' purpose. Synagogues were turned into storage, chapels were used as impromtu cinemas and chateaus became hen houses. The rest was demolished as a political statement.

Many towns lost their soul entirely. The regime stripped these places of their flesh and rebuilt them again in the aesthetic concept of the new ideology - bulky, grey and functionalist. Furniture, porcelain and works of art were confiscated. Some families removed their family heirlooms and hid them away in basements and cottages. Others jumped on the bandwagon and willingly burned their own antique furniture in a symbolic gesture of loyalty to the regime.

The advent of communism offered an opportunity to part with the past and make way for a better and more equal future. Yet, it was not enough to remove, destroy and lock away all signposts of aristocracy. The regime had to replace the past with a carefully contrived present, one where the Party anchored its supremacy over the collective through a heroic narrative.

Statues of Stalin, Lenin and home-grown leaders cropped up to penetrate the visual landscape of public spaces. Framed portraits of cult personalities hung on people's walls, in schools and offices. Streets throughout the country were renamed to suit the vision of the era. Soon they bore the names of key communist personalities, events and places.

Bratislava got Stalin's Square, Gottwald's Street and a street named after Victorious February, among many others. There was no hiding from the ideology, not even on the most remote street corners of rural Slovakia.

*Slovaks may be one of Europe's youngest nations, but the region they inhabit has a long and tumultuous past. In the last 100 years, Slovakia has gone through six regime changes: the collapse of the Empire of Austria-Hungary, the rise of democratic Czechoslovakia, the establishment of the Nazi Slovak State, followed by socialist Czechoslovakia to an independent Slovakia, that willingly ascended to the European Union.*

*All the structural and ideological changes have left their mark on the cities and towns of the region. Every single regime re-branded Slovakia as well. Bratislava, for example a city located at the crossroads of Europe, and regimes as the last century proved, has borne several names.*

*Hungarians called it Pozsony, while the Germans embraced it as Pressburg, but the Slovaks referred to it as Presporok. After WWI, it was nearly renamed Wilson's City, as a token of gratitude to the American President who backed the Czechoslovak liberation.*

*The city only received its contemporary name of Bratislava in 1919, in honor of the brethren union between the Czechs and Slovaks, in the newly-founded republic. The name can be interpreted as 'glory to brotherhood'.*

The grandeur of the imperial past and the beauty of the bourgeois taste and lifestyle were replaced by architectural brutalism. Massive concrete fortress-like structures became the new blueprint for building anything from ministries to kindergartens.

Living quarters and work spaces were to be first and foremost functionalist, not pretty or comfortable. Slovak town and cities are still a visible reminder of what it looks like when an ideologically informed - construction fever grips a society.

> *Freedom Square in Bratislava is one of the most intact displays of this architecture mania. Flanked by stark buildings, its focal point is a fountain, a large stainless-steel structure weighing over 12 tons in the shape of a massive linden flower.*
>
> *The communists skillfully leveraged culture symbolism into their propaganda. The hijacking of national codes was also a useful tool for embedding their messages into the collective subconscious.*
>
> *The totem of the linden weaves its way back to the pre-Christian era. It is a cultural emblem that continues to be celebrated as the sacred tree of Slavs, as well as the national tree of Slovakia. It is no surprise that the Party reached for it to brand and validate itself.*

No town was left untouched, but it was indeed the Slovak capital of Bratislava that was to become the showcase of communist achievements in Czechoslovakia. A drastic architectural make-over turned into more of a botched-up surgery than a beautification project began.

First, Bratislava received a lofty new title: 'the city of peace'. This slogan also served as a subconscious reminder to whom the Slovaks were indebted too. Their liberation from Hitler and good fortune had not come on its own.

In accordance with this vision, many doves of peace in various forms, shapes and sizes were placed throughout the city. From road signs flanking the highway coming into Bratislava, to large and small monuments and sculptures, the dove of peace appeared everywhere. However, in the cauldron of fear and insecurity, nothing could go smoothly.

When dove signs were put up, the icing on the cake of the re-branding effort, they were facing the wrong direction – the West. This caused an uproar among the apparatchiks.

Although we may never know whether this 'mistake' was done unintentionally or as an act of silent and defiant protest, the Party did not take its chances. Whether deliberate or innocent, it was too loaded with geopolitical double-meanings to not correct. Swiftly, the dove sculptures were re-oriented to face Moscow.

A great many new socialist landmarks were lavished on Bratislava to make the new regime more visible and the past as insignificant as possible. The most controversial of them was the Slovak National Uprising Bridge, nicknamed the UFO, due to its flying saucer shaped tower. Across the Soviet bloc, it was celebrated as a masterpiece of communist architectural achievement. The bridge was officially opened in August 1972 and marked the 28th anniversary of the Slovak revolt against the Nazi regime.

But, the bridge came at a high price to the historic heritage of the city and the country. Much of the Old Town had to be sacrificed to make room for its modernity. It was also a testament to the ignorance and brutality of the regime.

The original idea put forth was both innocent and pragmatic. A new bridge would be erected to unify the city on both sides of the river. The structure would merge with the architecture of the city and cause minimal damage to the core of the capital's ancient heritage.

This proposal was rejected on the grounds of being too costly. Instead, a much simpler, less time consuming and most cost-effective construction was approved, in the true spirit of communist rationalism. After all, the bridge was not meant to be beautiful, but to serve a utilitarian purpose. Little did it matter that it would cut its concrete trail through a neighborhood dating back to the glory of Habsburg Austria and the glitz of the Kingdom of Hungary.

To top it off, the structure and roadway running through it destroyed an area that was once the beating heart of the city's famous Jewish quarter. It had been the home of one of Central Europe's most iconic synagogues and pilgrimage places of the Jewish faith.

The communists gleamed at the thought that the new bridge and road would pass right by St Martin's cathedral, a coronation beacon of many Hungarian kings and queens.

> *The communists had their eyes set on exactly this location for a reason. They despised reminders of the aristocracy, just as much as they disdained any group that did subordinate completely. Jews were the emblem of the bourgeois, a source of imperialist capitalism and cosmopolitanism.*
>
> *Enveloped by a once lively Jewish quarter, the area north of the cathedral became the underbelly of Bratislava following the Holocaust. With the Jewish population mostly annihilated, the neighborhood soon fell into squalor. The empty houses attracted the city's poorest inhabitants, as well as a seedy red-light district.*
>
> *In dire need of rehabilitation, it was no longer held in high regard by the public. The cadre counted on this apathy and even encouraged it when putting forth its new architectural plan that would destroy its legacy and rock the foundations of the Cathedral, the icon of the city.*

In its final version, the bridge was admired by many a local and even praised as 'the Slovak Building of the 20th Century'. Abroad, the bridge was revered as a mark of modernity. It even inspired a copy-cat in the Soviet state Latvia. An almost identical UFO bridge can be seen in the capital city, Riga.

*Today, the bridge houses a sought-after restaurant with spectacular views of the Danube, the second largest river in Europe. However, it was not supposed to be there according to the original plan. The government feared it would plant the wrong idea in people's heads.*

*Looming 1,000 feet above ground, Slovak restaurant diners would be offered a unique vantage point of nearby Austria, a gateway to the free West. It was so temptingly close ... How difficult could it be to escape? With so many defections, the Party was serious about taking all necessary precautions. It even banned paragliding in Bratislava.*

Another such architectural gem for people to marvel at was the radio building shaped like an upside-down pyramid. It is a symbolic testament to the ideology of communism. It turned the old world order upside down. Communism inverted the past social hierarchy of society. It was to be the rule of all, the peasants and workers. The building that still houses the national radio broadcast made its way on a list of the 30 ugliest buildings in the world. So much for the communist's architectural tastes. The collective forgetting also took a more subtle turn.

In order for the population to denounce their past, family histories had to be erased especially those that bore any trace of aristocracy. The state exercised pressure on individuals to forget who their predecessors were. To make sure inconvenient memories would remain forever buried, access to genealogical information was systematically disrupted.

Precious birth, death and marriage certificates, which tracked family histories for centuries, were stored in appalling conditions. State archives were intentionally left damp and humid, a perfect environment to permanently damage the fragile registries. There was no central registry and documents were scattered across the country to make it difficult for people to access them. As if that was not enough, the archives were every now and again flooded or even set on fire.

Eventually the tactics achieved their objective. By the time communism collapsed, most Slovaks with ties to nobility were unaware of their origins. Even today, that is many Slovaks today, do not understand why anyone would even like to know where their roots come from. What is the point, they ask?

# BETTER SAFELY FORGET THAN BE SORRY FOR REMEMBERING

*Having a Hungarian name meant having a problem in interwar Czechoslovakia. Having an aristocratic Hungarian surname in communist Czechoslovakia was a very bad idea.*

*After 1918, people were incentivized and even forced to 'Slovakize' their surnames. It made their lives easier and careers possible. Hungarian-sounding names were simply unwelcomed in a republic striving to build solid and purely Czechoslovak foundations.*

*The era of forgetting continued in socialism. Any connection to the ruling aristocracy, nobility or landed gentry was a nuisance. These people were seen as exploiters of the workers and peasants and the bedrock of inequality, according to communist ideology. As a result, memories that survived the first wave of the national memory-wipe, took another hard hit after WWII.*

*Here is a story of one family forgetting. The town of Vrutky in northern Slovakia was an important railway junction at the time of the Austro-Hungarian Empire. Back then, it carried the name Ruttka, in honor of an important noble family that owned lands and stately homes even outside the region.*

*After 1918, the dynasty first hid the family's crest. When the communists took power, the family disremembering escalated. Some members of the Ruttkay family changed their surname to Rutkovsky - much more Slovak and ordinary. Better safe than sorry. The legacy and heritage of the elite family was not talked about or passed down to the next generation. Little by little, the silence buried the memories. It is only now that surviving family members feel safe to begin re-discovering the fragments of their past.*

# MEDALS AND COSMONAUTS

Fear is a powerful tool, but people also need a little cheer, a little hope and a lot of faith to keep going, working and building the communist dreamland. But, how could the regime ignite a colorless and passionless mass? By striking the timeless chord of competitiveness and the human desire to be better than everyone else. The Cold War offered plenty of opportunities to make Czechoslovaks proud to belong to the communist East, or even be better than the rest of it.

This was the era of the relentless race for international prestige, where the East and the West both obsessed about outperforming their rival. Czechoslovakia too was gripped by the Cold War fever, proving who was the strongest, the most progressive, the most ingenious and the most visionary.

The international competition for global dominance took its most spectacular turn in the field of science. Little by little, heavy investment in research and development began to catch up with the achievements of the industrialized West. When the USSR developed its own atomic bomb and successfully detonated it in remote Kazakhstan in 1949, it ended the security of the American monopoly.

The Cold War game was about to get very serious, and it would not stop with the arms race, although each side put in a lot of effort keeping up with and out-stocking the other in deadly weapons.

LONG LIVE SOCIALIST INTERNATIONALISM

*Once the Soviets upped their innovation game, the power equilibrium shifted in their favor. Now, there was no longer one, but two nuclear super-powers, each armed with enough weaponry to annihilate the other.*

*The US and the USSR prevented planetary catastrophe through the precept of the MAD (mutually assured destruction) doctrine. If either side was attacked by the other, it would retaliate with equal or greater measure, resulting in total destruction and unacceptable losses, on both sides of the equation.*

*That calculation kept global peace and the Earth in existence. The entire globe was crossing its fingers, hoping the gentlemen in Washington D.C. and Moscow never went MAD.*

Matching the enemy was not enough; Soviet leader Nikita Khrushchev set his sight on the sky and beyond. The Cold War catalyzed an unprecedented space race between America and the USSR.

The Soviet vision came to fruition when the USSR became the first country to launch a satellite into space. The triumph was soon followed by more victories. The Soviets managed to get the first man into space in 1961, followed by the first woman just two short years later. Yuri Gagarin and Valentina Tereshkova became the heroes of the USSR and of the entire communist world.

Sending the first man into the universe forever immortalized the Soviet Union as the conqueror of the cosmos. Gagarin became an international hero and a token of communist success. It would take another 8 years for the Americans to respond to the challenge, by landing the first humans on the Moon in 1969.

# THE FIRST CZECHOSLOVAK IN SPACE

*Czechoslovakia also staked a claim in the cosmos. Vladimir Remek, the perfect embodiment of Czechoslovakia with a Slovak father and a Czech mother, was hand-picked by the Soviets as part of the wider recruitment activity run in the countries of the socialist brotherhood. Vladimir was inducted into the Interkosmos program and relocated to Moscow, where he trained at the space research facility 'Star City'.*

*On March 2, 1978, Vladimir was the first cosmonaut from a country other than the US or the USSR to be sent into the solar system. He remained in flight for a total of 7 days on the space ship Soyuz-28, carrying the Czechoslovak flag into the cosmos. In an unforgettable message to the people of Earth, he stated: "we have a good chance of living in peace for a long time" via a live transmission.*

*Some say that sending Remek into space ten years after the 1968 occupation was an appeasement effort by the Soviets when anti-Russian feelings were still rampant. The Soviet and Czechoslovak leadership were quick to utilize this incredible achievement as political capital. During the live transmission, both Brezhnev and Husak proudly greeted the young astronaut from Earth, to which Husak boasted, "long live socialist internationalism!".*

The quest for the stars captured the imagination of the globe and ignited political ambition. The space race soon became a space war. Launching large rockets into the dark abyss of the unknown, became a regular ritual accompanied by much political ado. Each accomplishment, and also every failure, spoke about the military might of the contestants, leaving no one in doubt about who ruled the day and the planet.

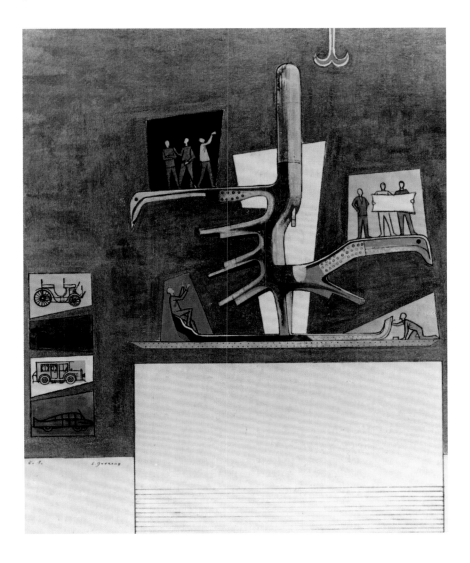

The Cold War was a battle in the arena of technology. Both East and West were anxious to have the better and shinier toys paraded as the only and the best. The competition brought out the worst of men's egos, as the pendulum swung between arrogance and genuine joy when something was achieved that was previously unthinkable. It was a grand ideological show off that rocked both camps.

Grooming the next cohort was a meticulous effort.

The entire Communist Bloc prided itself on the achievements of its sport superstars and focused much attention and care into their grooming from very young age. The most talented prodigies were hand-picked and entered into special programs crafted to develop their excellence to new heights. To be scouted as a potential representative of the nation was a big deal for children, and an even bigger deal for their parents.

The Soviets and their allies took sporting perfection very seriously. The international success of Eastern Bloc athletes validated the legitimacy and superiority of the regime. Athletic prowess was synonymous with virility, health and the potency of the communist population. Sports schemes were generously financed to grow winners, in all disciplines.

Coaches, physical trainers, injury therapists, psychologists and top of the range athletic infrastructure were made available to future athletic champions - anything to beat the wimpy imperialists.

*It was not only sports men and women who were expected to keep fit. Being active, in sport and in nature, was part of the prerequisite of being an able-bodied, hard-working, well-rounded socialist citizen, able to defend the motherland.*

*The medals and trophies of Czechoslovak athletes inspired the youth of the republic to keep healthy, strong and fit. Even if they would not make it all the way as national representatives, their physical stamina would feed into the military and economy. This would make the country and regime all the more powerful.*

WE MUST SET **EVERY WORLD RECORD!**

Gold medalist and world champions affirmed the superiority of the Eastern Bloc, not just in ideology, but in the biological supremacy of its human capital. Eastern Bloc representatives had to be the best, the fastest, the strongest, the fittest and the shiniest.

Every time an athlete stood on a prestigious international podium with a gold medal, it was not only their individual victory but one for the entire communist world. The USSR and its satellite states amassed an impressive amount of Olympic gold medals, world championships and world record titles during those 40 years.

The Soviet Union outperformed the USA by 78 gold Olympic medals between 1952 and 1988. The Eastern Bloc also ruled over the ice hockey world with unquestionable primacy. For over twenty years, the world knew only two ice hockey champions - the USSR and Czechoslovakia. It was as if the gold was reserved for them, and them only.

*The Eastern Bloc was not without its doping scandals, which the communist governments all over the world explained away as false accusations. They were but conspiracy theories born out of the West's jealousy over the athletic prowess of the East. In the socialist world, there was no such thing as per-formance enhancing steroids. Athletes were only given 'vitamins'.*

Needless to so say, ethics and good sportsmanship were not high on the priory list. What took precedence was achievement. The regime created athletic machines to win medals for the socialist league of nations. The greater the competitive advantage, the better.

As far as Czechoslovakia was concerned, the Eastern Bloc was the world's no.1 at everything. Nothing else would do.

# THE CHERNOBYL TRAGEDY

*Failures and imperfections were hushed up. It might seem humorous and at most times it was, but every now and again this cocktail of arrogance, ignorance and downright immaturity cost lives. The tragedy of Chernobyl in April 1986 is a sad reminder of what happens when the stubborn obsession to 'pretend' to be the masters of the universe grows out of proportion. The environmental disaster would affect Czechoslovakia in a very tangible way.*

*Following the nuclear explosion late in the night on April 25 and the release of a deadly radioactive cloud upon Europe, Moscow weighed its options. It concluded that warning the world was politically inconvenient and a threat to Soviet perfectionism. The health and lives of millions of people seemed like a small price to pay for protecting the political pride of the regime.*

*The Kremlin hoped that if it did not acknowledge the event in northern Ukraine, no one would ever find out about the catastrophe. And so, the communist leadership armed itself with silence, as the radioactive wave spread across Europe.*

*It was Sweden that first rang the alarm, when it detected heighted radiation levels on its territory. A national investigation followed and the Soviets were forced to admit that something had indeed happened in their part of the world. Although the communists had to admit to an accident, they were still not prepared to recognize the tragedy in its full and gigantic proportion.*

*Initially, the concerns of the West were formally dismissed as banal, or as an exaggeration by imperialists. According to Moscow, there was nothing to be feared. The explosion was a minor accident that was being promptly and effectively managed. All was under control. The Kremlin then released an official statement. The brief was to make people believe that the Western panic was all but a storm in a teacup:*

> *There has been an accident at the Chernobyl Nuclear Power Plant. One of the nuclear reactors was damaged. The effects of the accident are being remedied. Assistance has been provided for any affected people. An investigative commission has been set up.*

*The Czechoslovak government dutifully reported the same version of the 'incident' to its citizens, gambling with their nation's health. But the people knew it was a lie. News of a disaster of high magnitude spread far and fast.*

*Ukraine also neighbored Czechoslovakia, and the people could see the effects of the greatest nuclear tragedy in history for themselves. They saw the color of the sky change, while their laundry drying outside turned a toxic grey. All were signs that something was wrong despite what the Party said.*

*Equipped with little knowledge and tools with how to handle such a catastrophe, they tried their best to protect themselves from the rising radiation. A rumor spread that covering the roof of one's home with mustard would protect the dwelling and its inhabitants from the radioactive cloud floating above.*

*Of course, the magical mustard fell short of its promised effect. The number of miscarriages in the months following the nuclear explosion spiked, as did depression and thyroid gland diseases. At the time, these findings could not be officially linked to the tragic event. We may never actually know just how much the Chernobyl affected, and more importantly how it still affects, the population of Eastern Europe.*

# KEEP THE (COLD) WAR GOING

With time, the East and the West settled into their familiar roles at the opposite poles of the Cold War. This duality became a status quo that reduced the complexity of the world into easy to understand categories of good and evil, friend and foe.

Once the commerce and arms contracts were well established, the arrangement became quite comfortable. It suited many interest groups, on both sides of the divide. However, public opinion still had to be swayed. Hence, a state of permanent tension, danger and urgency had to be created and maintained.

The Cold War was the Golden Age of espionage.

Without any real desire to take to arms, but nevertheless unwilling to back down, the East and the West grew chronically paranoid of one another. What do you do in such situation? You spy and you plot to be on top of the game.

The ideological battlefields of the Cold War created plenty of opportunities for spying and an endless supply of enthralling spy stories.

Clandestine operations, ideological assassinations, code names, beautiful women and evasive double agents were the lore of the era. But the tensions were real, and the need to scope out the other side gave rise to the spy dramas that are still so poignantly captured on the silver screen today.

*A great many spy stories from the era remain disputed. One of them talks about a secret CIA surveillance station located just across the Danube River, in free Austria. High atop an unsuspecting hill, the American intelligence services set up a satellite system to eavesdrop on neighboring Czechoslovakia. Their target was*

*Hotel Borik, a high-profile Bratislava venue, still open to guests today.*

*Back then, the hotel was frequented by the most prominent communist officials. This is where the strictly classified folders were analyzed and gentlemen's agreements were arranged. Few knew about this undercover meeting ground, and even fewer about the Western infiltration.*

*The alleged station was also a violation of Austria's political neutrality. The unsavory topic has still not been discussed.*

Czechoslovakia would not miss out on the excitement, providing its fair share of actors for the Cold War melodrama. The STB were busy deploying intelligence officers left, right and center. These men and women would gather information for their motherland, but also for the Kremlin.

At the top of the spy hierarchy were the mysterious agents operating beyond Czechoslovakia, also referred to as 'satellites'. Only the best of the best were sent to the forbidden West. They were not only to collect intelligence material, but also to destabilize Western states through various influence operations in social, cultural, and scholarly arenas.

Subverting the dominant paradigm, instigating local tensions and corrupting decision makers, in addition to financial and electoral systems, were all part of the mission. Human vices, such as sex, money and power, were exploited, while threats, black mail and exposure were control tactics in every agent's arsenal.

*Once abroad, the potential for defection or of being recruited by the other side increased exponentially. Those not prepared to sacrifice their lives for their values could be easily seduced by*

*the sweet fruits of capitalism. That is
why they were rigorously monitored, by
their own people first and foremost.*

The Eastern bloc was rumored to have had some of the best agents in the game.

They were true masters of tradecraft. The clandestine intelligence services needed operatives who could think fast and act even faster. Men and women who could take action on their own initiative, and show no qualms when deception was required, were highly sought after. At the same time, the regime needed spies who also proved reliable when it came to following orders, ideally those who were loyal to the idea of communism.

The career of a spy started with a careful selection process. Those who applied to the STB directly were viewed with suspicion, as was any pro-active civilian behavior. The state preferred to handpick its spies, according to specific profiles. University grounds were amongst the most popular selection grounds. Top performing students, that demonstrated a certain character predisposition, were hand-picked by prospective handlers.

The entire headhunting process was a class act. After all, the intelligence community was made up of individuals with the highest IQ quotas. The process included a senior intelligence officer, a gentleman with a grandiose presence of sophistication and authority, being deployed into the terrain. There he would approach an unsuspecting student, who had already been pre-vetted by the apparatus months in advance.

The mostly male recruits would be invited to attend a special meeting, where an offer would be made to them. In return for using their skill, talent and intelligence to protect morality and peace on the planet, they would receive unheard-of rewards. These included travel, money, status, power and the glamourous lifestyle of a covert operative.

As an agent, they could play an immensely important role. The Cold War was more than a battle of ideologies, it was a battle for civilization. The candidates were told their objective was to contain the advances of the West, and eventually put an end to the senseless greed of the imperialists. The youth were promised the world in turn. The only drawback was that they could never tell anyone about it.

It was a tempting proposal that would make many a young person's head swirl with excitement. Enrolment was a big commitment. Once the offer was made, the recruit was given time to think. Should he or she refuse the offer, their free will would be respected. However, they were to forget that this meeting ever happened.

Those who accepted the offer subscribed to an initiation process that was rolled out across several stages. The beginnings were gentle. Student recruits were expected to keep up with their usual appearances. They were to continue with their normal lives and complete their higher education.

Upon graduation, the spy training swung into full gear. The future intelligence officers had to absolve a special two-year program conducted at a secret academy in a remote location. They were also obliged to learn new tradecraft and technology, and acquire a minimum of two foreign languages equivalent to native speaker fluency.

> *Once a spy, a normal family life was out of question. Secret agents could have many sexual partners, but they were to never surrender their heart and soul to anyone. Their allegiance and loyalty went to the Party. Love was an undesirable weakness and a high-risk liability.*

A life lived in perpetual secrecy had its drawbacks. For many the prolonged social and emotional isolation grew unbearable with time. Some coped with alcohol or drugs, in controlled bouts and micro doses, so that the substances would not affect their performance.

Others became consumed with their profession, moving up the hierarchy at every opportunity. Indeed, some spies ended up marrying, but forever lived double lives. Their spouses and children had no idea what their husband or wife, father or mother did when they were away from home.

# A DOUBLE SPY:
## FROM BRATISLAVA
## TO WASHINGTON

*Bratislavan Karel Koecher is one of the Cold War's most infamous KGB spies. He was one of a very few Eastern Bloc agents to have infiltrated the CIA. Karel was first deployed to the United States as a mole, or a sleeper agent, in 1965. After a few years of inactivity abroad, his loyalty was put to the test when Czechoslovakia was invaded by the Soviet military apparatus.*

*Infuriated by the betrayal of Moscow, Mr Koecher tried to get himself hired by the FBI, proving that even the toughest of spies have emotions. His application was denied. At the time, the FBI was concerned with containing the American mafia and other domestic issues; the small landlocked Czechoslovakia, was not high in their agenda.*

*Spies do not give up easily and Karel's perseverance paid off eventually. His skillset was eventually acquired by the CIA in Virginia, where he was to act as an interpreter and analyst. This thrust the spy for the Soviets into a unique vantage point.*

*Karel gained access to the agency's classified documents, including insights into their strategic tactics, global alliances and covert operations. Ironically, one of his tasks was to identify Soviet officials and affiliates in Latin America, who proved willing to turn coats and work for the West. This was a position he had sought for himself, when he had personally approached the FBI some time before.*

*Once the emotional charge of the Soviet invasion subsided, Karel was back to his old bag of tricks. Like a true opportunist, he decided to continue working for his previous employer, while also collecting a salary from his new one. Double agent Karel would trade information across both sides for many years.*

*Finally, in November 1984, some twenty years after his relocation to the America, Koecher was apprehended and eventually tried for espionage. He pleaded guilty and was given a life sentence. When Moscow learned of the verdict, they decided to reclaim. Karel was too precious to be locked away, luckily for him.*

*Tense negotiations between East and West ensued. Eventually, Karel, his wife and eight other prisoners, were returned to the Eastern Bloc via Berlin, in an iconic exchange of spies. Back in Czechoslovakia, Mr Koecher received a welcome worthy of a Soviet hero. A house, a Western car and a prestigious job were immediately granted to him.*

*Though the mills of God grind slowly, they grind nevertheless. After the fall of the Iron Curtain, the anti-hero Karel disappeared into the abyss of forgotten history. Such is the destiny of spies.*

# PART
# THREE

# FROM RED CRADLE TO RED GRAVE: EVERY DAY LIFE IN CZECHOSLOVAKIA

THE ULTIMATE WEAKNESS OF COMMUNISM IS THAT IT ROBS MAN OF THAT QUALITY WHICH MAKES HIM A MAN.

*MARTIN LUTHER KING JR.*

What was it like to live in a regime that was desperate to control everything and everyone?

For those who have never experienced a totalitarian regime, it might be difficult to understand how a single Party was able to hold on to power for so long. Foreigners often ask why the Czechoslovaks allowed this to happen, and why they allowed it to continue for over four decades? What would it take for them to say 'enough', take their power back and reclaim their freedom? After all, it was millions against a few.

Communist Czechoslovakia was a paradox.

Czechoslovakia was a highly-advanced country, with an educated and cultured population, that caught itself in an invisible cage of fear and manipulation for decades upon decades. The story of Czechoslovakia is a sad tribute to the most sophisticated manipulation and control strategies that communism came up with.

For those 41 long years, the state employed elaborate techniques to break the hearts, minds, bodies and spirits of the people, day by day, and year by year. Yet, it was not all doom and gloom. There was also sweetness, innocence and genuine togetherness that seeped in to sooth the unbearable grey reality.

> *The ideology of communism elevated the collective above the individual. The 'we' always came before the 'me'. Society was to be ruled by the whole. A single individual could not and should not make decisions concerning the greater good of all. The individual's purpose in society was to find his or her place in the 'we'. In the communist vision, this meant blending in and repeating what everyone else did. For better or worse, the collective always knew better. End of discussion.*

How was it possible to survive in a society that invalidated your individuality, feelings and needs? What was it like to be constantly role-playing – at work, at home and at play? Was it possible to create any kind of a safe space, a sanctuary, to shield from the strict, inhumane and controlling regime? The answer is yes. Against all the odds, the people continued to laugh, love and care for one another.

The worst of humanity also brings out the best of humanity. This is why we invite you to explore with us, to find out what it was really like to live in communist Czechoslovakia, from womb to grave. Together, we will relive the good, the bad and the fascinating aspects of waking up and living in communism.

Through the daily grind, we will experience the funny, silly, painful, harsh, exciting and dull moments in a life prescribed by a political party. Take what you read with a grain of salt, but above all, feel for yourself what it was like to make due in a cage of illusion, false promises and ideological verses.

# BIRTHED into Communism

Without people, there are no countries or empires. More tangibly stated, without people, there is no one to rule, nor govern. The Communist Party of Czechoslovakia extracted its power from the number of its subjects, which is why it feared nothing more than depopulation.

The Party was seriously concerned about running out of people to preside over. What is more, Czechoslovakia was lacking in human resources. The shortages in skilled workers was particularly acute for the economy. This was due to the losses of WWII. and the population swaps that saw millions of people leave the republic.

Every newborn Czechoslovak child was a future indispensable cog to the maintenance of the system. The economy needed workers to operate its machineries, just as the state needed clerks to manage its institutions. How else could the system grow? The communists understood early on that human capital was indispensable to their dreams of global expansion.

The bottom line was mercilessly pragmatic. The Party had to incentivize Czechoslovaks to populate the republic. The birth-rate in Czechoslovakia was dropping. The initial excitement that the war had ended brought quite a few little boys and girls to the world, but the baby booming years were short lived.

With the advance of industrialization and the emancipation of women, female subjects were less concerned with giving birth and raising children. They were more attracted to self-actualization in the new jobs and sectors made available to them.

There was also another problem. Although living standards were improving fast, it was not fast enough. Many young Czechoslovaks did not feel inspired to bring new human beings into the grey world they inhabited. Economically speaking, the situation was far from rosy and children were expensive.

The concerned Party was desperate to find a solution quickly. They wanted to find the magic wand that would boost birthrate statistics. But, the reality was blatantly clear. The social, economic and cultural state of Czechoslovakia did not motivate people to pass on their genes to the next generation.

Despite its best propaganda, the state learned it could not order its citizens to procreate on command. Annoyingly enough, there are areas in human life that defy the logic of central planning.

With no other option available to them, the government opted for a long-term investment. Its strategy was to incentivize young couples to birth babies, by providing a more supportive environment to them. It took them a couple of decades to work out the nitty gritty of the process, but finally in 1968 they found the right formula.

Gustav Husak, the man entrusted by the Kremlin to reign in the republic, was the face of a mediocre and passionless communism to the public. However, Husak, was also exceptional when it came to handling crises. It was his policies that marked the beginning of the most significant baby boom in the region.

The Party unleashed a charm offensive as a way to help people forget the unpleasantness of the invasion. Love, the greatest force of all, was weaponized because Husak firmly believed that productive copulation would cement the future of regime.

He rolled out pro-population policies, including longer maternity leave, attractive state loans for newlyweds, and a generous child allowance.

The strategy was as successful as it was expensive. Soon, the state ran out of money to support the costly procreation operation. With incentives withdrawn, the artificially inflated birth rates began to drop again. Alas, some things cannot be forced.

What was it like to be born into communist Czechoslovakia?

Cosy birth wards with comfy armchairs, pink walls and comforts for mommy and baby did not exist to ease the arrival of future generations of the proletariat. Home births were out of control of the state and so a big no-no. Czechoslovak hospitals were dark, sterile and gloomy. Long corridors, stark rooms and a general air of strictness offered mothers-to-be little solace or sense of security. The outdated medical practices did not help either.

> *Daddies were nowhere to be seen. Child birth was a female matter and a man holding his partner's hand during it was unheard of. All young fathers were to wait respectfully outside of the ward and sometimes even the hospital. If a child was born outside of visitation hours, the women could only show their newborn sons and daughters to proud fathers through the hospital room windows.*

Unless a woman was lucky to be blessed with a quick delivery or the partner of someone with connections, giving birth in communism required hours of lying on a table, or in an equally uncomfortable position on a cold hospital bed. Birthing wards tried to maximize on space. At busy times, there would be several women laying side by side, giving birth in the same room.

Empathy was not on the practical to-do list. It was not out of the ordinary for the laboring mothers to experience neglectful and even harsh treatment at the hands of doctors and nurses. Plus, the entire hospital system placed the patient in an inferior status. Hospital staff always knew best and did not have to waste their breath explaining anything to anyone.

Sometimes, those in labor would overhear hospital staff joking and gossiping amongst themselves, as they tried to push through their contractions. Ignored by them, her concerns would fall on deaf ears. The right to move her body was restricted, because medical textbooks stated that women gave birth on their backs.

*Although all socialist mothers were expected to produce children, some segments of the society were more encouraged than others. The state struggled with the 'gypsy question'. Despite their efforts to 're-educate' the Romany population, to cut down their impressive re-production rate, success was negligible. Unfortunately, widespread enforced sterilizations of Romany women occurred, some of the most horrific examples of human rights violations under communism. If the state could not solve the problem, they wanted to eliminate it, with little concern for the people.*

Once a child was born, the insensitive ordeal was not over. Babies would be immediately separated from their mothers and placed into a special ward. There they would lie, crying side by side with other infants, without much attention or care. Physical contact between the mother and baby was kept to a minimum. From day one, the state had the upper hand.

*In 1948 Czechoslovakia had one of the longest life expectancy rates in the world, ranking in 12th place. However, by the end of the regime in 1989, the country fell to 27th place on the ladder. Overall, and in the process of 41 years, the lifespan of the average Czechoslovak was 4 years shorter, compared to the average life expectancy in the West.*

Yet, despite all its gory sterility and lack luster approach to patient care, the Czechoslovak healthcare sector improved. Doctors became more accessible to the masses. While there was only one physician per over 700 Czechoslovaks in 1954, there was 1 per 278 civilians by 1985.

# from TOYS to OATHS

## "GIVE US A CHILD FOR 8 YEARS AND IT WILL BE A BOLSHEVIK FOREVER."

VLADIMIR LENIN

To cultivate the next generation of good workers and to ensure a smooth continuation of its reign, the Party started drilling the fundamentals of the ideology into individuals very early on.

Naturally, this shaped the offer of toys in Czechoslovakia as well. There were no capitalist Barbie dolls, nor was there any Lego. Communist children were not spoilt by products that did not contribute to their proper socialist development.

Toy production was directed by the state and each and every toy on the market had to tick ideological boxes. There were wooden and metal construction toys for boys. These cultivated a sense of dexterity and technical understanding, as the cars, tractors and cranes were pieced together. Toy kitchen sets and baby dolls were made available for girls, alongside the gender-neutral doctor kits and wooden puzzles.

> *Children raised in communism, especially during the less harsh second half of the era, did not necessarily come into contact with restrictions or hardships of the regime.*
>
> *As kids, they went to school, and after school they went to their various activities, before they returned home to have dinner with their parents. For these youngsters, the world was calm and stable. In a sense, communist children were protected by the controlling regime from the many perils of modern life, including drugs and street violence.*

On the surface, communist toy stores were akin to any other in the world, but in a planned economy, the goods were always limited. The selection of models, dolls and colors would not differ or evolve from year to year. Instead, every child had the same toys available to them, year after year.

It was never too early to start teaching kids, by example, what communist equality meant. But try explaining that to the little ones. Receiving the same toy on Christmas and for one's birthday was not thrilling. It was also a very real material limitation that all parents had to face at some point.

A black toy market prospered. Many parents would go to unimaginable lengths in the quest of finding that special western toy for their beloved son or daughter. If that was not possible, they tried their best through conventional methods. Even securing a state-approved toy car or toy vacuum cleaner was a grand challenge because there was not enough.

Christmas presents were a true test for every family. Shopping fever meant standing in lines for hours, sometimes starting at dawn, to get that coveted item. The more proactive parents were not deterred by local shortages and hunted for their prizes for months across the entire republic.

Being a child in communism was not just play. Kids were expected to help their parents with household chores, garden work and look after their younger siblings. Most families had working routines, and cleaning Saturdays were a must for every household, including changing bedsheets and scrubbing bathrooms.

The daily routine of washing dishes and taking out the garbage was standard, as was picking strawberries and plums in summer and harvesting potatoes in the autumn. Just because you were a child did not mean that you did not have to do dull adult things.

All in all, participating in labor was a normal part of the Eastern European childhood experience. Forget about receiving pocket money as a reward, unless you were very lucky. Every child was expected to do the work and to do so willingly and joyfully. Even though they would much rather be running around with their friends than harvesting apples, good and obedient children were not allowed to resist their parents.

As life rolled on, children moved from toys to books and entered into the state educational system, a well-oiled machine producing little communists. Building a heaven on earth required women to participate as well. No excuses. In order to facilitate their return to work as soon as possible, the state provided nurseries for children as young as one-year old and preschools for toddlers three years of age and up.

Even in these playpens, it was impossible to escape from the ideological indoctrination. The state did all it could to make sure that the torch of communism was passed on to trustworthy and competent hands. It was never too early to begin instilling a devotion to the ideology in the population.

Different programs marked various stages of ideological rites of passage.

From infant to child, from teen to young adult, the next generation of communist human capital was cultivated into committed socialist adults. Men and women who were willing to lay down their blood, sweat and tears, alongside knowledge and skills, for the greater vision.

The integration into communism kicked off until full gear once children reached the age of six and passed through the gates of primary school. This was where the seeds of a strong socialist identity were planted into young and malleable minds with the utmost precision and consistency. To start the day right, school children were required to rise and greet their teacher with a unified 'honor to work', the ultimate communist greeting.

Under the guise of fun and play, the regime went even further. It encouraged and expected children to join after-school clubs to learn more about the superiority of communism, the importance of the party, and the magnificence of its leaders, in contrast to the evils of capitalism.

*By the 1980s, each Czechoslovak child spent 10 compulsory years in education. Those with a clean track record, politically reliable parents and intellectual ambitions could enroll in high school.*

*Even in communism where education was free, secondary education was not accessible to everybody. High schools also served as a spring board to universities. That nevertheless remained open only to those with spotless records and reputations.*

*Like in every economy, the schooling system was designed to match the market need for human resources. Slovakia was an agrarian society, going through a process of industrialization. It was also an economy that needed more workers than thinkers.*

*Vocational school were made available for the less intellectually ambitious. This was also where unsavory individuals received an education. They armed youngsters with technical skills and produced cooks, plumbers, stokers, miners and factory workers.*

Boys and girls joined the *Little Sparkles* at the age of 6 years. They would then continue the process and enter the cool *Pioneers league.* A teen's fifteenth birthday marked accession into the *Czechoslovak Union of Youth*, where young Czechoslovaks could remain until the age of 35 when they become fully-fledged adults according to the system. But most dropped out earlier, as soon as they finished high school or enrolled in university.

Do not think for a moment that these were voluntary clubs. Most children wanted to join them so as to be like everyone else, but memberships were more or less mandatory. A child's active participation in such organizations was critical to getting a good job as an adult or going to a desired university.

To become a *Little Sparkle* or a *Pioneer*, each little boy and girl had to take an oath. This included memorizing the core principles of each program. Being a child builder of communism was a serious task as well as a great privilege.

Because it was such an important and momentous undertaking, little Czechoslovaks had to look their part. The *Little Sparkles* wore blue shirts and a badge in the shape of a red star. The *Pioneers* presented themselves in light blue pressed shirts, with dark blue shorts for boys or dark blue skirts for girls.

To complete the outfit and to mark their childhood transition towards the next level, each growing boy and girl was upgraded from a red star to a red scarf. The iconic relic of the era, the red scarf, was the holy grail for millions of children. It was worn proudly around the neck of dignified young pioneers, repeated 'honor to work' to comrades all over the country.

**A PIONEER BUILDS THE SOCIALIST HOMELAND!**

WE WILL
RAISE
A GENERATION
SELFLESSLY
LOYAL
TO COMMUNISM

*A sparkle always says the truth.*

*A sparkle wants to know and explore more.*

*A sparkle likes to exercise, sing, draw and play.*

*A sparkle works hard and helps their parents.*

*A sparkle wants to become a pioneer.*

The point of these youth organizations was to provide activities for children and prevent them from getting into drugs and alcohol, being lazy or, even worse, idle. One gets all kind of ideas when they have plenty of time on their hands.

The Little Sparkles and Pioneers programs, in addition to hobby clubs, were a welcome relief to busy parents. Working mums and dads across the republic were happy to have their offspring occupied.

Each club organized fun activities for the little members, including singing and dancing to communist songs, mural painting, live theatre and sporting events. By far, the most exciting were group outings into the mountains, lakes and forests of Czechoslovakia. The outdoor activities fostered healthy habits, physical strength and natural resilience in little communists.

To keep the children motivated and disciplined, every pioneer was required to keep a journal. In it, girls and boys jotted their goals and aspirations. Make no mistake - these were no private diaries. Each journal was surveilled by a pioneer leader, keeping an eye on the personal development of Czechoslovak communists in the making.

*A pioneer is dedicated to their socialist homeland and to the Communist Party of Czechoslovakia.*

*A pioneer is a friend of the Soviet Union and a defender of progress and peace in the world.*

*A pioneer reveres the heroism of work.*

*A pioneer helps to build the socialist homeland with their actions, learning and work.*

*A pioneer is proud of the Pioneers Organization.*

*A pioneer prepares for the Union of Socialist Youth.*

On very special occasions of communist festivals, such as International Women's Day or the many foreign delegation visits into Czechoslovakia, the Little Sparkles and Pioneers were paraded before the public.

During these processions, the youngsters recited endearing verses that affirmed their devotion to peace in the world through the building of socialism. The pageant would not be complete without a solo recital or singing performance. This was a great honor for the chosen youth, and many a child aspired for this minute of red stardom.

The little communist played a cute and critical role in cementing the valor of communism and the people's obedience to it. During key ceremonies, handed out quintessential red carnations to women, foreign officials and domestic Party leaders. How could you possibly object to a regime that is seen doing that?

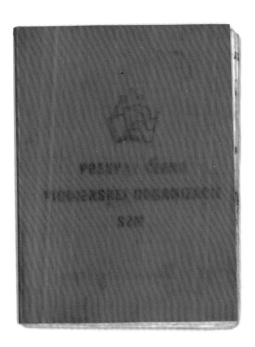

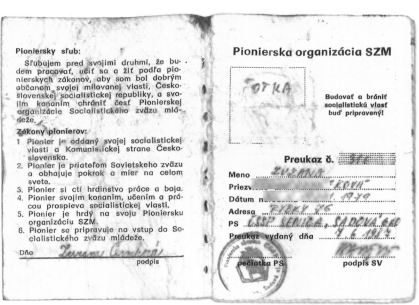

## PionÍersky sľub:

Sľubujem pred svojimi druhmí, že budem pracovať, učiť sa a žiť podľa pionierskych zákonov, aby som bol dobrým občanom svojej milovanej vlasti, Československej socialistickej republiky, a svojím konaním chrániť česť Pionierskej organizácie Socialistického zväzu mládeže.

## Zákony pionierov:

1. Pionier je oddaný svojej socialistickej vlasti a Komunistickej strane Československa.
2. Pionier je priateľom Sovietskeho zväzu a obhajuje pokrok a mier na celom svete.
3. Pionier si ctí hrdinstvo práce a boja.
4. Pionier svojím konaním, učením a prácou prospieva socialistickej vlasti.
5. Pionier je hrdý na svoju Pioniersku organizáciu SZM.
6. Pionier sa pripravuje na vstup do Socialistického zväzu mládeže.

Dňa ........................................
podpis

## Pionierska organizácia SZM

Budovať a brániť
socialistickú vlasť
buď pripravený!

Preukaz č. ....................

Meno ...... ZUZANA ......

Priezv...... "KOVÁ"

Dátum n...... 1. 1979

Adresa ...... RYBKY 76

PS ...... LSSP SENICA, SADOVÁ 660

Preukaz vydaný dňa ...... 11.5. 197...

pečiatka PS                  podpis SV

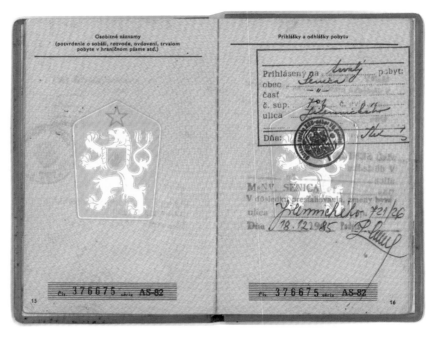

*When Czech and Slovak children turned the big one-five, a very special document was entrusted to them in a very stiff initiation ceremony.*

*The Czechoslovak ID was so much more than a mere identification document. It was a little red booklet that contained one's name, date of birth and address, as well as stamps tracking their employment or education history, year by year. The ID was to be carried with you at all times, and to be treated with great care and respect.*

*Receiving an ID was a moment that marked a person's 'buy-in' into the system. From that moment forward, police officers could stop you in the street and demand your identification document. It was a tool that allowed the authorities to know everything that was needed.*

Upon leaving the *Pioneers*, one proceeded to join the *Union of Socialist Youth* to further strengthen their communist resolve. This is where things became a little more serious and play turned to work. The young adults would be called on to participate in various forms of manual labor, in an effort to increase the productivity of their socialist homeland.

Akin to a team building exercise, these labor excursions were organized by the state and regarded as critical to fostering a healthy character and good work habits.

The outings were organized in military fashion. Every participant received a badge and wore the same blue shirt. Young women and men 'voluntarily' participated in the building of public roads, schools, railways and water works. Potato or other crop picking brigades were a standard exercise every autumn. These activities would take place on weekends and during school and university holidays. The hard physical work was spiced up by communist debates, presentations, lectures and games.

All in all, schools and clubs worked in unison. They were all part of a wider social engineering effort that manufactured an allegiance to communism. The new human capital was to be programed and molded into optimal performance.

The social network enabled the system to catch any prospective rebels and re-program them, when their minds were still young and impressionable, to avoid any future havoc.

*Youth organizations were nothing new. In fact, they were a counter-response to the imperialist Boy Scouts, a tradition that finds its origins in South Africa, during a time when the English were wrestling with the Dutch for power.*

*According to one story, it all started when the Dutch sent their children to go spy on their English peers. Once the Brits found out, they applied their shrewd military thinking and created the Boys Scouts, a youth organization with military foundations.*

*It taught young boys how to survive in the woods, navigate in the wild, lay traps and make fires, but also how to work together, follow orders and take leadership. Step by step, it turned boys into capable and reliable young men, promoting British interests.*

*Hitler used a similar model and founded the Hitler Youth organization, to prepare young German boys and girls for military service, and ultimately to fight for the Third Reich.*

Once students in vocational school finished, they went straight to work. For students in academic high schools, they could either then join the work force or go to university. However, only those who checked all the right boxes in their ideological personal development diary, as well as a clean family record, could consider attending university.

Although education was free, Czechoslovak universities could only admit a certain number of students per year. All schools had a strict quota to observe. The regime needed skilled people who could manage, advise and strategize the making of a better tomorrow. At the same time, the Party also feared anyone who used their brain.

Knowledge has always been the most powerful of weapons, and the Party was acutely aware of the risk of having a knowledgeable population. To keep matters under control, the Party decided to only educate as many people as was necessary, and not one more.

Just like that, a free spot in a university program became akin to hard currency. It was traded left, right and center. Parents would not stop short of passing bribes to cadre office clerks to fight for the precious placements of their children.

Parents, especially those who did not have the opportunity to study themselves, wanted to give their progeny the best possible start to a socialist future. The perks included a comfortable office job, carrying a leather briefcase to work, and liaising with important people much to the envy of friends and neighbors.

> *As much as access to education was weaponized as a control tactic, it was nevertheless free and accessible to all (with an untarnished record) on an unprecedented basis. More children who had come from illiterate families could hope for and acquire university degrees. Although communism damaged the life chances of those who had been on top, it also gave wide reaching opportunities for those on the bottom.*
>
> *In a remarkably short time, the regime cultivated not one but two university educated generations. Armed with new knowledge, they also helped to address the significant skills and knowledge gap that were prevalent in the Slovak part of the republic.*

Not even the halls of universities were spared from ideological infiltration. Every study program was entwined with communism. So much so that in the 1950s, students spent the entire first semester in factories, so as to get closer to their comrades, the workers.

A freshman year usually began with a very special two-hour lecture. All eager students were summoned into a lecture hall to be briefed with some hard facts about the state of the world. In a nutshell, they were encouraged to continue to build-up the anti-imperialist sphere, alongside their Soviet comrades.

Students were also reminded that the socialist republics were under threat from the imperialists. The West simply could not stand the moral ideals of communism, the socialist brotherhood or the social equality the Eastern Bloc represented. The lecturer then went on to elaborate on the various sinister methods used by the enemy to destroy what they had built.

Media was a major culprit the lecturer would warn. Western music and films crept on up on the vulnerable minds of the unsuspecting Czechs and Slovaks, impregnating them with faulty ideas about life and greedy consumerist desires. These were all examples of weaking the force of communism from within.

The Americans would even spy on the innocent people with advanced satellites, continued the lecturer. These were so powerful, they could zoom in from the Earth's orbit and read the very words in the newspapers that unsuspecting civilians were reading over their Sunday breakfast.

No place was safe, everyone was at risk. The Party was entrusting students with this information because it believed that they were now mature enough to handle it, and act accordingly. Other than that, a university experience would be filled with laughter, mischief and memorizing for exams to make your parents proud and professors satisfied.

*Law is one of the most popular and respected professional disciplines in the region today, but it was not always the case. Far from an exciting battle of bluff, skill and wits, there was hardly any glory in strictly following the book of law and solving minor civilian disputes during communism.*

*Justice lost its appeal in an era of show trials, when verdicts were based on the whims of the Party. During this time, no innovative policies were crafted, and no new cases rose before the courts, to challenge the status quo. Or state.*

*And so, it was not law, but rather medicine that was most sought after by students and parents alike. Being a medical doctor during socialism meant prestige, respect and power for some. On the other hand, the ultimate say over life and death was a potent aphrodisiac for others.*

*The culture of giving one's power away to an all-knowing doctor infected the entire Czechoslovak health sector. With power, rose arrogance, and doctors were notorious for taking bribes.*

The good news about being a university student meant that you were pretty much guaranteed to graduate. As university places were limited to a certain number every year, those who filled them were also expected to graduate. There were five-year plans for universities too, and no one wanted to compromise them by failing students. The pressure to push students along resulted in exams being passed even when they should not have been.

However, if you dared to show signs of being too wild, liberal or, worse yet, anti-regime in ideas, you would be quickly and unceremoniously kicked out from the institution. Quota or no quota, the state had zero-tolerance for insubordination.

With a university degree in hand, you were more or less set up to live a good life. But, it did not necessarily amount to a higher salary. Despite the lack of material compensation, degrees were seen as a mark of social status and prestige, in a society that could never before study so widely and freely.

If university education was not for you, then it was time to step into the real adult world. This meant entering permanent employment, including executing the infamous five-year plans. However, if you showed any signs of being a rebel or you happened to have untrustworthy parents, your career path was limited.

For compromised individuals, going to highly sought-after secondary schools and consequently to universities was out of the question. The prospect and dream of having an attractive professional career went up in a puff of smoke and a grim reality of becoming a cook, a stoker or a plumber set in.

# GROWING into a MAN

Life in socialism was as simple. Everything could be organized into neat little black and white boxes, including gender stereotypes. Women were to be women, and men were to be men. Only when they fitted into the clearly outlined boundaries of manhood and womanhood could they step into their role in the socialist society and meet the expectations of the regime.

Growing up as a boy, you were expected to be both tough and tame. Being too rebellious was a red flag, even though it would secure a lot of attention from girls.

No long hair, tattoos or piercings were allowed. Boys with questionable locks would be given a compulsory haircut. A boy's hair could be no longer than the width of a teacher's fingers, who periodically ran their hands through heads in random check-ups.

And it was best to keep hands off cool clothing like cowboy boots or Levi jeans. Such tastes would raise eyebrows over one's commitment to socialist ideals. They were a red flag.

> *It was not only the rebellious youth that were pushed, but also their parents. Without delay, mothers and fathers would be brought in for questioning. A self-examination would be required, asking them to review where they had failed in the political upbringing of their offspring.*

As a boy, you were expected to do well in school and to attend all the communist clubs and activities. All boys took special 'boy' classes that focused on engineering and agriculture. From early childhood, they were encouraged to recite pro-socialist poetry, obey their parents and do anything that the regime asked of them. The goal of the system was to raise strong, resilient and complacent workers.

A MAN IS
A FRIEND,
COMRADE
AND BROTHER
TO A MAN!

As a man, you were expected to talk, walk and smell like a man, whether you were wearing the omnipresent blue overalls - the uniform of the proletariat - or the shapeless Eastern Bloc grey suit. No respectable male aspired to be a pretty boy, a bohemian artist or a high-flying activist in those days. Boys were raised to be efficient workers, active community members and responsible fathers who would one day provide food and shelter for their children.

To toughen them up, the regime devised the much despised and feared mandatory military service. In the eyes of the state, it was a necessary rite of passage to manhood. After all, the socialist republic was under constant threat by the West. It had to be ready to defend itself against any insidious attack, and so all young man had to serve for two years of military training after finishing high school, or, for one year upon graduating from university.

LONG LIVE OUR ARMY –
WITH THE PEOPLE, FOR THE PEOPLE!

Should one refuse the honor the patriotic duty to protect the motherland, he would most likely find himself in the coal mines as punishment.

Do not confuse this mandatory service with being recruited into a professional army. These young men were not well fed, and they lived in poor conditions. Their uniforms all but fitted them and were insufficient for winter weather conditions.

Duties included peeling potatoes in damp wet basements, enduring pointless bullying by superiors, cleaning toilets and attending ideologically driven seminars. Plus, they underwent training, exercising and general toughening up. So much so, that many a man returned with damaged health, with health conditions that would plague them for the rest of their lives.

The only escape for the soldiers was drinking, and if that was out of reach, the desperate young men would numb their misery with a special brew. Horse-strength black tea was used to knock themselves out of reality for an evening.

Some could not cope with the harsh physical and psychological treatment and took their own lives to end the torment. Intellectuals, artists, pacifists and young men used to the comfort of their homes withered away or hardened to the point of non-recognition.

Young men who feared the prospect of being bullied by officers and fellow recruits proved willing to do anything to be granted the holy grail of an exception from military service. The notoriously known 'blue book' was not easy to get, especially if you did not a have a friend or a relative in a position of political influence, or in the ranks of medical staff.

Men would resort to faking illnesses, pretending to be mad, or breaking their own limbs to avoid the ordeal of mandatory service. Clearly, they did not believe in the 'honor' of serving for a Socialist Czechoslovakia.

For those who survived service, life would continue to unfold in a very predictable fashion. Before they even realized, many a young man slipped into the familiar routine of their fathers.

They went to work, came home, read the newspaper, had dinner with the family and sometimes went to the local pub for a drink with friends and fellow comrades. The routine was repeated Monday to Friday for the rest of one's work life, save for weekends, which were left empty to mend cars, fix leaking sinks and loosen door handles.

It was rare for men to help with household chores, or to be actively engaged in child rearing on daily basis. The socialist daddy was mostly a passive parental figure, unless it came to discipline and logistics. It was a father's job to handle unruly offspring, and to drive the family around on ski trips and summer holidays.

By and large, masculine creativity was channeled into building and improving the domestic shelter. The lack of construction services and products available created an exceptionally skillful male population. Czechoslovak men mastered plumbing, plastering, planting, carpentry, electrical work, construction and fixing malfunctions of all kinds. They had to.

A man's worth was measured by his dexterous nature and skillful hands.

Building a house, something that most modern people cannot even imagine doing, was a normal way of providing one's family with a nest. Czechoslovak men would manage to build a house, in addition to their regular job. Construction took place after work, on weekends, and during holidays when friends, neighbors and family came together to build one another's houses.

> *To get at least a little taste of freedom, men carved out some 'escape' time for themselves and their friends and took to the woods.*

*The 'tramps' packed their rucksacks and tents and headed into the wilderness on weekends. These trips were not just an escape from daily life, but also a way of coming to terms with who you could trust. If you really wanted to get to know someone, it was best to spend three days with them in nature.*

*Away from urban conformity, genuine life-long friendships were born. Men grew so close that they were willing to put their necks on the line for one another in life.*

*However, the authorities felt uncomfort-able about groups of men gathering in the secrecy of forests. The clubs were treated as dangerous political organiza-tions. Belonging to such a society carried a promise of grievances, both at home and at work.*

# Blooming into Socialist
## WOMANHOOD

The advent of communism brought many ailments to Czechoslovakia, ones which the subsequent generations still need to heal. However, it also institutionalized equality between men and women. Differences between the genders were downplayed in the true spirit of socialist universalism. Not just men but also women were expected to be active builders in their socialist homeland. Women were to work just like men. But there were some 'perks'. A limit was set on how much a woman could carry.

Growing up as a girl, you had more opportunities in communist Czechoslovakia than ever before, but not at the cost of neglecting the traditional mother role. You would have to handle both your workload and your household. The regime prepared girls for their role with a line of toys and free-time activities. This is how little ladies could rehearse for their future role as wives and mothers, including cooking and cleaning. To make sure they got it right, girls attended special classes on cooking, sewing and childcare. Such subjects were a part of the standard curriculum.

The government put considerable effort into improving the educational status of Czechoslovak women. The number of women who completed higher education jumped significantly over a short period of time. The additional years of schooling saw the professional status of women take flight. As the doors of the labor market swung open to them, women could suddenly be anything, from shop assistants to cosmonauts.

Under the surface of the rhetoric and hypothetical opportunities, the East was no different from the stigmatized West. Women struggled to balance being mothers, citizens and working professionals. Regardless of the regime and what the communists would like us to believe, the gender equality pattern was the same in most developed nations, from Czechoslovakia to the USA.

Despite the fact that nearly 90% of working-age women were employed in the mid-1980s, seeing a woman in a top decision-making position was still rare. Career ambitions were by and large reserved for men. Moreover, females still earned less than their male counterparts in the exact same positions.

A woman's job was also to beautify the republic. As a lady, you were supposed to look after yourself, but not too much. A woman's beauty routine was not to interfere with looking after her children or doing good for her nation.

> *From village to city, the unofficial home uniform of Czechoslovak women and a signpost of adulthood was the iconic 'apron'. It was a symbol of a diligent mother, wife and homemaker. The communist apron was a dress-like, button up, sleeveless garment that was made from synthetic material, so that it would not wrinkle. It was highly functionali and made all women look the same. Those who refused to look like their grandma and mother-in-law were seen as vain and gossiped about.*

A proper communist woman was to look strong and healthy, but never too provocative in her dress or demeanor. Modesty was in vogue. Wearing make-up or a mini skirt was out of question. In the greyest of times, even using nail polish could be interpreted as inappropriately cosmopolitan.

In addition to contributing to the good of Czechoslovakia through their labor, women were praised as critical national assets, for they birthed the new generation of socialist human capital. The future of the Eastern Bloc was dependent on them.

*To make sure they gave life to a healthy new generation of builders of communism, women in reproductive age were required to attend regular gynecological check-ups. These were not done to just to keep an eye on their healthy inner workings, but also to monitor for any undeclared pregnancies.*

*Giving birth was political, which is why the secret police worked in collaboration with hospitals to make sure the pregnancy cycles of women were monitored from conception straight through to the delivery room.*

The double role of women as comrade and mother was appropriately celebrated on 'their' day.

International Women's Day (March 8) was a big day for the ladies of the East. Employers organized office parties and special festivities were held in the towns and cities of Czechoslovakia. Every woman received a red carnation, the iconic flower of the era, while political leaders recited lengthy speeches in honor of their female comrades.

Men were reminded to treat their better halves with a bouquet of flowers, and both sexes were encouraged to join the merriment of work parties, which usually ended late at night with one drink too many. These celebrations produced countless new spicy stories to gossip about in the office.

International Women's Day was as much about thanking women for their work, as it was about maintaining stereo-types and boasting about the success and marvels of communism. It was both a ritual and propaganda statement, showcasing the progressive gender equality of the Eastern Bloc.

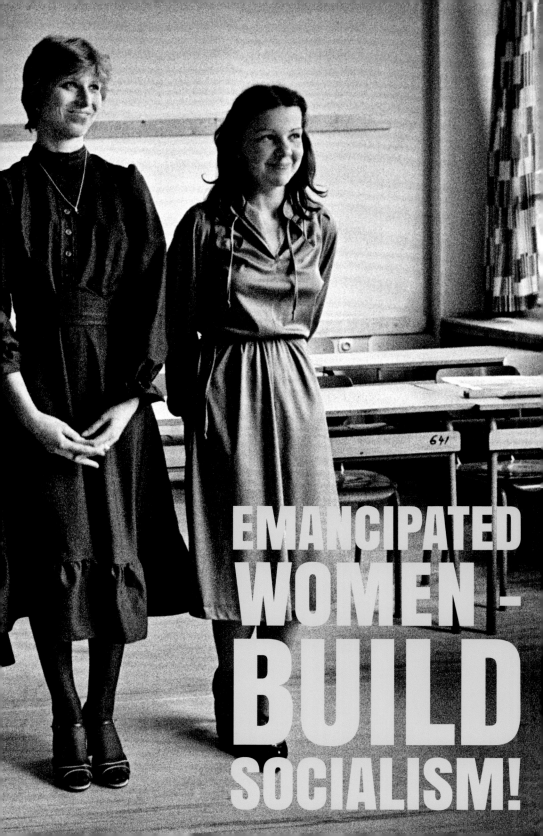

EMANCIPATED WOMEN –
BUILD SOCIALISM!

*Women across the world celebrate 'their' day on March 8th every year. Although the first Women's Day was observed on February 29th, 1909, in New York, it only received international attention a few years later, when on March 8th, 1917, the women of St Petersburg congregated amidst the turmoil of WWI to voice their demands of peace, bread and basic human rights.*

*The day marked the beginning of the Russian Revolution and with it, the rise of communism. Just seven days later tsar Nicholas II abdicated. A provisional government was established in place of the monarchy, and women were granted the right to vote. To show their grateful-ness, the Bolsheviks made March 8th an official holiday.*

*As the Iron Curtain befell upon Europe, International Women's Day spread across the entire Eastern Bloc, bong before it was adopted as an official holiday by the United Nation in 1975.*

BUILD YOUR HOMELAND, BUILD PEACE
COME JOIN US AT A FACTORY
FOR THE HAPPINESS OF YOUR CHILDREN!

# ROMANCE, LOVE AND SEX

Love and romance are the source of softness, gentleness and sweetness. In a world so preoccupied with meeting targets and chanting propaganda slogans, love was a healing force that brought joy, happiness and relief to the hearts of a controlled population.

However, the Party adopted a much less elevated approach to love. Finding a suitable partner was highly encouraged by the state, not so much to make people happy, as to widen the ranks of dutiful Czechoslovaks.

What did the dating scene of communist Czechoslovakia look like? Let's first clarify what 'dating' meant.

The entire concept of 'dating', as in getting to know each another better, was quite foreign. Romances were not really about giving love a try, testing the waters so to speak, and discovering for yourself what kind of partner suits you best through it. In communism, dating nearly always meant serious courtship, one that would end with marriage and, shortly after that, the birth of a first child.

Young people met in school, at university or at work. The next best thing were Saturday discos, when the halls of local culture centers were emptied of their usual rows of tables and chairs, to make room for the energetic youth keen to let off some steam.

Dancing in a sterile space normally used for Party gatherings or school lunches, draped with red curtains and propaganda posters, was not exactly like rocking it out to the latest Western music in a cool nightclub. Yet, there is nothing that a little bit of intimate lightening and imagination could not fix.

Swaying to the rhythm of Czechoslovak pop, many a heart fell in love, but the dating ritual looked quite different from what we know today. Limited cash flow posed serious constraints on activity selection. Taking your sweetheart out for dinner, or a drink at a fancy bar, or hip a festival, were but dreams, and not options for the people behind the Iron Curtain.

Instead, taking leisurely walks in the woodlands or chatting over a homemade lemonade in grandma's garden would have to do. A trip to a local cinema or to the dance hall in the next village would be a highlight of one's dating experience.

Once the spark of attraction grew, the couple would enter a relationship. If a woman got pregnant during the dating phase, marriage was a must. Half of all marriages happened because there was a bun in the oven.

To counteract undesirable sexual contact, the Party whipped up a series of anti-singlehood policies. The matter of getting civilians to copulate was approached from the perspective of bone-dry pragmatism. Remaining single was highly un-profitable, while rewards for getting married and producing children were showered upon the fertile population.

*As egalitarian as communist Czechoslovakia aspired to be, certain class divides still revealed themselves in the most surprising places. For example, not every-one could afford to have an extramarital affair.*

*Office workers, the administrative elite of the era, had more time and money on their hands. They also had more liberty with their whereabouts than their com-rades serving on factory lines, which made it easier for them to sneak off to a hot encounter.*

*Most affairs took place at work or behind countryside hay shacks. At the very top was the communist leadership. In a lea-gue of their own, they had privileges, status and power that made them big beacons in the eyes of many attractive women.*

*They were the only ones who could afford to also have a mistress on the side. The leadership was notorious for their extra marital affairs, and their ability to main-tain multiple mistress arrangements.*

The Party and its propaganda mouthpieces were painting an image of a moral, prudent and responsible Czechoslovakia. Officially, there was no pornography, let alone prostitution, but of course they existed.

No matter the culture or the era, the human fascination with sex has always been a powerful lure. In Czechoslovakia, it was made even more attractive by the fact that it was not as easily accessible.

Pornography was one of the most popular smuggled goods, and although prostitution was suppressed, it still existed. There were even a small number of officially tolerated prostitutes, who were often recruited as agents, true to the script of popular Cold War spy dramas.

# WORK HARD, PLAY a LITTLE

After the war, the Czechoslovak government prioritized kick-starting heavy industry. To meet the grand goals of the Soviet vision, all the human capital of the country had to be plugged into the economy. Every able-bodied Czechoslovak was required to work long hours and weeks.

It might sound harsh, but it was a real improvement compared to what Czechoslovaks were used to before. Prior to communism, people were only eligible for a maximum of eight days of holiday a year. To get those precious few off days, they had to work continuous 6-day weeks, for a total of 15 years. After 1954, workers were entitled anywhere from two to four weeks of paid holiday per annum. Now, that's a paradigm shift.

As time went by, Czechoslovaks were even treated to a generous two-day weekend. Behind the revolution of the work week stood no one else but the liberal hero, Dubcek. He first introduced the 'weekend' idea in 1968. To pacify and distract the people, it was implemented at all work places after the invasion of 1968.

> It was symptomatic of the regime that jobs that held the power apparatus together were generally better paid then jobs that required advanced knowledge and special skills. The communists took care first and foremost of themselves, paying each other comfortable salaries. A communist apparatchik or a police officer could earn twice as much as a senior manager at a hospital.

Communists took the saying 'idle hands are the devil's workshop' very seriously. When people were suitably occupied, they had little time to think about the bigger picture, let alone take action against the regime that controlled every minute of their life. An occupied mass was an obedient mass.

Every Czechoslovak had an obligation to work, there was no such thing as being unemployed. Refusing to work towards a better today was punished by a prison sentence. At work, people were kept occupied at their assembly line or desk.

Busily meeting the unrealistic five-year plans was task enough. But, every now and then they would attend conferences and award ceremonies, where members would gather to pat each other on the pack as per their bogus achievements. Diplomas and medals were handed out to make the ritual seem more real.

The Party paid close attention to spotlighting outstanding members of the working class, to inspire others to follow in their noble example. Year after year, the best workers who did not just meet their quotas but exceeded them were paraded and awarded before the public.

> *The 'Hero of Socialist Labor' award was the highest civic order in Czechoslovakia. It was granted to outstanding workers in the form of a gold star. The ceremony was grand and unforgettable. Performed by the President himself, at the Prague castle, it was a highlight of one's professional achievement. The gold star award also came with a once-in-a-lifetime opportunity, to see the cradle of Czechoslovak communism for oneself. Prague was the political and decision-making center of the country.*

The very best of overachievers became idols of the era. Their faces and success-stories were plastered in newspapers and magazines, much like the successful entrepreneurs of today. Collectively they spoke of their passion and dedication to the ideals of communism. They were true heroes of the regime.

Those not catapulted to proletariat stardom received their validation from the state in more subtle ways. Countless framed 'thank you' diplomas from the Party adorned the walls and hallways of state institutions, as well personal abodes. For some, they remain a touching personal exhibition of one's pride, worth and professional achievement.

> By the 1970s, the Czechoslovaks developed a peculiar approach to work and productivity. Some would call it slack work ethic. The motive behind 'going to work', especially office work, was more about role-play than performance. Czechs and Slovaks would go to work, sit at their desks, push papers around and call one another's offices to be 'seen' doing something.
>
> The regime preferred status quo to change and innovation. Workers were not allowed to apply their creativity or individual agency to solve problems. With the lack of freedom and motivation came boredom, idleness and apathy.

Accolades went beyond paper certificates. Diligent workers were also rewarded with experiences, like a week-long stay in a premiere domestic spa or national mountain resort. Some got lucky to even venture beyond the borders of Czechoslovakia. This was not a holiday where they were free to use his or her time to their liking, however…

The purpose of time away from work was to restore the bodies of workers, and increase their performance upon return. Spa holidays followed a rigid structure of 'productive' free-time activities and compulsory bonding with fellow holidaying comrades. Mandatory treatments, group exercising, and evening dances/ concerts were all part of the program. Educational day trips to nearby castles and museums made sure everyone was occupied with worthwhile activities.

The Party had a peculiar approach to relaxation. It just did not believe in the idea of 'free time' and so a way to occupy the Czechoslovaks' idyll weekend time had to be found. The government recognized the attachment Czech and Slovaks felt to nature. In an act of compromise, it supported and spread the much older tradition of small garden allotments to the people.

Citizens who lived in apartments were assigned narrow parcels of land by the state, on which they could grow fruit and vegetables for their own private consumption.

It was a clever move.

It filled the now longer, 2-day weekends with digging around in the ground. With their energy spent, they would not have time to conspire against the regime. They were too occupied. These little plots of land were also able to compensate for the shortcomings of the centralized economy. Harvesting their own apples and potatoes gave people some sense of food security in a time of shortages and long lines for food. In fact, homegrown produce made a significant difference in the economy.

Even a small allotment produced enough potatoes, carrots, parsnips and other long-lasting vegetables to see a family though winter, without having to rely much on the local grocer.

Nothing went to waste in Czechoslovakia. An organic barter system existed between neighbors, friends and relatives. For centuries in the predominantly rural Slovakia, communities survived by working together. Extra preserves, compotes, eggs, potatoes or alcohol were traded for other goods and services in a mutually beneficial, symbiotic system of help-outs.

These private gardens were many people's pride and joy too. They were an escape from the dreary grey reality of communism. Digging their hands into soil, while working on their land, brought comfort and solace to people who had very few opportunities for relaxation and nourishment.

CELOZÁVODNÝ VÝBOR KOMUNISTICKEJ STRANY SLOVENSKA V *ZVL, k p. Skalica*

UDEĽUJE

# ČESTNÉ UZNANIE

za dlhoročnú a obetavú prácu
v straníckej organizácii v podniku

v Skalici, 13.3.1985

PROLETARIAT
TARDOM!

OKRESNÁ POĽNOHOSPODÁRSKA SPRÁVA
OKRESNÝ VÝBOR ZVÄZU DRUŽSTEVNÝCH ROĽNÍKOV

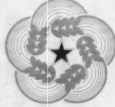

PREPOŽIČIAVA ČESTNÝ TITUL

*vzorný pracovník*

POĽNOHOSPODÁRSTVA OKRESU

za dlhoročnú obetavú prácu v socialistickom
poľnohospodárstve

PO 1. mája v Senici
udeľuje

# Čestné
# uznanie

z príležitosti
životného jubilea

V Senici 4.8.1950          predseda PO

Vedenie podniku, CZV KSS a ZV ROH pri k.p. ZVL Skalica

udeľujú

# Čestné
# uznanie

pri príležitosti 50 narodenín

V Skalici 10.3.1955

ZV ROH          CZV KSS          RIADITEĽ PODNIKU

*Fruit that was not fit for consumption or canning was used for an alternative purpose. The imperfect produce was distilled into alcohol. Any fruit would do, but plums were, and still are, an old-time favorite distilled into Slovakia's signature alcoholic beverage, slivovica.*

*Illegal home distilleries supplied slivovica to friends and relatives in cities. Every now and then, there would be a police raid on these 'establishments', but it was worth the risk. The plum brandy was more than a readily available sedative. Slovaks swear on its healing properties, while foreigners regard it as deadly. given the minimal 50% alcohol content.*

*Slivovica continues to be a part of an ancient bonding ritual. It is still custom in Czechoslovakia to offer a shot on the occasion of a wedding, a birth of a child, a newly finished home or just to welcome Friday. Clinging shot glasses brimming with the liquid inheritance of the ancestors is a sacred moment. When offered to newcomers, it is a symbolic gesture of welcoming them to the family and culture.*

So, you had a job, a family and cottage. What next? The truth is, that was pretty much it. It was unusual for people to change employers or experience any significant ups or downs before life took them under.

In a merry-go-round of working Monday to Friday, pottering around on your allotment on weekends, or organizing family outings in the forests and mountains, your aim was to sail smoothly into retirement.

That is when you could start living 'the life'. On half of your wage as a pension, you could not exactly splurge. But you had all the time in the world that you could now spend in your cottage, and of course looking after your grandchildren. Your daughter or son expected it.

# HOLIDAY-MAKING in a cage

The ways to spend your holiday in Czechoslovakia was geographically limited to domestic destinations, for a great majority of people. The Party preferred to not lose sight of its citizens. And so, most Czechoslovaks did not really have a choice and could only vacation at home.

The state provided its people with affordable facilities where they could recuperate and regain their strength. Modest chalets, basic camping sites, and austere hotels encouraged Czechoslovaks to explore all that their republic had to offer. Indeed, the political elite holidayed in luxury away from the masses, and also abroad.

Despite being provided only with rudimentary hospitality services. Castles, palaces, chateaux, museums and galleries all across the republic were open to all, mostly for free. That is privilege seldom found in the West. This was not only to provide people with something to do, but also to foster pride in the nation and trust in its political leadership.

Communism also made going to the spa, mostly seen as a luxury in other parts of the world, widely accessible to the public. Such retreats truly made the most out of Czechoslovakia's world-renowned natural resources, her clean air, green forests and healing springs.

Here, women, men and children alike were sent to take preventative care of their bodies, but also to recover from serious injuries, illnesses and surgeries. Which is why lengths of stay sometimes lasted even several months.

The regime really did take good care of the bodies of the working population. After all, their hands were required to build a bright new future. Mud treatments, massages, breathing therapies and mineral baths were carefully compiled into comprehensive healing programs.

The spas were places to heal and recover, so as to get the people back work as quickly as possible. But, they were also a source of great adventure. They offered a rare opportunity to meet people from across the republic, and even the exciting abroad.

> *The spas became renowned for romantic escapades. Far away from home, family and friends, spa guests suddenly found themselves experiencing a new and precious source of privacy.*
>
> *A doctor's prescription for spa therapy gave a green light for many unconventional activities. Rehabilitation procedures did not take up the whole day, leaving plenty of time for socializing in a relaxed atmosphere. New connections were established, some warmer, others hotter. Who knows how many women returned pregnant to their unsuspecting husbands...*

True to the spirit of collectivism, company holidays became immensely popular, and sometimes the only accessible way to travel. The government encouraged collective leisure time and was in charge of organizing domestic and foreign trips of workers.

This way the comrades could keep one another in check. Extra eyes assured that everyone would behave appropriately, keeping holiday excesses and affairs to a minimum. Czechoslovak holiday-making was far from hedonistic indulgence into the pleasures of life.

> *Even before the arrival of communism, Czechoslovaks were a collective people. They enjoyed spending their free time within their wider family circles. Collective leisure time was therefore not far removed from what had always been normal. Although many people today do not miss communism, they miss the social bonding*

*and comradery that was encouraged in a culture that valued the group over the individual.*

Most people never made it beyond Hungary or Poland. The Czechoslovak cage only opened its gate very rarely, and to a very few. On the other hand, it gave birth to a uniquely Czechoslovak phenomenon.

On weekends and holidays, the nation's towns and cities were left empty as families jumped into cars and trains, heading for their cottages in the countryside. These second homes were a Czechoslovak cult hit. Akin to sanctuaries in nature, they allowed people to better cope with the humdrum of the grey days that awaited them, upon return to regular life.

Nowhere else in Europe has the trend of second-homes been so widespread among the masses, and not just reserved for the more affluent groups of society.

Escaping the city to spend free days improving one's holiday home was a great resource for families. Children could run loose, as their parents' picked mushrooms in autumn and berries in summer. Huddling together by a log fire in winter was a great anti-depressant for the people, even helping them to forget their caged lives behind the Iron Curtain.

These scared spaces were also where Czechoslovaks could realize themselves more. Away from the prying eyes of their neighbors, they could feel more relaxed. People lived their private lives in their weekend cottages. This is where their hearts were.

And then there was the forbidden abroad. For over 40 years, it was reserved for the luckiest of the lucky. Those who crossed the national borders to make it to Poland or Hungary, or even wander off as far as East Germany, were considered true adventurers.

To leave the territory of Czechoslovakia was quite an achievement and required you to tackle an impressive pile of paperwork. First of all, it was unlikely to be successful, as an individual traveler. Package holidays with a cohort of

fellow holiday makers were more realistic. Such excursions, where everyone was followed by the keen eyes of everyone else, were deemed much safer.

Being monitored by a group meant that people were less likely to succumb to temptation and defect.

What were the pre-requisites? Going abroad required a clean personal record and influential connections, in addition to the approval of several different layers of the bureaucratic apparatus. After the required papers and stamps were collected into a neat pile, the final permission slip was that of bank. You needed to have proof of foreign currency, of which there was never enough.

Getting all those stamps in order, within an administrative system that moved at a sloth's pace, took quite some time and required patience. Those who persevered to the end were rewarded with a special temporary grey passport.

> *Implemented in Czechoslovakia in the 1980s, the grey passport was to serve as a 'red flag'. It was a means to alert border officers in Yugoslavia, the most favorite and only available sea-side destination to Czechoslovaks, that the 'tourist' standing before them could be trying to illegally cross over into Italy or Austria. Sound complicated? Life can get messy when we micro-manage and try to control everything...*

Going to Hungary was particularly exciting for the caged Eastern Europeans. Renowned as the Soviet Bloc's 'little West', everyone wanted to go there. The country was run on a much less severe form of communism. There, the 'goulash' communism allowed some forms of private ownership and entrepreneurialism to exist. Hungary even traded with the West.

But, it was Yugoslavia that was the great treat and destination dream of many. It was not only its beaches that Czechoslovaks, a landlocked people, sought out. The regime in Tito's Yugoslavia was more relaxed than in any other country in the East. It meant one thing – an easier escape to the West.

> *Presiding over the seaside haven was the strong-willed Josip Tito, the President of the Socialist Federal Republic of Yugoslavia. He had defied Moscow's hegemony and broke his country free from Stalin's steel grip. How was this even possible? Some people say, it was due to the fact that the Yugoslavs had managed to liberate themselves from the Nazis, without much help from the Soviets. As a result, they were not politically or energetically indebted to Moscow for their freedom. More practically said, the apparatchiks could not sway public opinion to justify the Soviet's presence in a land they did not liberate.*

The seaside 'escape corridor' of Yugoslavia was no secret. The Czechoslovak Party was well aware of its temptation, which is why only the most reliable individuals were granted the right to travel there. Only pre-approved loyalists could taste for themselves whether the sea water really was as salty as they heard.

> *The seashores and quaint towns of former Yugoslavia hold a curious story. As the Soviet invasion in the summer of 1968 was underway, quite a few happy Slovak holiday makers became refugees overnight, stranded somewhere on the Balkan coastline. To return to their occupied homeland was foolish, maybe even suicidal. But they also realized that they could not stay in Yugoslavia either.*

*Although the country practiced a looser form of communism, it was nevertheless an ally of Moscow. With no country to return to, there was only one thing left for them to do: go West. Austria and Germany became home for many Czechoslovak 1968 refugees. Others set their sights further. They aspired to go to the land of the great unknown and braved it all the way to Canada and America.*

Chronically paranoid of being overthrown, the Party restricted access to foreign currency, so as to keep the people financially vulnerable. Czechoslovaks lacked access to international currency, which meant they couldn't engage with the world. Exchange rates were manipulated so that only a few citizens could get their hands on limited sums.

In addition, Czechoslovaks could only take a certain amount of cash out of the country. This action was justified by the fact that the Trade Unions used to pay for the package holidays, so the people did not need to use much money while abroad.

The intention behind this policy was to prevent over-consumption. The government did not support the splurging of their citizenry's hard-earned capital on imperialist goods. They also did not want to encourage poor habits, like partaking in the forbidden pleasures of capitalism. Heaven forbid they would bring any of these new products home and start a revolution.

Czechoslovaks were only allowed to leave with such a small amount of cash that it was not enough to buy even the most basic food supplies once abroad. To defy the limitation, the people resorted to hiding money wherever they could, in the hope that it would make it to the other side of the border control, unchecked. Bras were a popular hiding spot for women, as was underwear for men. The most dexterous would even construct their own false bottom suitcases.

Getting more money through certainly helped, but Czechoslovaks had far from enough capital resources to sustain themselves. Everything was more expensive in the West. With limited cash at their disposal, even from their undergarments, holiday makers sought other ways to survive.

Czechs and Slovaks packed their cars full of food and provisions from home, enough to last for their entire holiday. Canned meats, pickles, salami and potatoes and apples from the garden were holiday staples.

Few could afford to stay in a hotel, and most had to make do with tents, pots, plates and gas stoves. Do not think for a moment that this tradition disappeared with communism's defeat. Old habits die hard. Thousands of Czechs and Slovaks still load up their cars with provisions and set off to Croatia as notoriously stingy holidaymakers.

*Czechoslovak leadership did everything to contain the threat of the West, but it could not resist the temptation of foreign money brought in by Western tourists. Czechoslovakia was a cheap and exotic travel destination for adventurous foreigners.*

*Those who worked in the hospitality sector benefited most from these international exchanges. The problem was that this money was difficult to spend. Surplus cash stimulated suspicion and unwanted attention from the secret police.*

*People had to get creative. The most inventive ones travelled to other towns and cities to buy goods away from the gaze of their neighbors. This was also the heyday of smuggling Russian gold. But, the beautiful golden earrings, rings and necklaces screamed for attention and had to be worn sparingly.*

# SHOPPING: a symphony of cries and whispers

Life in communist Czechoslovakia gave one plenty of opportunities to cry, both from laughter and frustration. You might think that shopping therapy would surely help to lift the spirits behind the Iron Curtain and take tired minds off the propaganda theatre. Not really. Life in communism demanded an entirely different attitude to life and wealth.

More often than not, shopping resembled a chase of the proverbial wild goose. Even such a mundane thing as grocery shopping became a real mission that required some solid patience and unwavering determination.

Things one really, really, really wanted were usually the ones difficult to get. They took time and a master plan to acquire, especially when it came to non-essentials items. These were considered bourgeois goods of convenience or beauty. Having a roof over one's head and something to eat was important. Anything else, like skirts in different colors or pretty photo frames, were frankly silly demands of a spoilt generation.

Shops across the country sold the same goods at the same prices. People were given little choice when it came to buying anything. All the items had to be produced within the Eastern Bloc or from befriended countries. Despite the consistent assurances of the leadership, not everything was of top quality. Far from it, in fact.

To illustrate this point, children's tights were only available in four colors – pink and white for girls, blue for boys, and brown as a unisex option, and had the most annoying tendency to roll down and collect at the ankles of little socialists. Children learnt to cope with the slight discomfort, but the perils of shopping in Czechoslovakia did not end there.

Many girls could not go to sleep at night out of the sheer excitement of wearing their brand-new red winter boots to school the next day. Their joy dwindled when they realized that half of the class was wearing the exact same boots, as there were only two styles available that winter.

Even more irritatingly, it was not always easy to buy a shirt, a dress or shoes in your size, as all production was planned according to 5-year schemes. This meant that if the republic ran out of something, there was little that could be done about it, until the next production cycle was orchestrated by the Party. Factories and production lines had very little sovereignty.

> *No deficit was more annoying than that of the perennially missing toilet paper. All it took was one of the few factories producing it to experience some unfortunate event. A fire or mechanical malfunction, and the production of the much in demand tissue would be halted.*
>
> *Czechoslovaks had to adapt to the circumstance. Newspapers and magazines were cut up to replace the missing toilet paper. Using the propaganda stories about Soviet progress or the faces of Czechoslovak leadership for this unique purpose gave a sense of satisfaction to many.*

Cut off from the rest of the world and governed by a centralized economy - that was far from flexible and adaptable to the demands of the market - meant that Czechoslovaks experienced legendary shortages.

Each and every one tested the inventiveness of the population, willing to queue for hours on end to obtain what they needed. Waiting in line, sometimes for miles, was a daily reality. Whether one wanted beef, fruit or a cassette recorder, the people knew they had to wait in front of shops long before they even opened.

For much of the era, goods such as tropical fruits were only available once a year at Christmas. The Party recognized the holiday as a very important ritual. It was the perfect time to show the generosity of the state by stocking fruit & veggie shops with exotic, sought after delicacies.

Still, getting bananas and oranges at Christmas required some connections or patience. It was as if the entire world rushed into shops, desperate to secure this special grant for families. You still would have to wait and hope for the best, because it was far from certain that there was enough for everyone. Czechoslovaks learned to take care of their own, and shop owners would set aside the special fruit for close family and friends.

On the other hand, the lack of options also had its perks. One did not have to do too much thinking when furnishing their modest home. The choice of a kitchen layout was limited to a few models and a couple of colors. Indeed, there were only really two house styles to choose from. When it came to creature comforts like sofas and armchairs, there were only a couple designs to choose from. Best to keep it simple.

> *Cars were the true luxury item of the regime, which is why very few people had them. If you did, you would only have one per household. The automobile selection was limited to mostly Eastern Bloc brands, including the iconic Trabant, Skoda, Ziguli, Varburk, Volga and Lada. Buying a car would always mean putting your name on a waiting list and then waiting and waiting and waiting.*

Yet, the regime was not completely heartless. For items that were not available consistently, waiting lists were compiled to please the hardworking citizen. As they say, hope dies last. The men and women of Czechoslovakia were led to believe that they could have whatever they wanted.
Eventually. Maybe.

The waiting lists for a sewing machine, a TV or even a red dress were endless. If queuing obediently or getting their name on a waiting list proved futile, people looked to alternatives. Many turned to the black market, but that involved some serious risks, including imprisonment.

Yet, Czechoslovaks found a way of softening the rules. The system was still operated and enacted by people. When the lady behind the counter noticed a young mother standing in line with a crying baby in her arm, or an older gentleman struggling to hold himself upright on his crutches, she would let them to skip to the front of the line.

# ŠKOD

Creating micro-alliances with shop-assistants and cashiers became something of a national sport. There was nothing more upsetting then having waited in line, all morning, only to enter the store and find its shelves empty. Without a 'friend' in a shop, who could hide the prized and sought-after goods under the counter, your chances of getting what you wanted were slimmer.

There was also another way to compensate for shortages - to steal from your place of employment, which by default meant stealing from the state. Although this practice was condemned on the surface, employee theft was seen as a necessity by most citizens. So much so that it gave flight to a popular saying: "those who do not steal from the state, steal from their own family".

Western brands were the dream of many, but accessible only to the few. They had the longest waiting lists of all, and their purchasing cost was exorbitant compared to local wages. You might ask whether anyone at all could afford, for example, such a car. Truth be told, prominent party members and their close friends and relatives all had them. Having a foreign car was a reward for their loyalty. It was also a symbol of status and power.

*Everybody's business was everybody else's business in Czechoslovakia. In a culture where the state-encouraged neighbors to eavesdrop and report on one another, unique creations were created to facilitate it.*

*The birth of the Czechoslovak iconic shopping bag, is a case in point. The net-like, see-through bag was not a trendy fashion item. Although sturdy and convenient, it also revealed the contents of everyone's shopping experience.*

*In an era where privacy was a liability, the bag exposed what people were up to. Carrying a lot of fleshy meat, bananas or fancy bottles of liquor raised an alarm in a society that suffered from shortages all the time.*

*Having more than was usual meant that the culprit either had a special relationship with the shop assistant, or else bribed his or her way to the oranges. Officials were concerned about such dealings. Each time someone took more than they should, the system in which everybody was supposed to have the same was destabilized.*

The stores themselves ranged from small individual bakeries, fruit & veggie shops to shoe repair stands and entire department stores. Regardless of location, they all looked the same in form. As nothing was privately owned, shops could not bear a name, or any type of personalization or market branding. The sign above a shop entrance would simply read 'Grocer', 'Butcher' or 'Florist'.

Many of these shopping 'jewels' of the era can still be found across the region. They offer a glimpse into bygone times. They can be easily identified by their iconic and very dated window displays and notoriously confusing, maze-like layouts.

*The atmosphere of the Dunaj Centre, the premiere shopping complex in Bratislava, is the perfect specimen of the former shopping shrines. Back in the day, it was a sought-after shopping destination.*

*It also housed a store that sold dreams – a special boutique where foreign clothing could be purchased. The imported items arrived from Italy every Wednesday, at noon. This was a well-known secret among the fashionable crowd of the capital. Women would sneak away for an early lunch, to get there early. Everything would be sold out within two hours of arrival.*

361

# TAX-AND DUTYFREE STORES

## Tuzex
**CZECHOSLOVAKIA**

At the top of the shopping hierarchy presided the iconic chain *Tuzex*. These shops were the only official source of western goods in the republic. They were the home of luxury and opulence. *Tuzex* shelves overflowed with chocolate Kinder eggs, quality cacao, boxes of fancy washing powder, and toys never seen before, as well as stamps, jeans, cassette players, foreign cosmetics and Adidas sneakers.

> *The **Tuzex** was the only place where you could buy jeans. Denim was the quint-essential American material; as such it was also an implicit symbol of freedom. This made jeans, a mundane reality in the West, a mark of cultural rebellion in Czechoslovakia.*
>
> *Wearing denim to school would make you the coolest kid in the neighborhood, and a thorn in the eye of your teachers. Countless teenage boys and girls across the republic spent sleepless nights trying to make their denim dream happen. How? By nagging, begging and negotiating with their parents.*
>
> *Wearing jeans was more than a political and a philosophical statement. It also meant getting a girlfriend or boyfriend.*

The *Tuzex* shopping experience offered a blissful respite from the regime approved selection. In an economy where all production was planned by the state, there was only one collection of suits, bras and shoes available to shoppers.

*Tuzex* was unique. These shops were proof of what wasn't supposed to exist, an exemption from all the rules of the controlled economy. True to their outlier status, the shrine of foreign treasures did not accept the local Czechoslovak crown, but only special *Tuzex* 'bons'.

'Bons' were coupons that the government implemented

to replace the impossibly to get hard foreign monies, which the Party did not want to circulate freely on its territory. Getting *Tuzex* 'bons' was a tricky process. You could not officially buy as many as you wanted or needed to make that jean purchase for your son or daughter. That defied the communist logic of equality, and the desire to protect the country from the amoral influence of western consumption habits.

One of the only sources of 'bons' were Czechoslovaks who worked abroad. These were mostly diplomats, highly qualified workers, entertainers and of course agents. They were workers that were paid in 'bons', to limit their purchasing sprees and freedom when abroad. Nor could they return to Czechoslovakia with a bag of foreign currency either. Hence, 'bons' were a happy medium and control tactic by the state.

Unless you were lucky and knew someone who had just came back from abroad, you had to resort to the thriving black market to procure the coupons. Dealers, often older unassuming ladies, sold them on shady street corners, at inflated prices, that once again made them accessible to the very few.

*Wherever you went, all shops sold the same stock. The general lack of fashionable items and the scarcity of quality materials such as cotton or silk turned Czechoslovak women into very capable and imaginative seamstresses.*

*Inspired by smuggled-in magazines from the West, or the regime-approved Burda, a sewing journal from East Germany, they would stitch up their own hand made imitations.*

*Many standard Soviet dresses and blouses were turned into beautiful, trendy and provocative creations. The contemporary Czech and Slovak shops selling fabric, buttons, threads and lace are a reminder of the era when the latest fashions were an unattainable item.*

Prvoděv

# FOR SOCIALISM AND PEACE!

ZA SOCIALIZMU

# FEEDING the Regime

Communism reduced everything in life to its pragmatic bone. The attitude permeated every sphere of life, and reached deep into the very hearts of Czechoslovak households - their kitchens.

Cooking and eating was stripped of any 'meaningless' decorative presentation, complexity, fun or color. The ceremony of cooking and sharing food with others, going back centuries into the recesses of the lost kingdoms of Austria and Hungary, fell into disfavor.

Food, a vehicle that had been bringing people together for millennia, was suddenly treated with deep suspicion. Anything with the potential to connect people and create a space away from the gaze of the Party raised red flags. And so, the ritual of sharing a common meal, which had helped human beings foster a bond with one another, had to be curbed.

To reduce the political risks and interpersonal bonding over a meal, the regime decided to reduce culinary pleasures, and with that wipe out the colorful Central European culinary culture. Whether they liked it or not, the age-old eating rituals had to adapt to the new world order.

The new ideology came at a cost: it altered the rhythm of life and family eating routines in Czechoslovakia. The systematic industrialization of Slovakia also played a role. No longer could a family meet over lunch, as they had once done before. Neither was there time to spend a whole day preparing elaborate delicacies.

A shared meal was moved to dinner time, to allow all good citizens to dedicate their daylight hours to enthusiastically building the Socialist Republic. Gone were the days of the opulent banquets of the aristocracy, or the sophisticated dinner parties of the bourgeoisie. There was simply no time in the busy socialist work schedule for such debauchery. Nor was there space to host such gatherings in dinky socialist flats.

Just like that, Czechoslovakia lost its rich food culture. Cooking became a socialist duty, rather than a nourishing or playful activity. The crusade against food was thorough and merciless. In the general suppression of individual creativity, meals became nothing short of mundane.

> *Wives and cooks alike did away with anything that would vaguely ring of the bourgeoisie, aristocracy and, above all, capitalism. Certain ingredients quickly disappeared from shop shelves. Asparagus, held in high esteem by the public as a regal vegetable, was too close to the narrow zone of communist comfort.*

> *Long story short, asparagus had to go. There was no place for such multi-textured, rich, elitist delicacies in the new sprawling concrete jungles and tiny kitchen units. The only reminders of a diversity of ingredients, and the skills of chefs, were old cookbooks, melancholic remnants of an era that seemed to have never existed.*

There were also many positive sides to the socialist take on the equality of food supply. Up until the arrival of communism, meat was a precious commodity in most households. After their ascent to power, the Party regulated prices of all foods, including meats, which made them affordable to all. Undercover inspectors screened markets to make sure no seller was offering their produce for a few crowns more than the official price.

Communists also introduced food standards, and diligently enforced them from Prague to Bratislava and beyond. A schnitzel would taste and weigh the same in whichever restaurant you ordered it at.

One thing that did not change was the deeply ingrained

belief that home cooking was a job for women only. Cooking was not something that any respectable socialist man would devote time to. Women became an extended feeding hand of the regime, while also being expected to follow a strict work routine.

Being plugged into the machine of the marvelous planned economy, they could no longer spend hours in their kitchens, like their stay-at-home grandmothers were used to. The Czechoslovak culinary manual for households was simple and straightforward.

A proper meal had to be filling, affordable and quick to prepare and eat. Workers were not to spend hours cooking, nor indulgently eating their creations. That was in bourgeois taste, a bad habit and act of pretention.

The industrialization of the society and the rising living standards also ushered in a new era of large but frugal portions. The habit of frying everything and anything in sunflower oil proved to be a highly effective means of turning cheap ingredients into filling meals. Deep-fried cheese and cauliflower were complimented by heaps of potatoes and rice. It created a feeling of abundance of sorts.

Winters were long in this part of Europe and the planned economy was unpredictable. Whilst buffering food shortages, long lines, and a lack of diversity in stock, the Czechoslovaks proved resilient and impressively self-sufficient.

Almost everyone either had access to or knew someone who had a garden allotment or a cottage. From these precious pieces of privately-owned land, fruits and vegetables flowed onto the plates of the republic.

Not all was eaten straight away. In the true spirit of the country, most of the harvest was kept for the time when trees where not laden with ripe apples and pears. The only way to make the garden produce last for months was by preserving it in glass jars. Big freezers were an innovation that was yet to come.

As soon as harvest started, a preservation fever gripped every diligent lady of the household. Skillful hands worked together; sisters, mothers and daughters, aunts and nieces clustered together to turn the fresh fruits into jams, marmalades and compotes.

Cucumbers, corn, cabbage, mushrooms and indeed the Slavic staple sauerkraut were all pickled. Tomatoes became puree or ketchup. The hard-working Czechoslovak ladies pushed themselves to their limits and did not rest until their home shelves and pantries were full to the brim.

Preserves and pickles became a vital part of barter trade, and gift-giving, that was a normal part of Czechoslovak relational life. No grandma would turn up in town to visit her grandchildren without a basket full of glass jars full of strawberry jam, blueberry compote and of course pickles.

Together, Czechoslovaks cushioned the shortcomings of the planned economy. No matter the fiscal restraints, one always had enough to survive.

*It was inconceivable to throw food out in communism, a belief and practice that lends itself to the strong rural heritage of Slovakia. The Slovaks have always had respect for nature, and the fertile soils that had sustained them over the centuries. In Slovak eyes, every berry and every pepper were a gift from God and mother nature herself.*

*Moreover, the fickle Middle Ages and the two world wars of the 20th century brought periods of starvation into the homes of many. Hunger was a fresh memory for the population. Therefore, to have enough food to eat meant a family was safe.*

*Pickles and preserves, stored apples, carrots and potatoes were synonymous with survival through the winter. They were the treasures of a family and something to be circulated between friends and neighbors. Giving them to one another was a sign of love and affection. Little has changed since.*

Monotony and repetition were to be expected at home and outside, as everyone was supposed to eat and dine in the same fashion, whether they liked it or not. Even the most creative cooks had their wings clipped by the limited range of ingredients and continual shortages.

For example, stores offered only two lemonades, one yellow and one pink. A basic selection of spices, meats, fresh fruit and vegetables was all locally sourced during their natural growing season. Needless to say, foreign influences, especially those coming from the imperialist West, were kept to a minimum.

Drinking Coca Cola, which would have had to have been smuggled from abroad behind the backs of vigilant border guards by some fluke, or bribe, was an act of a true political rebellion. Instead, most exotic goods came from the East.

But these too were few and far in-between. A curious exotic powder broadly referred to as 'curry', a token to the befriend-ed Asian socialist republics, was as exotic as the imports ever got.

*Since western brands were forbidden from entering the market, Czechoslovaks created their own versions of iconic capitalist products. Czechoslovakia's very own version of Coca Cola was, and still is, called Kofola. Made of ground coffee beans, the drink was actually a healthier and less sugary version of the western legend.*

*Czechoslovakia also had its own signature hot drink: Granko, the nation's hot, instant, chocolate beverage of choice. Far from a fancy hot cocoa, it tasted similar enough, and it was beloved by Czecho-slovak children. Decades later, and with access to the best cocoa goods available, Slovak and Czech offspring still prefer their beloved Granko.*

EVERYDAY
WORK
IS A STEP
TOWARDS
COMMUNISM!

Day in and day out, Czechoslovaks were faced with the same select dishes. No wonder the excitement of eating vanished into thin air. The options were: meat with rice or potatoes, then again sweat cakes, fried cauliflower or goulash. The weekly rote was combined with a slightly more diverse portfolio of soups.

These were the times when a luxury meal consisted of a slice of meat, accompanied by a scoop of rice, as well as a handful of potatoes. A combined side was a mark of a very special occasion.

The Sunday lunch became the embodiment of the era, and its stiff, uniform eating rituals. Wherever you went in the Republic, you would be served the same Sunday menu of beef or chicken broth, schnitzel or roast chicken, and a mandatory portion of rice, or potatoes, spiced up by a serving of compote.

A break in the routine was a cause for concern – could the family not afford schnitzels or was it harboring revolutionary sentiments?

Away from home, the state took over and made sure its human capital was properly fed to perform. School kitchens and work canteens dished out set menus, guaranteeing a warm lunch to everyone. There was no such thing as a vegetarian option. Such special food requirements were nonsense, not to be catered to.

The main concern for school and work kitchens was the quantity of food and not its quality. Little did it matter where that mandatory calorie count came from, as long as no one left feeling empty in the stomach.

Children, at critical points of growing and in need of important nutrients, were fed the usual combo of potatoes, rice and meat. Let us not forget about meatless Fridays, when sweet buns or rice pudding would make a regular lunchtime appearance.

Meals would be washed down by the quintessential sweeten black tea, ladled out from a large pot by lunchroom ladies. These women were the true matriarchs of public food spaces. Their commanding and often large presence was only superseded by their robust serving proportions.

*Salad did not feature high on the socialist menu. Czechoslovakia was dependent on locally grown, seasonal vegetables that were simply not available throughout the year. The precious fresh summer salads of garden tomatoes and cucumbers were replaced with pickles and compotes for the remainder of the year.*

*Moreover, the pragmatic communist cuisine saw salads as too fiddly, and nowhere near as filling as potatoes. Green leaves were written off as impractical.*

*Still, many sighed with relief, when summer brought back fresh lettuce. It was the only leafy vegetable that was accepted into the Slovak food pantheon. Served with a sprinkle of icing sugar and a drizzle of concentrated lemon juice, it was a true seasonal treat. Unfortunately, this is there the imagination ended, when it came to alternative salad dressings.*

The socialist period was certainly not a treasure trove of culinary delicacies.

However, its culture of the delicatessen was brought to a level of communist perfection and cold buffets became an icon of the era. These boasted a proud selection of mayonnaise spreads and other delights. Czechoslovaks loved to replenish themselves on their mid-morning breaks with a small bowlful of one of these mayonnaise-heavy spreads, served with a bread roll. Life was simply unimaginable without these little pieces of heaven.

At the heart of it all were the famous Czechoslovak open sandwiches. No wedding reception or humble birthday party was complete without a selection of open sandwiches. They were so popular that a special type of bread, something between a baguette and a loaf, was invented to satisfy the Czechoslovak sandwich craze.

> *The Wallachian Salad, a popular snack food, became the undisputed king of Czechoslovaks delicatessens. But, the story of the commie's favorite salad goes back to imperial Austria-Hungary. The original recipe was an invention of the owner of the very first delicatessen founded in 1911. It did not take long and the 'salad', which was more of a spread, made its way into the bellies and hearts of Czechoslovaks as a staple.*

> *The pioneering delicatessen did not escape the consequences of the regime change either. The shop was confiscated by the state, but the stubborn family refused to share their recipe with the government. The Wallachian Salad was to forever remain a family heirloom. Out of fear of a public uproar, the comrades created their very own version of the famous salad. That socialist spin on the traditional recipe is the one that people still use today.*

*chlebíček*

*An unwritten rule prescribed what a proper sandwich looked like — on top of a base layer of butter or mayonnaise spread, there was a slice of ham, a hard-boiled egg and pickled cucumber. The mosaic was incomplete without a sprinkle of grated cheese to top it.*

The regime altered the culinary architecture of the republic. Work-places and schools all opened their own in-house cafeterias to feed people quickly. Restaurants seemed to disappear from the urban landscape, one by one. Some closed down, while others converted to quintessential buffets or prudent canteens, serving ready cooked meals.

Eating out was far too bourgeois of an experience to the communist liking, as was finding pleasure and delight in any act of consumption.

The few restaurants that miraculously did remain served more or less what people cooked at home. They were a source of little excitement. For that, you would have to visit one of the handful upmarket restaurants. These catered to high Party officials and their close circles. Inaccessible to the masses, they were the only opportunity to escape the greyness of food in communism.

These restaurants were places to be seen and served. Some modern European delicacies, including snails and frog legs, sourced by local entrepreneurial school children that caught and peddled them to restaurants for pocket money, were also available.

*Cooking beautifully and imaginatively was unnecessary and so there were only a handful of celebrity chefs in communist Czechoslovakia to tickle the taste buds of foreigners and high Party officials.*

*Restaurants employed people who could cook, bottom line. The waiting staff was there simply to bring you the food ordered. Any customer service beyond that, a smile or an expression of politeness, was hard to come by. This legacy proves hard to shake off, even decades later.*

*The imprint of over 40 years of very 'basic' cooking is still felt in the region today, especially outside bigger cities. There, restaurant menus look curiously similar to those of the past. The same could be said about the restaurant service.*

# THE ART OF ENGINEERING THE HUMAN SOUL:
## CREATING A HOMO SOVIETICUS

Nothing could exist in Czechoslovakia without the approval of the Party. Art was no exception. Its purpose was neither to aesthetically please nor to provoke thought or discussion. Instead, artists, from painters to writers, were integral to the propaganda effort. Stalin himself referred to them as *"the engineers of the human soul."*

The quote continues and reveals what a tremendous role that the arts played in totalitarianism: *"the production of souls is more important than the production of tanks, which is why print is the sharpest and the strongest weapon of our party."*

The job of the creative class was simple - to celebrate the regime and the ideology and to damn capitalism and democracy. A new genre was born that became known as socialist realism. It was the only permitted form of artistic expression, in the early years of communism.

From sculpture to literature, all art was expected to glorify the working class and to sing praises to the ideology that brought emancipation to the proletariat.

The epic struggle for justice, equality and better working conditions, while exposing all the ailments of their rival ideology, was the chime of the day. The exploitations of imperialism, the moral corruption of bourgeois decadence, and the multicultural cosmopolitan lifestyle were properly demonized.

On the other side of the spectrum, the virtues of the political East and the purity of the proletariat were flaunted without a drop of modesty. A new model of the perfect human being was created - Homo Sovieticus was born to permeate all forms of artistic expression.

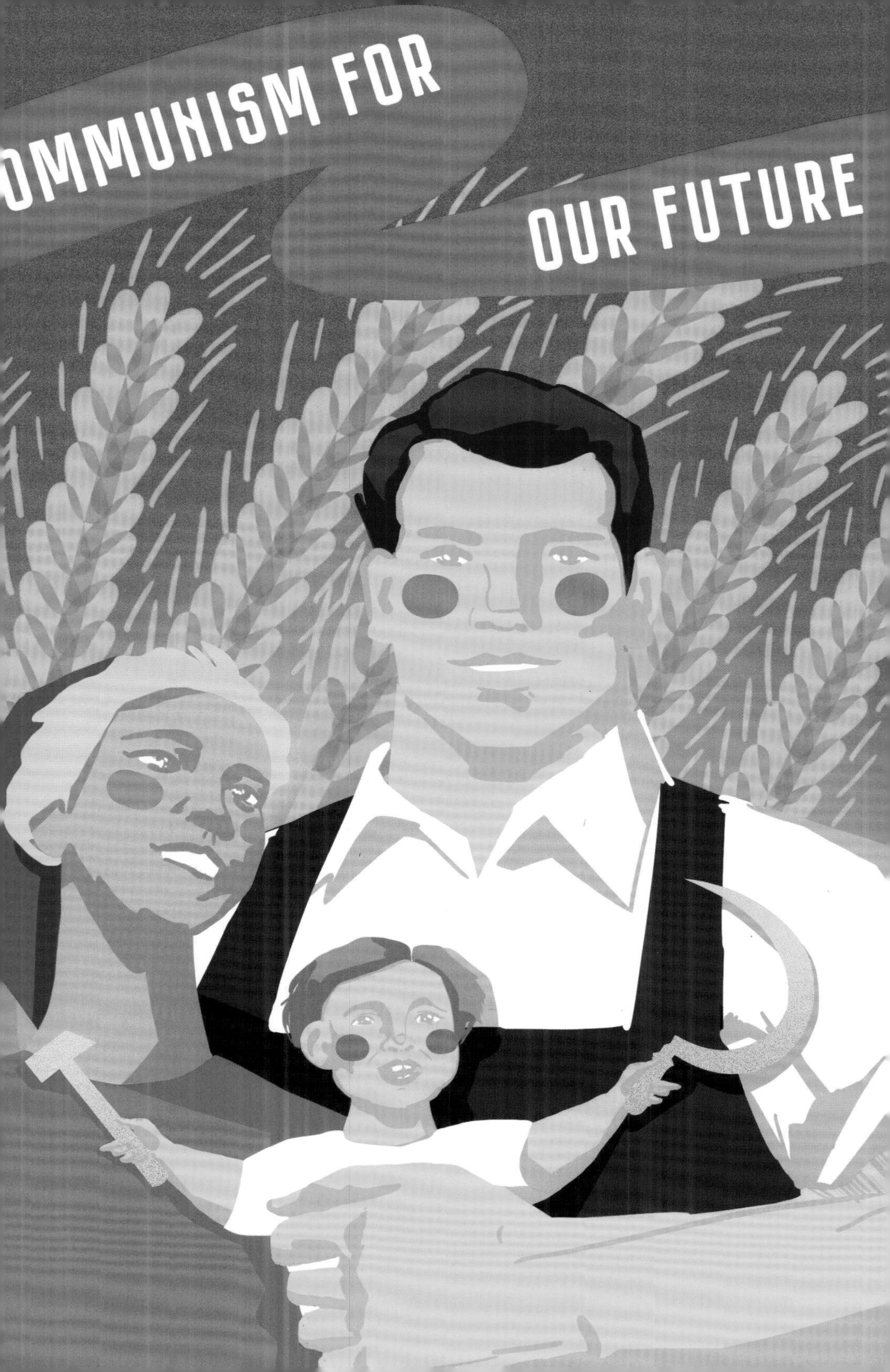
OMMUNISM FOR
OUR FUTURE

In the world viewed through the lens of communism, all was very black and white. Reality was based on material values, numbers and hard science. There was little space for imagination, fluffy emotions, or even beauty for that matter.

Socialist realism demanded of the artist to re-create a truthful representation of an idealized reality. This meant also replicating the stark and somber reality of communism.

The omnipresent Party gaze was suffocating for all, but it was most unbearable for artists.

All artistic production, including books, songs and films, had to pass strict censorship criteria. The desire to create freely drove many artistic souls to flee to the West. If they did, all their work, be it a book or a film in which they had a minor role, were permanently banned from the country. When a singer fled the regime, his or her songs would disappear from Czechoslovakia, as if they had never existed.

*Censorship was always tight in Czecho-slovakia, but it became flat-out absurd after the Soviet invasion in 1968. Everything was meticulously scrutinized for double meaning. The potential tongue in cheek subtext was most feared.*

*For example, a popular Czechoslovak singer had one of his songs banned from the airways in the 1980s. The authorities believed that the song lyrics were too provocative. Why?*

*According to the lyrics, a man flipped a coin to describe the sincerity of the love he felt for his romantic interest. This was interpreted as an insult to the Czecho-slovak currency. Talk about political insecurity.*

No children's playgrounds and public park were spared from the visual reminders. The omnipotent statues and busks of domestic or Soviet leaders kept vigilant watch over streets and squares of the Republic. Memorials celebrating the Soviet liberation from the Nazis, by far the most popular art topic, dotted the public landscape and imagination.

Most of these memorials survived the fall of the Iron Curtain. Countless reminders of the past are still present in Slovakia and the Czech Republic today. Take a wander anywhere in the country and you cannot be mistaken, for they all look very similar. The square, solid and strong features, with perhaps a statue or a plaque in the middle, express the gratitude of Czechoslovakia to the Soviet Union for its liberation.

*While cities boasted grand monuments and sculptures, the regions received more subtle displays of the Soviet friendship. They depicted soldiers standing on a column.*

*Back in the day it was Virgin Mary holding a baby Jesus that crowned those pillars. Now it was army men flocked by children, looking up to their strong masculine saviors.*

*Art, beauty and godly devotion, whether to a spirit in the sky or the ideals of an ideology, were merged into one. This is how the propaganda built on the symbols of Christianity, and the Roman Empire in Czechoslovakia. In doing so, it tapped into the collective subconscious and fortified its social conditioning.*

**COMMUNISM, A COMMON THING FOR ALL PEOPLE!**

Literature became one of the most popular avenues of infiltrating the minds of the population. This made writers into precious national assets. Today, their stories sound almost charming in their blatant propaganda, but back then they were to be taken seriously.

Regime-friendly publications aggressively promoted the Party and its vision. They were not meant for leisurely reading. On the contrary, they were the literary expression of the communist doctrine.

These books taught the population how to think, behave and even dream. Reading them was not only encouraged, it was expected. Mandatory reading lists followed one's life from school to employment. Read on to immerse yourself in the signature plots and storylines of the communist writing period.

A young Czechoslovak orphan girl was born far from beautiful. Growing up in an orphanage, she had no friends and was not popular at school. Despite her familial misfortune and physiological disadvantage, she was strong and perseverant in character. She aspired for nothing more than to become a good citizen and the best milkmaid in the republic. To achieve her heart's desire, the girl sets off on a mission to read all the book about cows and the different techniques of milking them that she can lay her hands on.

To prove that hard work, in the name of the republic, would never go unnoticed, the girl receives an internship to the USSR. Upon her return back to her home village, she becomes the best milkmaid in town, as well as the most popular girl around. Unfazed by the attention and fame, she chooses to remain humble and shy. Having achieved what she wanted, she sets herself a new ambition - to teach the rest of the local women how to milk cows the best way possible, the Soviet way!

It does not take long before the most handsome man in the village takes notice of her devotion to the ideals of communism. He falls in love with her instantly. The story ends with a big kiss and a noble promise: the milkmaid and Mr. Handsome will continue to build socialism together.

*There was little room for romance or intimacy in communist literature. Couples had far more important matters to discuss. The future of the regime depended on their devotion to work. However, this story, along with many other similar inspirational pieces, always carried many sexual innuendos to encourage copulation between Czechoslovaks. The expression of love, or lust, were to never to step out of their firmly prescribed borders. Love and sex were weaponized and re-directed towards the vision of building a better world: man, women and child, the holy trinity shining for a better tomorrow.*

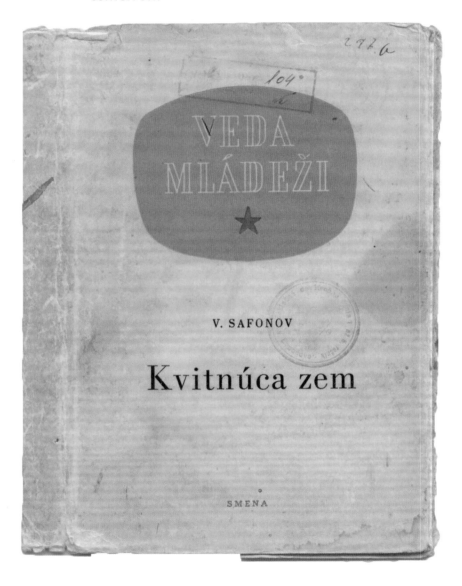

The story begins with a murder. The plot revolves around a young communist boy, sitting peacefully on a branch, while enjoying the sweat taste of a juicy pear. All of a sudden, a stick comes flying through the air, hitting the boy on his head and knocking him to the ground. The owner of the pear tree, a horrible and ugly man, could not stand that somebody else was consuming what belonged to him. The tree and all its pears were his, and the boy had violated his private property. A young communist boy is killed by an evil and greedy capitalist for the innocent act of climbing up a tree and taking a bite out of bountiful nature.

Although the capitalist did not intend to kill the boy, that is exactly what happens. The boy falls to the ground unconscious and dies in the hospital several days later. At the funeral, the devastated mother, who has lost her son, her only child, also has lost all hope for life. Just as she decides that there is nothing to live for, the national anthem of the Soviet Union fills the wake. Wiping her distraught eyes, the woman gathered herself. At that moment, she realizes that she does have something to live for after all - the great rise of the socialist vision.

# The SOCIALIST
## ENTERTAINMENT INDUSTRY

TV is an influential medium in any era and country. Most Czechoslovak households eventually owned a television, but their precious apparatuses only broadcast two TV channels, and both were propaganda mouthpieces of the Party. No surprise there.

Documentaries, television series and films became elaborate commercials for the regime. They celebrated the successes of communism and its supremacy over democracy in pretty much everything. No opportunity was missed to remind Czechoslovaks of their good fortune of living in the Eastern Bloc. Propaganda was shoved down the people's throats.

> *Indeed, only Eastern Bloc products, cars, tractors and helicopters, as well as washing powder, biscuits and mayonnaise, could ever appear on Czechoslovak screen and films. These artificially planted commercials were inserted uncreatively, and often came at the cost of the plot.*

Czechoslovak TV catered to all the builders of socialism. Public indoctrination required it, from toddlers to pensioners, and no cohort was spared.

Every day at 7.15pm, the TV belonged to the boys and girls of the republic. A 15-minute program called 'Little Evening' became the television version of endearing bed-time stories. The short cartoon was to imbue young children to core human but also socialist values, right before they slipped off into the unconscious.

Truth be told, the program was done very well. It was an audio-visual treat that standardized bedtime for the republic's little darlings. All the while, each episode also contained a powerful moral parable to learn from. The little program was a valued education tool.

> *The creators behind the children's show Bambulka were tasked with a grand vision in 1982. They were to program the next generation to swear their allegiance to the expansion of communism. The end goal was noble – a more just world for everyone. But, to achieve that, the regime needed to secure the 'buy-in' early on.*

> *The show introduced young children to the Slovak way of life, and it immediately became a big hit thanks to its playfulness and heartfelt messages. Every episode ended with a lesson learned. Unlike the empty propaganda of the times, Bambulka really did add value to the life of both children and parents.*

Fridays were dedicated to paying tribute to the liberators of the country, in what became known as 'Soviet Admiration Night'. Every Friday evening the content, including news, sitcoms and movies aired in the country, was imported from the Soviet Union. The enforced 'Soviet Admiration Night' was an opportunity to refresh the Russian language skills of the Czechoslovaks. It also helped to renew respect and gratitude for their ideological leaders.

Weekends belonged to extremely popular entertainment shows. These followed a carefully prescribed format of comedy acts and musical performances. Only state approved singers and actors could ever appear in them.

Entertainment that was not produced at home or within the Eastern bloc, was more or less banned. This meant that the Soviet world had to produce its own versions of what was popular in the West, including its pop-culture, Wild West epics and iconic cartoons - anything to stop the people from reaching over the barbed wire for the forbidden fruit.

The strategy worked, and for a while the entire Eastern Bloc was smitten by the handsome native American hero - Winnetou. Appropriately, Winnetou was born in the head of Karl May, an East German who never set foot in the Americas. Yet, his character went on to become the greatest Wild West legend of the Eastern Bloc.

From a series of books to a series of films, Winnetou inspired an impressive cult following that no Western blockbuster would be ashamed of. Many Czechoslovak men, who were only boys when the Winnetou mania hit the communist world, still base their ideas about Native Americans on Karl May's television tales.

On the other side of the empire, the Soviets created their own version of the emblematic cartoon 'Tom & Jerry'. Their series was called 'Nu Pogodi' and revolved around a very similar narrative to the Warner Brothers plot. A wolf was always trying, but perpetually failing, to capture a rabbit.

The regime did not stop at films and TV shows. Music has always been a powerful tool of control or liberation. In order to keep Czechoslovaks happy and obedient, many western hits were reproduced into Czechoslovak covers, with Party approved lyrics.

The Eastern Bloc even had its very own version of the Eurovision song contest. *Intervision*, an annual Soviet-bloc song parade, grew much bigger and more popular than the original. People commonly think that the first competition was held in Poland in 1977, but that is not entirely true. The roots of the contest are a little bit older and purely Czechoslovak.

The very first edition of *Intervision* was a baby of the Czechoslovak National Broadcaster. It was founded with the intention not to rival Eurovision, but to nurture a connection between the West and the East in a pan-European talent show.

The very first edition was held in 1965 at the time of increasing relaxation of the regime, but its tradition was short lived. The invasion of 1968 spelled the end of the ambitious project. There was no room for such an East-West endeavor in the world of renewed soviet totalitarianism.

The second edition opened in 1977, not so much to connect to the world, but to show off. The communists wanted to prove to the West that the East was beyond progressive. The contest was opened to all countries in the world, regardless of their political regime.

The popularity of Intervision was not attributed to its regular contestants. What caught the people of the East's attention were the intervals in-between the performances. They were filled with the exciting performances of acclaimed western artists, the names whose work was otherwise banned from entering the Czechoslovak territory.

Thanks to the exceptional platform of Intervision, people from Bratislava to Vladivostok were glued to their television sets watching the legends of the world music scene, too afraid to blink, so as to not miss any detail of the rarity. The multinational song contest of the Soviet world offered a window into an otherwise forbidden West. The curtains were lifted once a year only.

*Despite its far-reaching success, Intervision experienced an abrupt end, only a few years after its creation. In 1980, Poland, the traditional host country, was going through turmoil. Solidarity, an anti-communist movement, grew from strength to strength. It even orchestrated strikes in the Gdansk shipyards, just a stone's throw away from where Intervision was being held.*

*Exhausted workers were asking for more freedom. In an act of solidarity and protest, the Polish contestant came on stage and sang 'Our house is burning'. That was the last straw that broke the camel's back. Martial law was declared in the country as protesters clashed with police, backed by large tanks that appeared out of the blue.*

*Moscow decided an example was to be made of the 'Polish incident'. There would be no more Intervision song contests.*

Although the Party was more than just reluctant to air anything not made in the Eastern Bloc, there were special occasions in which a few films were broadcast. They became a secret and highly seductive weapon, unleashed during important religious festivals.

To stop people, mostly Czechoslovak women, from going to church, the communists proved willing to comprise on their otherwise strict moral code. Angelique, a much-loved French film series that followed the adventurous love escapades of a beautiful *femme fatale*, would surely keep the ladies of the republic at home, and away from God.

Yet, it was not all doom and gloom. The restrictions of the era pushed human creativity into new and unexplored areas.

Anything other than the glorification of the regime became untouchable. The creatives had to find new ways to express the grand themes of the arts.

The artists who did not want to sacrifice themselves on the altar of a brave political statement turned to ordinary life for inspiration.

Their stories did not offer superheroes or suspenseful conspiracy plots, but they were deeply touching. Films and songs that explored the extraordinary and bittersweet themes of the more mundane, but no less remarkable, cycle of life including love, death and friendship. These were outside of political commentary. To this day, they constitute the golden vault of Czech and Slovak cinematography.

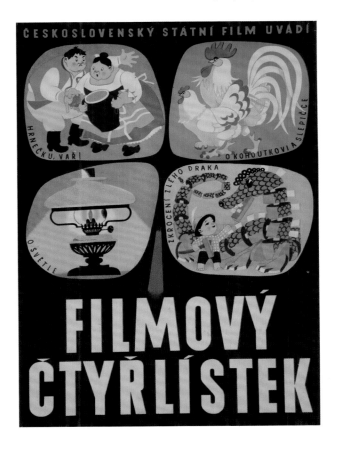

# THE SHOOTING STAR OF
# EASTERN BLOC SHOWBIZ

*Karel Gott was born in Pilsen to a normal family of a clerk turned factory director. An outlier from the very beginning, the young boy had ambitions beyond leading a normal and boring life behind the Iron Curtain. First, he wanted to be a painter, but the national art schools would not have him.*

*Denied his creative outlet, he then enrolled in a standard vocational school to train as an electrician. But his larger than life personality could not be satisfied by the excitement of a communist class room, or the promise of the manual job that came after it.*

*As a teenager, the pro-active Karel designed an escape plan coded 'Journey to the North' together with his best friend. Their plan was to flee to the capitalist West via the corridor of Eastern Germany. It failed, and the boys were caught by the police. Life was not looking up for the young Karel; with this serious blemish in his records it went from bad to worse.*

*Nevertheless, he remained resilient. He found an avenue to shake off his disappointment by channeling his creative energy into his personal passion: music. Starting at the very bottom, he attended singing competitions and sung at local clubs and coffee shops. An electrician by day, a singer by night, this double life soon became exhausting.*

*Karel decided to take the risk and pursue singing professionally. At first, the Czechoslovaks were not quite sure what to make of him. His lively, playful, flirty, personality driven performances did not fit into the rigid blueprint of the late 1950s. But then swing arrived in Czechoslovakia and took the music scene and dance floors by storm.*

*The political thawing of the 1960 worked in Karel's advantage too. He seized the opportunity in a spectacular fashion. His first smash hit even got him a singing engagement in Las Vegas. Those were the days!*

*Having harvested success in the US, Canada and Western Europe, Karel returned to Czechoslovakia to release his first album. His career skyrocketed from then on. Fame and the adoration of girls and women followed. East Germans were fainting at the mere sight of him. Thousands upon thousands of fan letters and sold-out mass concerts, both at home and across the Eastern Bloc, became the norm.*

*Karel was living his dream.*

*The young man was so loved that the regime simply had to follow suit. Compromises had to be made and the dashing Karel became the mascot of communism and the darling of the Party. He also made a lot of money for them. Some rumors say that he only too willingly collaborated with the system.*

*Who knows the whole truth, but it is beyond a doubt, that if he wanted to protect his career in a regime that was not keen to support the success of such gigantic dimensions, there would have to be some bargaining.*

*Gott's success peaked in the 1980s. As the dissident movement was growing and people left, right and center were signing the Charter 77, a manifesto of freedom, Karel Gott made a questionable move. He was the pop cultural icon who signed a counter-charter created and circulated by the Party.*

*The fact that he never defied the regime and collaborated with it instead tainted his record in the eyes of the public. After 1989, many Czechoslovaks would reproach him for being spineless. But a great many more continued to love his music. Regardless of ideology or era, Karel's career continued to flourish into the 21st century.*

*Karel Gott was the legend of Czechoslovak music and an undisputed king of Czech and Slovak hearts.*

# Give Them
## BREAD and GAMES

Live spectacles are a critical part of human existence. They feed the primal impulse for passive gaiety and are therefore an expedient tool of population control, by appeasing the needs of the masses.

The Romans understood and mastered this technique with their famed gladiator contests. These circuses were used to keep their vast empire satiated and distracted for centuries. The greatest empire on the planet survived and even thrived because it gave the people what they wanted: 'bread and games'.

This *modus operandi* has since been replicated by different regimes, and then communism offered a truly marvelous take on the principle. To cater to the most basic nature of the human being, the leadership across the Eastern Bloc rewarded its hard-working population by putting on opulent parades.

Among them one stood out. It was the Iconic *Spartakiada*, a mass 'sporting' display of the best of what Czechoslovakia had to offer - her human capital.

The ceremony took place in Prague once every five years. Only the best of the best were invited to participate, physically perfect boys and girls, men and women, as well as soldiers. The lucky ones, carefully pre-selected, prepared for their performance for an entire year. They practiced their routine after completing their school and work duties.

On the last Spartakiada in 1985, over 200,000 gymnasts took turns performing a synchronized gymnastic routine before some 1.2 million spectators. These included some of the most important officials in the communist social hierarchy.

The display was nothing short of spectacular, as thousands of bodies moved as one living organism, in a celebration of physical perfection. Row after row twirled, bent, jumped and stretched in unison. The synchronized movements demonstrated the prowess of the collective over the individual. All in all, it was truly a sight to behold and its emotional impact was undeniable.

*Sokol, or Falcon in English, was a Czechoslovak sporting organization that was established in the 19th century. Very popular in the first republic, its bedrock values were that of physical activity and collectivism, which it viewed as essential ingredients to a healthy lifestyle and society. The organization also supported nationalism and the forbidden concept, democracy. Needless to say, Sokol, with a membership of over 1 million people at the time of the communist coup, posed a major threat to the regime. Sokol was therefore banned.*

*Nevertheless, some of the popular Sokol activities were adopted by the regime, who had a similar appreciation for sporting excellence. The iconic Spartakiada was a Sokol practice, snatched up by the regime. The Party recognized it as a useful tool to tap into the hearts and minds of the population.*

EACH OF US
IS A SPARK,
TOGETHER WE ARE
A FLAME!

**JUST LIKE ANY GOOD RELIGION, COMMUNISM TOO HAD ITS RITUALS: GATHERINGS, MARCHES, SLOGANS, SALUTES AND FLAG CEREMONIES WERE ALL PART OF THE ARSENAL.**

Another national treat day was Labor Day. Its processions and festivities took place every year on the 1st of May. Although Labor Day was a public holiday in the republic, everyone from children to senior citizens were expected to be seen on the streets, attending the string of grand processions that passed through every Czechoslovak town and city.

The most impressive was always held in the capital. Shop and flat windows were adorned with flags of the Soviet Union and Czechoslovakia. Red carnations, little socialist verses and posters with communist slogans were also on display during the 'mandatory' day of merry making.

In the Slovak capital of Bratislava, the procession culminated at the Slovak National Uprising Square. This was where Party head honchos greeted the parading workers. The leaders, always elevated from the crowd, would watch the procession from a tribune. After a succession of lofty but standardly boring political speeches, a cultural program would follow for all to enjoy.

To make sure no one had any superficial excuses as to why they could not be able attend the national celebration, extra buses were mobilized to bring people from the suburbs of the capital into the center.

Not being seen on the 1st of May ritual meant failing to attend to one's socialist duties. The fearful stories of what happened to social deviants in communism, as well as the promise of yummy delicatessen and other scarce goods made available on the celebrations, as well as the attractive cultural program, kept people in line and in attendance.

# HONOR TO WORK!

**PROLETARIANS OF ALL COUNTRIES, UNITE!**

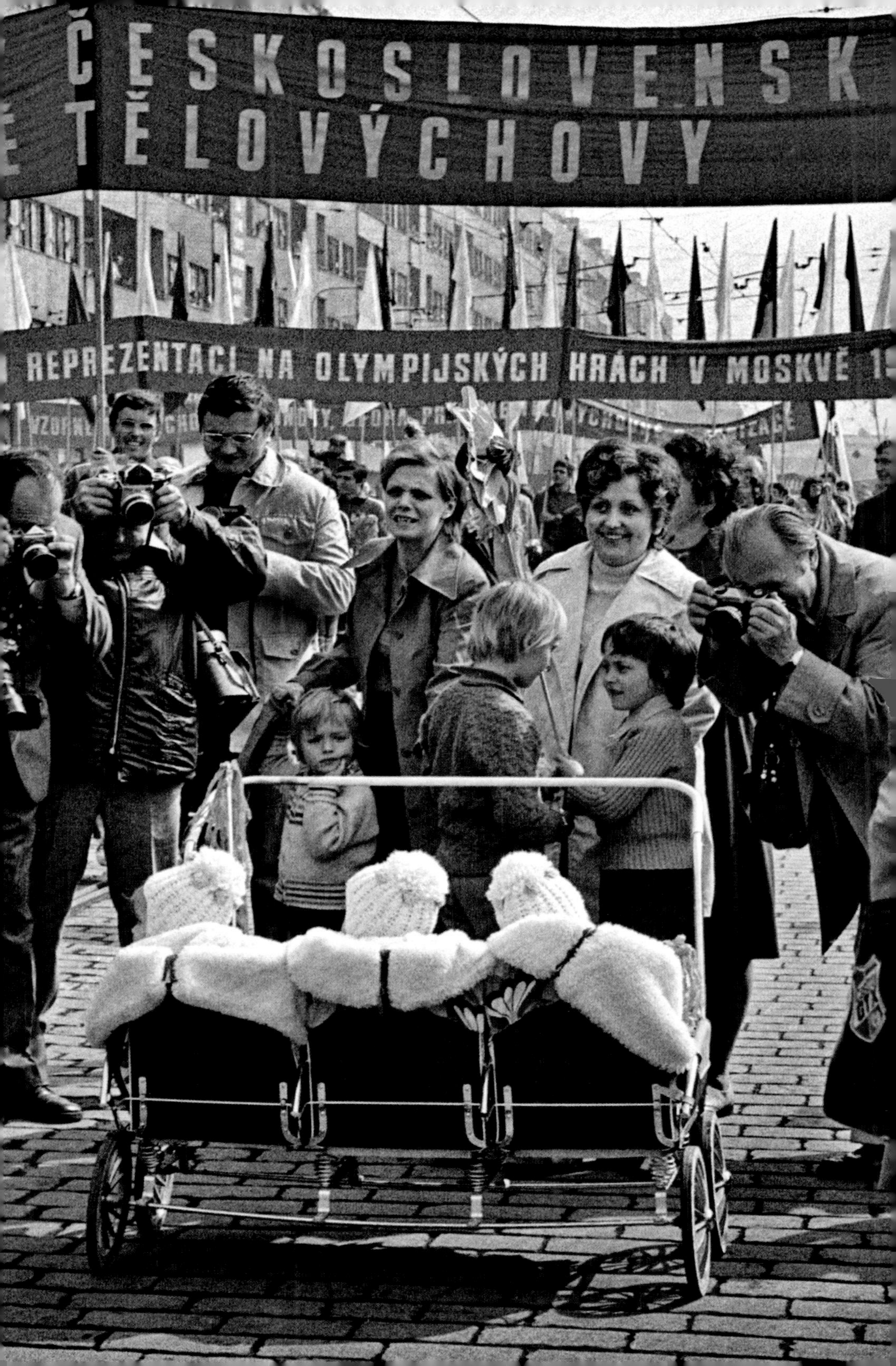
ČESKOSLOVENSK
TĚLOVÝCHOVY
REPREZENTACI NA OLYMPIJSKÝCH HRÁCH V MOSKVĚ 1

# PART
# FOUR

# The
# RESISTANCE

# COURAGE IS MASTERY OF FEAR, NOT ABSENCE OF FEAR.

*MARK TWAIN*

The communist regime did all it could to convert everything and everyone to its gospel, yet human nature is unpredictable. We are simply far too intricate and complicated. In any climate of suppression, a resistant counter-culture is bound to rise.

Not everyone in Czechoslovakia submitted to the ideology. The Party was powerful, but it could not crush the dreams, ideals, determination or memories of every single Czecho-slovak. A community of dissidents, from artists to nuns and everyone in between, put their careers, futures, even lives at risk to take a stand for freedom.

These people could no longer bear living in a climate of fear and suppression. They saw through the lies and grew tired of being governed by absurd and unjust norms and practices. They had enough of the propaganda and censorship and wanted to help liberate the people from being told what to do, how to think and what to say.

But, with no way of voicing their concerns and criticism openly, they resorted to covert ways of expressing themselves to subvert the regime that controlled them.

Under the foot of the communists, a rebel community was born. It fate was to live life outside the mainstream norms and their influence. The resistance movement birthed its own identity and thousands of Czechoslovaks lived and breathed the defiant counterculture, for the most part covertly.

This elusive community was also a haven where everyone knew everyone. United by a vision, as well as a common enemy, the underground network served as a shield against the all-surrounding and all-pervading control of the Party.

It was a source of hope fiercely dedicated to maintaining seeds of freedom and diversity.

However, it would be wrong to assume that all anti-regime protests were a manifestation of this intellectual circle. On the contrary, people from all walks of life found small and big ways of expressing their dissatisfaction with the state of matters in their country.

The beating heart of the underground ecosystem could be found in Prague. Its Slovak version centered in and around Bratislava was more humble. One of the reasons for its smallness had to do with loyalty to communism. After all, the regime – particularly in Slovakia - had upgraded the lives of millions of people.

Bratislava was one of very few cities in Slovakia to have an organized and active circle of rebels. But, the dynamism of the Slovak counter-culture was very different from that of Prague. This underground community was a perplexing anomaly.

In Bratislava, the official culture of the state and the parallel culture of the would-be revolutionaries blended into a curious mélange. The Slovak resistance movement brought together people who were neither ardent communists, nor uncom-promising anti-communists. People working for the regime, those who used to work for it, as well as those not in agree-ment with it, met face to face.

The regime was less brutal in Slovakia too.

One of the reasons was that Slovakia did not have enough qualified human resources to run itself. The percentage of qualified or educated human capital was tiny in comparison to the peasants and workers.

The Slovak communists were also Slovak nationalists, vis a vis the Czechs. They understood that Slovakia, a nation of 5 million, could not afford to lose the few knowledgeable professionals it had, if it wanted to sustain its culture. This also meant a compromise.

*Slovaks, already a minority in Czecho-slovakia, was a part of the Kingdom of Hungary for 1,000 years. A people that had already survived an attempted at their colonization were not ready to throw in their towel, just because the republic had turned red.*

*A silent agreement was struck among the Slovak officials of the regime; they would take a more lenient approach when it came the suppression of their professional capital. Some critical assets had to be preserved.*

Still, many Slovak intellectuals lost their jobs during communism or were forced to work in manual jobs and saw their lives crumbled into ruins because of it. Many others continued in their public sector professions, while also remaining on the periphery of the dissident movement.

It was not ideal as far as the Party was concerned, but there hardly was a choice. In small Bratislava and Slovakia, everyone was pretty much related to everyone, in one way or another. This meant party and position expulsion was also more sticky and difficult. Over time, a rather large grey zone formed and the Party decided to turn a blind eye to the nuisance.

Slovak communists chose to sacrifice their strict principles in favor of national survival. With the way things were going, how long would it take for the existing Slovak culture and language to blend into Czech customs completely? Probably not very long they thought.

# WHAT WAS CHARTER 77?

*Charter 77 was a civic initiative that was catapulted to fame following the state interception and later imprisonment of the Czech underground rock band, 'The Plastic People of the Universe'.*

*Ironically, the musicians were not strongly politically orientated. The rock group did not so much want to revolt as play their music before an audience. Nevertheless, they defied everything the regime stood for, refused to politicize themselves and their music, and chose to ignore the old structure and embody their freedom by dressing, acting and singing the way they wanted to.*

*After the crackdown and jailing the band members, a petition was crafted in their honor. To the dismay of the Party, 'The Plastic People of the Universe' became the ultimate emblem of the resistance movement.*

*The petition grew very quickly as prominent figures of the political and artistic underground lent their names to the campaign. At the head of it stood Vaclav Havel, the darling of the resistance movement.*

*Created in 1977, the document's official purpose was to cite the human rights violations of the regime.*

*The movement openly spoke about the unjust practice of university admission, and students being denied education on the basis of their parent's political records. What made this document unique was that it boldly and openly reprimanded the Party via a signed petition. It was the first serious public action against the Party, since its rise to power nearly 30 years prior.*

*The original document, carrying the names of 241 signatories from all walks of life in Czechoslovak society, including former members of the Communist Party, was confiscated when Vaclav Havel and his colleagues attempted to deliver it to the government.*

*In consequence, the founding fathers of the campaign, as well as many of the signatories, were prosecuted for their bravery. Vaclav Havel, among others, received harsh prison sentences.*

The dissidents refused to bend to the dictate of communism and implemented many forms of non-violent resistance to invoke change in their homeland.

Some dissidents were more vocal, others more careful. Some held private theatre performances of Czechoslovak authors, and others took to music and set up secret radio stations. Writers used their skills as wordsmiths to sneak subtle messages of resistance into the mainstream.

Every act of deviance served its purpose. Many young people chose to ignore the commonly accepted codes of dressing and grooming as a passive act of resistance. Boys wore long hair and had their ears pierced. Girls put on make-up and shortened their skirts.

The underground activities were so diverse and clever, the tentacles of the Party had to work around the clock to keep up with and suppress the dissent.

Singers and playwrights, the most influential entertainers of the era, sneaked carefully coded protests into their songs and plays, right under the eyes and ears of the apparatchiks. Every single song, poem or play was an indispensable spark that kept the flame of freedom, no matter how tiny, alive in Czechoslovak hearts.

The bravest ones dared to explicitly express their opinion of the regime and the Party in an unmistakably bold and political manner. This battle was spearheaded and kept alive by many, but it was Vaclav Havel who became the its most renowned face.

*Vaclav Havel was a thorn in the communist eye from the very beginning. Born into an affluent upper middle-class Prague family, everything about his pedigree and artistic-intellectual inclinations reeked of bourgeoisie.*

*Not allowed to study at university because of his background, Vaclav nevertheless became a prominent underground poet, writer and playwright.*

*Havel was also a beacon of hope for the resistance movement, and because it, he was routinely hunted and imprisoned by the secret police. Although his health deteriorated in prison, his unwavering spirit inspired the people to vote him president after the fall of the regime. He was a true leader to the people.*

On August 4th 1975, Havel wrote an open letter to President Husak accusing the regime he represented of cultural genocide.

*Dear Dr. Husak,*

*If every day someone takes an order in silence from an incompetent superior, if every day he solemnly performs ritual acts which he privately finds ridiculous, if he unhesitatingly gives answers to questionnaires which are contrary to his real opinions and is prepared to deny himself in public, if he sees no difficulty in feigning sympathy or even affection where, in fact, he feels only indifference or aversion, it still does not mean that he has entirely lost the use of one of the basic human senses: the sense of dignity.*

*On the contrary, even if they never speak of it, people have a very acute appreciation of the price they have paid for outward peace and quiet: the permanent humiliation of their human dignity. The less direct resistance they put up to it – comforting themselves by driving it from their mind and deceiving themselves with the thought that it is of no account, or else simply gritting their teeth – the deeper the experience etches itself into their emotional memory. The man who resists humiliation can quickly forget it, but the man who can long tolerate it must long remember it. In actual fact, then, nothing remains forgotten. All the fear one has endured, the dissimulation one has been forced into, all the painful and degrading buffoonery and, worst of all perhaps, the feeling of having displayed one's cowardice, all this settles and accumulates somewhere on the bottom of our social consciousness, quietly fermenting.*

*Clearly, this is no healthy situation. Left untreated, the abscesses suppurate; the pus cannot escape from the body and the malady spreads throughout the organism. The natural human emotion . . . is gradually deformed into a sick cramp, into a toxic substance not unlike the carbon monoxide produced from incomplete combustion.*

*No wonder, then, that when the crust cracks and the lava of life rolls out, there appear not only well-considered attempts to rectify old wrongs, not only searchings' for truth and for reforms matching life's needs, but also symptoms of bilious hatred, vengeful wrath, and a feverish desire for immediate compensation for all the degradation endured.*

*Vaclav Havel*

Yet, it was not just the politically active and outspoken who challenged the regime.

Ice hockey was the pride and passion of Czechoslovaks and Russians alike. The 1969 World Ice Hockey Championship was an exceptionally high stakes sporting event. Less than one year after the 1968 Soviet invasion of Czechoslovakia, it was an opportunity for the Czechoslovaks to avenge themselves.

The small nation could not take on the military might of the Soviet Union on the battlefield, but they could take out their frustration on the ice rink. Czechoslovakian national hockey team had only one thing on their minds – revenge.

The love for their homeland and the pain of the Soviet betrayal resulted in an unforgettable face-off with the USSR.

Not once, but twice the Czechoslovaks beat the Soviet Union. They did not win the championships, 'only' claiming the bronze medal, but that did not matter. The team went to Stockholm, Sweden with one clear goal – to claim victory over Soviets. Nothing else mattered.

The triumph was not only satisfying, it was a miracle. The men in red had been the consecutive 'Champions of the World' for seven years straight. They were virtually undefeatable on ice.

However, the Czechoslovak team committed an act of political defiance by tramping the silent rules of the socialist brotherhood. They were not supposed to beat their Big Brother in anything, least of all in hockey, the national sport of the Soviets.

Moscow was furious.

The unexpected victory turned into an international political affair. Meetings were called, and the Communist Party of Czechoslovakia had much to explain to Moscow. The red lines were set, and the Czechoslovaks had dared to overstep them.

Despite their best efforts to bring the situation under control, Moscow could do little to stop the nation-wide euphoria that flooded into Czechoslovakia. Small celebrations grew into larger and larger gatherings. Eventually over 500,000 people came together in the towns and cities of the country to celebrate the win together. And to show the Kremlin the middle finger.

The joy of victory quickly turned into anger at the invasion. The event sparked a nation-wide protest against the occupiers, in what became to be known as the 'Czechoslovak hockey riots'. A rumor was later spread that these were incited by the Soviets, to justify the need for harsh treatment against the people.

Such was life in oppressive Czechoslovakia. It turned even the most passive citizens into potential enemies of the regime, at some point in their life. Political activism in its explicit, and more commonly implicit forms, was bound to happen as merely breathing and living as a human was considered a risk.

# A STORY OF A DISSIDENT FAMILY

*I NOW ADVOCATE TOLERANCE FOR ALL PEOPLES.*

MILAN SIMECKA SR.

*Although Vaclav Havel became the face of the Czechoslovak resistance and by far the most famous leader of the movement, the underground community was not built with one man only. One of the most prominent figures of the community, little known abroad, was Czech-Slovak Milan Simecka Sr.*

*A university professor dedicated to the ideals of egalitarianism, Simecka Sr. was one of the first to embrace communism and join the Communist Party. After the coup of 1948, his faith in the ideology was damaged and he lost all remaining sympathies for the ideology after 1968. By refusing to toe the Party line, he became a target. He knew all sorts of Party moves and secrets, which made him very dangerous.*

*Being formally castigated did nothing to shake Milan's resolve to speak out publicly against the regime, a passion that was set aflame following the occupation of 1968. That year, he was forced out of his job as a university professor, and reallocated to a menial position. That is also when he wrote his greatest work, a treatise against totalitarianism.*

*'The Restoration of Order' became a much sought-after book, both at home and abroad, as very few publications managed to document the normalization strategies in such a crystal-clear manner.*

*With the precision of a surgeon and without demonizing the regime and the individuals in it, Simecka described how the mechanism of normalization was implemented. Through a language and style that was accessible to everyone, he gave the silent and often tacit phenomenon of total control through psychological manipulation, a conceptual framework.*

*Thanks to his genius, the people could now comprehend what was happening to them and protect themselves from it.*

The book was a smash hit in the underground dissident community. The publication became a survival manual. The theories laid out in it were discussed late into the night in many living rooms and kitchens across the republic.

The West was delighted too. At last, the people on the other side of the Iron Curtain could get their heads around the mechanism of mute monstrosity that normalization was.

Such influential work could not go unnoticed by the officialdom. Simecka, once the shining star of the Party, was sentenced to prison for over a year. As upsetting as his fate was, many were shocked at the lenience of the prison term.

The state was not stupid. The communists knew how sensitive the Simecka case was thanks to his influence and popularity. The incident had to be handled with appropriate care. The last thing the Party wanted was to create a martyr who could stir a revolution or attract more attention from the West.

That is why the punishment of Simecka Sr, the rebel with a sharp pen, was symbolic more than anything. However, in the true spirit of subtle control techniques, it would go on to affect the life of his promising offspring. The regime went after the bloodline.

The regime had already stripped Milan Simecka Sr of his profession and status, put him in prison and forbade him from ever writing again. There was nothing else the communists could do to him personally, which is why they turned to his son, Milan Simecka Jr.

At the age of 14, the young Milan, who had a bright future ahead of him, was summoned to attend a meeting that was to decide his fate.

A senior Party official awaited Milan and sat him across a large mahogany table. There he offered the teenager an impossible deal. Either he formally denounced the activities of his father and separated himself from his dissident family, or he would never be allowed to attend secondary school or enroll for a university education. The unthinkable compromise demanded *a child to betray his own father or suffer if he did not, forever living on the periphery of society as a social outcast, just like his father.*

*Despite the assurances of his father that he would understand his son's choice, for the sake of a better future, Milan Jr refused to make a pact with the regime. How could he turn his back on the man that had raised him, and join forces with a government that had treated his family so unfairly?*

*This is how one of the brightest student progenies of the entire republic was denied the right to an education and had to become a boiler room stoker, as a result.*

*But, the will of the Simecka lineage proved too strong to break. Self-educated Milan Junior threw himself into the resistance movement and, following the collapse of the regime, he became a respected political thinker, journalist, editor and writer.*

*Today, his son follows the family legacy and calling. After studying at Oxford and working abroad, he has returned to his homeland to enter the political arena. He became one of the founding fathers of a new and progressive political party geared at reforming Slovakia.*

# INFORMATION
## Smuggling

> SINCE THE HAND OF THE STATE PENETRATES EVEN TO THE INSIDE OF ITS CITIZENS, EVERY GENUINE STRUGGLE FOR ONE'S SOUL BECOMES AN OPENLY POLITICAL ACT."

VACLAV HAVEL

As part of the ideological seclusion, the communists did not want any uncensored information to circulate on their territory. They viewed anything coming from the West as an unsolicited engagement. Not only was it amoral, it was a ploy to corrupt the moral integrity of the East.

To inform and engage became the priority of the dissident community. They sought to expose the truth hidden behind the lies of propaganda, by giving the population access to a counter perspective. The rousing of the sedated from their complacency and slumber proved to be a huge task to accomplish.

Everyone even loosely affiliated with the publishing or broader media world was monitored. Writers and translators were naturally the most closely watched groups. At first, they were threatened, but as the society developed, the Party could no longer resort to brute physical terror to assert its control.

Instead, the communists compiled profiles on key persons of interest. These were individuals capable of inciting social rebellion. Random unannounced 'visits' to publishing houses, newspaper offices and private homes of the red-flagged creatives became commonplace. Their aim was to destabilize and distract the resistance movement from any coherent and consistent activity.

The inspectors did not need to say much.

The mere presence of STB officers within the privacy of one's home or place of employment was enough to send shivers down the spines of all involved. Many a social and moral ideal were promptly swallowed and forgotten, following such violations of human rights and privacy. Some even conceded to the circumstance, arguing that fighting for justice just wasn't worth the risk.

The intellectual class certainly had the odds stacked against them. Despite the hardship, there were still plenty of courageous Czechs and Slovaks that rose to the challenge, with fearless grace and elegance.

It was an endless battle against the information blackout.

Books played a big role. The devoted few copied works of Czechoslovak dissident writers, as well as foreign literary jewels, by typewriter. Those without access to such tools even copied texts by hand. These precious manuscripts were then circulated among family, friends and fans to help them understand what was 'really' going on around them.

Milan Kundera and George Orwell, among many other talented writers, were personas non-grata in the communist world of literature. Nevertheless, their work was widely read.

> *In 1984, a young Dutch couple smuggled a printer from the Netherlands to Czecho-slovakia to help dissidents print their own newspapers, thereby distributing knowledge and supporting freedom of press. Given the tight border controls, their only chance of getting the printer across the Iron Curtain was to dismantle it into the smallest of pieces. The puzzle was then smuggled through a fake bottom on their caravan.*

> *Once pieced back together, the illegal printer had to be hidden in a series of safe houses, in addition to being relocated ever year. The dissidents couldn't risk losing such a valuable asset. Normal, nonpolitical active families volunteered to shelter it in their homes, at their own risk, all to help with the resistance. To this day, the Dutch printer is in the basement of a family home in Bratislava.*

Much needed assistance also came through foreign diplomatic missions housed in Czechoslovakia. Ambassadors, protected by the international accord of diplomatic immunity, were exempt from border checks. Many used this privilege to smuggle out manuscripts, photographs and anything else that could be used to raise awareness of Czechoslovakia's political situation abroad.

The West was also curious what it was like behind the impenetrable grey sheet that covered more than half the European continent.

News from behind the Iron Curtain was in high demand among the Czechoslovak expat community in Western Europe and North America. Those living in exile wanted to know how their friends and relatives at home were doing. They were also keen to finds ways of supporting the resistance movement. Wealthy Czechs and Slovaks abroad become critical to the homegrown defiance. Their financial support kept the under- ground network alive.

The diplomatic mail delivery service was another way the underground Czechoslovak writers could have their work exported to the free world, and published internationally. Once translated into French, German and English, more and more people could learn about the daily brutalities of life under communism.

Information was also smuggled into the country.

Keen to support the efforts of the oppressed, foreign diplomats went out of their way to indirectly contribute to the resistance effort. Embassies went as far as recruiting tourists to become temporary agents and information disseminators.

How was the information smuggled? Mostly through false bottom suitcases, where foreign newspapers and magazines, like the American *Time* and *Newsweek* were discreetly hidden. Once in Czechoslovak territory, these materials were quickly passed on to the established dissident network that knew exactly what to do with them.

As quickly as they could, these magazines, reports and books were duplicated. It was impossible to keep track of how many copies were in circulation. The dissidents did not really care about the exact numbers. Their mission was to get the information out to as many people as possible.

The rule of thumb was that once a contraband book landed on your desk, you only had one night to read it. This network was disciplined, organized and efficient. It also adhered to the code of 24 hours or less. That's how important it was to to circulate the vital messages and words of the free world with the rest of the underground community.

> *Young university students hoping for a better tomorrow often served as 'runners' for the Czechoslovak underground. They would carry documents taped to their bodies and they shuttled back and forth between Bratislava and Prague. Or else, unbeknownst to their parents, they allowed their family mail boxes to be used as 'safe havens' for passing further information. However, if caught, the Secret Police knew no remorse. Youth, innocence or even young motherhood did nothing to soften them from punishing the 'delinquents'. One young mother, who ran documents between two very prominent dissidents, returned home black and blue after days spent in a cell, refusing to speak about her experience.*

# "A NATION THAT IS AFRAID TO LET ITS PEOPLE JUDGE THE TRUTH AND FALSEHOOD IN AN OPEN MARKET IS A NATION THAT IS AFRAID OF ITS PEOPLE."

JOHN F. KENNEDY

Despite their best efforts to suppress it, the dissident culture persisted. The freedom-loving souls of the republic were highly imaginative when it came to spreading hope. Some set up dissident radio stations which streamed uncensored information, devoid of any state propaganda. These were regularly raided and closed down as well.

But not all could be silenced. Annoyingly, the dissident community resembled a hundred-headed dragon, spitting truth and dreams of freedom wherever it went. What was worse, when the Party chopped one head, three more grew in its place.

> To stop any radio transmission from the West, the USSR chose to use frequencies outside of the ones used by the West. These airways travelled just under the standard FM frequency, and catered to a tech radio hardware made exclusively for the East.

> However, all European radio signals were controlled by the International Telecommunications Union in Geneva. This meant that the institutions had to agree with using such radio signals. Was the West colluding with the Kremlin? Or was is just a matter of cold-hearted business, respecting the status quo and the post-war division?

It is not so easy to completely isolate a country that is located right in the heart of Europe. The Slovak capital of Bratislava is located just a stone's throw from the Austrian border. Due to its proximity, the Party could not prevent Slovaks from catching Radio Vienna or ORF, an Austrian television channel, intermittently.

The state knew about this and did what it possibly could to blur, interrupt and block the information transmission. The sound of the radio jamming became known as the 'Moscow boogie' and was cursed by many. According to the Party, they were protecting the citizens from disinformation campaigns orchestrated by the West.

The Cold War was not a time of rest in the West either. The British set up a Czechoslovak division at the BBC, and the Americans founded the iconic radio station *Radio Free Europe*. It went on to become a symbol of freedom all across the Eastern Bloc. Supported by the US government and made possible by the CIA, *Radio Free Europe* targeted the satellite states of the Soviet Union most actively.

Its first broadcast reached Czechoslovakia in 1950, and it started to send messages to its listeners in the Czech language as early as 1951. The words "This is the voice of free Czechoslovakia calling, Radio Free Europe" filled many a heart with renewed hope and optimism. *Radio Free Europe* aired forbidden music and news from the other side of the Iron Curtain, as well as information on what was going on within Eastern Europe.

The radio was a critical source of knowledge and offered the public a counter-opinion to what they had been programed to believe. This contrast of facts helped to alleviate the information blackout imposed on the country. It was *Radio Free Europe* broadcasting from Munich, West Germany, and staffed by Czechoslovaks who fled the country, that brought the news of the Soviet invasion in 1968 to the masses.

The radio station was a nemesis not only to the Communist Party of Czechoslovakia, but their Moscow leadership. The Soviets had a zero-tolerance policy to ideological contamination. In an elaborate counter-intelligence maneuver, the Soviets designed an infiltration strategy to silence the nagging of freedom forever.

Spies, who presented themselves as Czechoslovak dissidents fleeing the regime, were planted in the West with the objective of infiltrating the headquarters of Radio Free Europe. In addition to that, they were also directed to steal data, know-how and operation procedures.

When it came to it, the KGB would even resort to murders and open attacks. A Bulgarian service respondent was murdered in London in 1978, and a bomb was detonated at the Munich radio headquarters in 1981. To the great relief of the Czechoslovaks, Radio Free Europe persevered and once again freedom proved indestructible.

Music has always been and will always be a potent instrument to inspire, awaken and shake up humanity. A vibrant underground music scene developed in communist Czechoslovakia to circulate messages of freedom. Musicians met to play prohibited western songs, smuggle foreign LPs, or play their own dissident musical creations.

*One of the most famous songs by the legendary Beatles hides a code of resistance with a Czechoslovak imprint. Dezider Hoffmann, an acclaimed Slovak photographer and former RAF pilot, could not return to Czechoslovakia after the communist coup of 1948. He stayed in London and made his way up to the very top of the music industry in the free West.*

*In the winter 1969, a few months after the invasion, he was working closely with the Beatles. Outraged, frustrated and saddened by what was happening in his homeland, he screamed 'Piss off' in Slovak during the recording of the Yellow Submarine, the iconic Beatles' song.*

*This act of personal rebellion was left in the recording to become a covert message of defiance to the Soviets. The single sentence is a reminder of the many little deeds of heroism that penetrated the dark era.*

# The SECRET CHURCH

> **RELIGION IS THE SIGN OF THE OPPRESSED CREATURE, THE HEART OF A HEATLESS WORLD, AND THE SOUL OF SOULLESS CONDITIONS. IT IS THE OPIUM OF THE PEOPLE."**

KARL MARX

It is astonishing that well over half of the population still identified as Catholic in a country whose regime favored and promoted atheism by all means possible. It was not enough to confiscate the property of the Church or ban religious iconography from public spaces.

The Party shut down 216 monasteries and 339 convents in Czechoslovakia, while removing 2,400 monks and 12,000 nuns. They also held public show trials, prosecuted Christian leadership, and handed out death sentences and long prison terms. Ripping the faith of people was and is a messy business.

*The Catholic Church was too big, too powerful, too used to its own status and too organized to be tolerated. Its wings had to be clipped.*

*Ironically, when it came to the issue of Catholicism, Czechoslovak leaders were much more radical than Moscow. In fact, the Russians appeared liberal, compared to the dogmatic Slovak officials, who pushed for far stricter religious rules.*

*They were driven by fear as they knew just how powerful the Church was in this part of Europe. Slovakia had the highest prosecution rates of Christians, out of all the countries of the Eastern Bloc.*

The determination to eradicate religion had the opposite effect in Slovakia. It drew the Christian community into hiding, which only strengthened their persuasion and faith in God. What is more, these religious minded Slovaks saw many parallels with their plight and those of the early Christians, who had to endure similar mistreatment by the Romans in the name of Jesus.

> In 1943, a Croatian priest arrived in Slovakia. Tomislav Kolakovic came to the region not only to participate in the Slovak National Uprising against the Nazis. He came to issue a prophetic warning to the young nation. Kolakovic observed and understood that the geo-political alliances of Europe would be radically altered after the war.
>
> He foresaw that the Slavic countries would most likely fall under the Soviet sphere of influence. The Bolsheviks and their atheist ideology posed a threat to European spirituality, and the priest wanted to prevent Christianity from being erased from the continent. In order to preserve the sacred belief system, and as a preventative measure, he established the secret Church.

The brutal persecutions of Christians gave rise to the Christian resistance, and the creation of a very powerful institution and movement, known as the Secret Church. It became a haven for Slovaks who were not ready to deny their beliefs, but they would have to hide them.

An entire ecosystem of secret seminars, workshops and illegal seminaries prepared new priests to serve the underground community; it also became known as 'the family'. Those secretly ordained would carry proof of their initiation on a piece of cloth that was often sewn into an article of their clothing.

Nevertheless, the underground priests were forced to live double lives. They worked as clerks or manual laborers during the day, and preached the words of God to private audiences by night.

> *Some leading figures of the Catholic, Lutheran and Orthodox Churches, kept their religious services public. Records released after 1989 reveal that a portion of these individuals, officially and unofficially, collaborated with the regime. They helped to spy on church goers, in exchange for keeping their status. At the same time, the Party continued to mobilize their efforts to also disintegrate the religion from within.*

Leading a normal religious life and attending important Christian rituals was not easy in Czechoslovakia, for any believer. Religious practice came with a string of inconveniences. The comings and goings to and from church were monitored by the secret service and also by common people. They were persuaded that they were serving their country by reporting on those who turned up for Sunday worship.

> *Poland was home to a far larger Christian community. This is where religious publications were smuggled from and where Czechoslovak priests were ordained in secret consecration ceremonies. The members of the Polish underground Church were critical allies for the Slovaks.*

A handful of inconspicuous churches were consecrated right under the regime's nose. They were tolerated by the Party, partly because they were not explicit. The sacred spaces were housed in unsuspecting-looking modern buildings, to attract as little attention as possible.

To lessen the surveillance, Slovaks also resorted to attending religious services away from their place of residence, in neighborhoods where nobody knew them by name. Baptizing children was also an act of political defiance and many newborns had to be christened in secret, often miles away from their hometowns and villages.

Even though the communists could prevent people from practicing their religion outwardly, they could not take the faith away from them inwardly.

## OPERATION
# 'SQUANDER THE HOLY SPIRIT'

*The dusty national archives hide many devastating stories marking the perversions of the regime. One belongs to a Protestant minister who escaped to Italy to avoid prosecution. However, the Party was not satisfied with the man being abroad. It wanted the man to become an exemplar case of what happens to people who dare to flee.*

*The STB crafted a detailed plan to lure the minister back to Czechoslovakia, using his own family as bait. The unwilling members were forced to stand before the camera wearing their Sunday best to stage a photograph. There was a fateful letter that accompanied the print. It was written in the name of the reverend's wife, describing how the political situation in Czechoslovakia was beginning to change. The letter ended with an innocent remark, but one that tugged at the minister's heartstrings: the children were missing their father.*

*It was those words that encouraged the priest to pack his bags and return from exile. The man boarded the next train headed to Slovakia, excited to be reunited with his family and his homeland. A very unpleasant surprise awaited him upon arrival. Instead of his wife and children, he was greeted by secret agents. Their sinister plan had worked like clockwork. Confused and shocked, the priest was captured, interrogated, and tortured, before being sent to prison for a very long time.*

*The tragedy did not end there. The feelings of betrayal were far worse than the violence the minister experienced at the hands of the state. He was encouraged to believe the disinformation, and went to prison thinking that his own wife, the mother of his children, had conspired with the STB to deceive him.*

*A man of God, he even requested a divorce. Of course, the party only nudged on his un-Christian actions. Distraught and destroyed by the emotion of the drama, the minister did not even think to question his own jailors, and the lies they had fed him.*

*Such mind games were not uncommon. The ranks of the STB and the Communist Party attracted also the more heartless members of society, including psychopaths. In this case, the minister never found out that he fell victim to a plot. He never reached out to see his family again.*

In truth, the Party was correct to fear the Catholic Church. Not only was it a powerful force within the country, it was headed by the Vatican, the ultimate imperialist and decadent institution of the West.

In turn, the Vatican joined the fight against godless communism.

When a Polish cardinal, Karol Wojtyla, was elected to become the next - and first Slavic - pope in 1978, the event sent a strong politically-charged message to Moscow. It was also more than just a gesture of support to the Christians of the Eastern Bloc. It ignited spiritual resistance.

In the end, it was the Czechoslovak Christians who spearheaded the fall of the regime in the heart of Europe.

# HUMOR
## as Rebellion

The suffocating embrace of the Party left many with few other options than to comply with the dictate. The majority just wanted to live a life in peace, regardless of politics. They wanted to care for their daughters and sons, occasionally get together with friends, celebrate birthdays and anniversaries jovially, grow old with their spouses, and play with their grandchildren.

They were not thrilled by the idea of risking their lives for a principle and so they submitted to the status quo.

Yet, somewhere between the dull and repetitive flux of daily life, and the incessant political propaganda, people dealt with the absurdities of the regime by laughing. In Czechoslovakia, humor became a weapon for resistance.

*The last century of modern Czechoslovak history put the people through unimaginable horrors, trials and tribulations. The turmoil forged a unique reaction to oppression. People coped with life - by laughing. They made ingenious jokes that stripped the nonsense, violence, ignorance and suppression of the authorities to the bone.*

*Even before the arrival of the Soviets, Reinhard Heydrich, Hitler's right hand also known as the architect of the Holocaust, called the Czechoslovaks the 'laughing beasts'. One thing was for certain, the worse the conditions in Czechoslovakia, the better their jokes.*

There was also plenty of inspiration and material for jokes behind the Iron Curtain. The regime was an infinite source of absurdity.

The centralized economy and repression of anything that seemed to veer off the Party's hardline created inherently funny situations. Every single one of these jokes was politically sensitive. Some say they were necessary to cope with reality, others say they allowed the people some form of comic release.

In the tense climate, jibes that ridiculed the regime, its leaders and even the forefathers of the ideology, Lenin and Stalin, were also an act of political rebellion. Telling a joke like that was no laughing matter.

The egos of the Party apparatchiks were fragile, and they took themselves very seriously. Under no circumstances was the Party's leadership, a cluster of very important men, ever to be laughed at. Such jokes were treason and could be a ticket to a gulag or mine.

Such was the infantile reality of life under communism where role play and facades superseded integrity and authenticity. The jokes that made people cry with laughter as they humorously captured this way of life were many. Here are some of the best:

 As long as they pretend to pay us, we will pretend to work.

 Five precepts of Soviet intellectuals:

> ✖ Don't think.
>
> ✖ If you think, then don't speak.
>
> ✖ If you think and speak, then don't write.
>
> ✖ If you think, speak and write, then don't sign.
>
> ✖ If you think, speak, write and sign, then don't be surprised.

 The four degrees of comparison in Czechoslovakia: good, better, best, Soviet.

The Seven Wonders of Czechoslovak socialism:

> 1. Everybody is employed.
>
> 2. Although everybody is employed, nobody works.
>
> 3. Although nobody works, everybody fulfils the plan.
>
> 4. Although everybody fulfils the plan, there are no goods.
>
> 5. Although there are no goods, everybody has everything.
>
> 6. Although everybody has everything, everybody steals.
>
> 7. Although everybody steals, nothing is ever missing.

 What is the most neutral country in the world? Czecho-slovakia. She does not even interfere in her own internal affairs. (made after the Warsaw Pact Occupation of 1968)

 An American tells a Russian that the United States is so free that he can stand in front of the White House and yell, *"To hell with Ronald Reagan."* The Russian replies: *"This is nothing. I can stand in front of the Kremlin and yell, "To hell with Ronald Reagan"* too.

 A man walks into a shop and asks: *"I see you don't have any fish".* The shop assistant replies: *"You've got it all wrong. This is the butcher's. This is where we don't have any meat. Where they don't have any fish is in the fish shop across the road".*

 *"Dad, can I have the car keys?".*
*"OK, but don't lose them, because we will get the car in seven years".*

 *"I want to sign up for the waiting list for a car. How long is it?"*
*"Precisely ten years from today."*
*"Morning or evening?"*
*"Why, what difference does it make?"*
*"The plumber's due in the morning".*

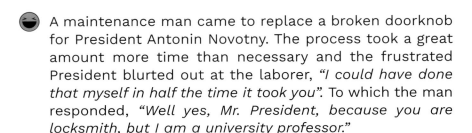

😆 A maintenance man came to replace a broken doorknob for President Antonin Novotny. The process took a great amount more time than necessary and the frustrated President blurted out at the laborer, *"I could have done that myself in half the time it took you"*. To which the man responded, *"Well yes, Mr. President, because you are locksmith, but I am a university professor."*

😆 "Who isn't a communist as a young person doesn't have a heart. Who is still a communist as an adult doesn't have a brain."

## NO JOKING IN THIS REPUBLIC, MAN!

*In 1967, a man told the following joke in a factory in Czecho-slovakia:*

*"Why is the price of lard not going up in Hungary? So that the workers can have lard on bread for their Sunday lunch."*

*To anyone behind the Iron Curtain, this joke hinted at the perennial material shortages in the East. So inaccessible were the most basic of goods that the local people were forced to replace their ritual Sunday meals - roast chicken or schnitzel - with lard sandwiches, because nothing else was available.*

*Unfortunately, this joke was overheard by a party ally, who immediately reported the worker to the officialdom. The consequences were swift and intense. The joke-teller was arrested on charges of regime defamation. But the hardship did not end there, as the employee was to be made an example of. He was fired from the factory.*

*However, justice surfaced in the most unexpected and human of ways. His punishment was reversed, because his factory comrades stood by their friend and persuaded the authorities that the party secretary had not heard his statement correctly. Or, more specifically, he had not heard the words preceding the joke: "I heard a very stupid joke yesterday."*

She might have invaded Russia.

# The
# ONLY OPTION
# WAS ESCAPE

## TODAY ON THE NATO LINE, [US] MILITARY FORCES FACE EAST TO PREVENT A POSSIBLE INVASION. ON THE OTHER SIDE OF THE LINE, THE SOVIET FORCES ALSO FACE EAST TO PREVENT THEIR PEOPLE FROM LEAVING."

RONALD REAGAN

Many Czechoslovaks yearned to leave the constraints of their homeland behind. Artists, intellectuals, ethnic minorities and religious groups were among those who found it hardest to adapt to the despotism of the new regime. They longed to go West. They desired freedom.

A better life lay within eyesight, especially in Bratislava, Slovakia's capital and the only city located on the Iron Curtain. Yet, the only way to leave Czechoslovakia was to escape. Doing that was considered the highest act of treason.

Austria was the most immediate gateway to the West, for the Slovaks. The border was sealed by a string of watch towers, guard dogs, military jeeps and border officers instructed to shoot at any trespasser.

Trespassing being a funny term, considering that these were not people trying to enter the country, but rather to leave.

*The Czechoslovak wolfdog, a hybrid dog, was created in communist breeding laboratories.*

*The obedience and trainability of the German Shepherd combined with the strength and stamina of the Carpathian mountain wolf created the most iconic dog breed of the era. The trainable but fierce attack dog suited the needs of the Czechoslovak military and STB perfectly. The wolfdog was used to secure the national border of Czechoslovakia.*

*However, merging the two species was not straight forward. First, scientists paired a male wolf with a female dog, but the wolf was not interested in cross-breeding with a different species. Then, they combined a male dog with a female wolf, but the dog did not manage to mount the stronger female. The experimentation found success when the scientists found a very dominating German Shepherd and paired it in a cage with a more gentle and submissive female wolf.*

Czechoslovaks who decided to risk it all to lead a freer life somewhere else did their best to cross this minefield.

They hid in cars, under trains, crawled under the barbed wire on foot and even swam across the Danube. Water escapes usually took place just under Devin Castle, which was where the distance between the Eastern Bloc and the free West was at its shortest. Others hijacked airplanes or tanks, took illegal paragliders or tried to dig their way to freedom through makeshift underground tunnels.

The banks of the Danube became a scene of many successful and failed escapes, and a witness to many human tragedies. Border guards were given permission to shoot at everyone and would even be guaranteed a reward, like a family vacation, when they succeeded at stopping people from making it to the other side. There were also cases of people torn to pieces by guard dogs.

*Czechoslovakia experienced two major exoduses. The first occurred after 1948, when 25,000 civilians illegally crossed the border to the West. Another one unfolded after the 1968 Soviet invasion, when another wave of 70,000 people fled by fall 1969.*

*All in all, it is estimated that as many as 300,000 people left Czechoslovakia and headed for the West in the decades following the invasion.*

*After the events of 1968, Western Europe, which had stabilized after the war and were prospering, were more compassionate to the Czechs and Slovaks. They were labelled political refugees and granted the right to stay and work.*

It is no wonder that most escapees preferred to flee alone. Mothers ran without their children, and men without their wives and families. Far from an egotistical act, crossing the Iron Curtain was dangerous and the less people involved in the operation, the better. Once on the other side, the defector could gather his strength and find a way to send for his wife and children. Or, so he hoped.

Under Devin Castle, where the free West and controlled East converged at their closest, border guards stood on alert. With freedom only a riverbank away, the Iron Curtain was further fortified by a series of watchtowers, standing several hundred meters apart. The entire fortification was lined by a track of sand that followed the length of the fence. The surface was painstakingly raked to expose footprints and alert the authorities of escapees.

There was a common 'joke' linked to Devin. On a Sunday afternoon a father and his son are promenading at Devin Castle. The young boy, unaware of the political climate around him, curiously asks his father "Papa, who lives behind the fence?" His father looks sternly at the horizon and replies "we do, son, we do."

Around 300 Czechs and Slovaks perished while trying to cross the Iron Curtain. Death by bullet, explosion, electrocution or drowning became a very real possibility for those who decided to risk it.

> *The brave men and women who crossed to the West believed they could send for their loved ones to join them. Despite the hardness of the Czechoslovak regime, the state made a special provision for the re-unification of families.*

> *The Czechoslovak Red Cross facilitated the reconciliation of mothers and fathers who had been split from their children. This was also a strategic move. A single-parent household was economically unsustainable and therefore a cost on the state. The defection of a parent also served as a reminder of escape. Such outliers were better to be done away with.*

Some opted for a slightly less dramatic option when fleeing the country, on holiday travel permits via the more relaxed Yugoslavia.

Czechoslovaks loaded their little cars with all they could take without appearing too suspicious and headed to Yugoslavia from where they hoped to continue to the West. In this scenario, it was important to appear as normal as possible. That is, like the average holiday maker. Nevertheless, car and bus searches were as thorough as they were merciless. The slightest hint of suspicion, like carrying your university diploma with you, would have you and your family denied exit.

However they escaped, the people knew that there would be severe repercussions for their family and friends who remained behind. The defectors' assets would be immediately confiscated, and their loved ones harassed by the state's secret police. It was the latter that made Czechoslovaks think twice about crossing the West.

Interrogations, career demotions, dismissals from work, and the denial of educational opportunities for the dearest and nearest of the emigrants were the usual means of torturing the souls of the exiled Czechoslovaks from a distance. It was a burden that weighed heavily on the conscience of many. To leave or not to leave was never a simple decision.

Once made, the departure from the Eastern Bloc was final. There was no coming back to Czechoslovakia, unless you were willing to put your conscience at bay and collaborate with the regime. It was not even possible to talk to your loved ones back home, on the phone. All incoming phone calls and letters were heavily censored, especially for any family that had a defector. These households were some of the most monitored.

# E S C A P E  and  R E T U R N

*In 1980, Yugoslavia's border with Italy was left unpatrolled at certain times of the day, and even when it was manned, border guards turned a blind eye to those crossing West.*

*During his summer holiday to the Yugoslav seaside, one young man decided to try his luck. With nothing on him but the clothes on his back, Adam left a hand-written goodbye letter for his parents and set off.*

*He waited until the dark of night to play it safe. With only starlight to guide his way, Adam crossed into Italy by foot, before hitchhiking his way all the way to Rome. A devout Catholic, he sought sanctuary in the Vatican. When the clergy turned him away, Adam found himself homeless in a foreign land. Alone and with no one to help him, he eventually decided to return back to Czechoslovakia.*

*His decision to flee, followed by his change of heart caused abroad, brought great political and professional discomfort to his high-ranking father. The defection of a son was a huge embarrassment for the family as well. Finally, his voluntary return was confusing even for the authorities.*

*At first, the Party did not know how to handle this incident. But soon, a brilliant solution was found, and a superb new narrative was crafted to accommodate its irregularity.*

*The young man became the face of a pro-socialist campaign. It proved that life in Czechoslovakia was so good, that people ran back home after seeing the exploitations of the West. The defector-turned-returnee was living proof that the grass was not always greener on the other side of fence.*

Once the barbed wire, watch towers, Czechoslovak wolfdogs, soldiers and their AK-47s were safely out of sight, a challenging new life awaited the Czechoslovak freedom-seekers. When the initial euphoria of having crossed passed, a tough new reality set in. Life abroad was far from a walk through a park of roses.

First came status. Once they left their source country, the fleeing Czechoslovaks became illegal migrants in the eyes of their host country. Documentless and vulnerable, their lives were now in the hands of foreign immigration authorities. And, at their mercy.

Austria received the largest share of incoming Slovak refugees, while Germany was the target destination for the Czechs. Refugee camps, similar to those built to house the Syrian migration wave in the 2010s, were set up to host Eastern Europeans running away from communism.

# LOOSING IT ALL TO GAIN IT ALL

*Edward was woken up by a call from his sister-in-law in the early morning on Wednesday the 21st August 1968. There were Russian tanks in front of their house in Bratislava.*

*What was going to happen next? Was Czechoslovakia to become another Soviet republic? The thought of continuing to live in the country was unbearable. All hope for progress seemed to have vanished.*

*Edward and his brother, and brother's family, got together to decide what to do. They went through an exhausting mental exercise trying to choose between two scary alternatives: risk living in a Soviet-like system, or to try to escape to the West. Running away, however, meant being middle-aged refugees, newcomers starting 'on the street' without helpful contacts, family, acquaintances, or money.*

*Considerations of the little group kept changing. Like a pendulum, they swayed from agreed decisions to doubts. Hesitation came to an end when the family finally escaped to nearby Vienna, in Austria. They landed in a refugee camp without any means to support themselves. All that they had in Czechoslovakia – homes, careers, friends and salaries-changed into a metal cot with a suitcase slid underneath, in a warehouse hall with about 200 unknown unhappy people. The future was terrifyingly uncertain.*

*But they were out of the Soviet orbit and at the brink of a new dawn.*

*Selecting the tough but vibrant New York, Edward Toran found himself in a new world to become a renowned architect and designer and later and acclaimed lecturer and a writer.*

With no money, networks and foreign language skills, these newly arrived migrants had to fight hard to establish themselves. Despite the obstacles, many Czech and Slovak emigrants rose to become leaders in culture, sport or politics. The perils of life in Czechoslovakia, paired with their tenacity and strength to leave an unjust regime, forged remarkably resilient characters.

Czechoslovakia paid dearly for the political exodus. The country lost some of her most talented citizens, from scientists to artists and from models to business leaders.

# THE STASTNY HOCKEY LEGEND

*Peter Stastny and his two brothers were outstanding Slovak hockey players. By 1979, they were already world ice hockey champions twice, and they had also experienced the euphoria of the Olympics.*

*When their domestic team, Slovan, won the 1979 Czechoslovak National Championship, it was an enormous and emotional achievement that overshadowed every other victory. But the Stastny brothers would not satisfy themselves with just that. They decided to get political about their victory and their entire team followed suit, taking a stand against the Communist Party and its cruelties.*

*The act did not go down well with the authorities. The three hockey stars were identified as dangerous political agitators. They were shadowed and harassed by the secret police and their entire families were added to the list of inconvenient subjects. With that, the Stastny children would not be able to attend university and their spouses would have to part with the idea of a career of any kind.*

*However, the biggest betrayal by the state was yet to come. The brothers were brought in for an interrogation and forced into taking back their words and opinions. They were told point blank: "If you refuse to do what we tell you, you will never again represent your homeland internationally".*

*It was a step too far. With their family in shame and their dreams crushed, the brothers decided to flee the unbearable communist cage.*

*The upcoming European Championships in Innsbruck, Austria, offered an opportunity that would not repeat itself. The Slovan ice hockey team knew that it had no chance in the international competition without its top players, the Stastny brothers. It seemed like a miracle when all three were given exit visas to represent the team.*

*Once in Austria, Peter Stastny took fate into his own hands.*

He picked up the phone and called one of his many professional recruiters, stating: "I am ready to go West". Although many NHL teams had tempted him with offers throughout his career, the young Peter had ignored them. He was a patriot and he refused to abandon his homeland. But, when push came to shove, even 'Peter the Great' had enough.

Within hours of the phone call, the top management of the Quebec Nordics flew into town. Another miracle. The Canadians did not hesitate. They knew just how valuable Peter could be for their team, and so they wasted no time putting their plan into action.

As soon as the escape blueprint was in place, two of the three brothers agreed to meet in front of a hotel where a car, and the Canadian delegation, would be waiting to take them away to safety. However, when Peter came he did not see his brother Anton anywhere. He did not know that the hotel had several entrances and Anton had been waiting at a different one.

Peter was paralyzed. He did not understand what happened and he feared for the worst. Had the KGB gotten wind of their plans? Did they take his brother away? Was he being interrogated or even tortured?

Winding through the Innsbruck streets on the way to Vienna airport, Peter gave up hope of finding his brother. That is when, out of the corner of his eye, Peter saw the silhouette of a man walking on the street. It was Anton!

In the end, Peter and Anton defected, while Marian, the third brother, returned back to Czechoslovakia on the bus with the Slovan team. He had three children waiting for him in Slovakia and he chose to return to them.

Once abroad, Peter was somewhat consoled by the fact that the Party would not dare to hurt his family. The Stastny dynasty was too popular to mess with. As a NHL player, Peter went on to achieve new career heights in the West, making any nasty moves against him or his family a public liability.

*Although more subtle than they would have wished, there was a punishment.*

*Mr Stastny, the father of the boys, went from hero-to-zero when his sons defected. The Slovak people went from looking up to him, to hassling and abusing him openly. What kind of a man raises his sons to betray the regime and everything the ideology stood for. But the Stastny family was one of faith and they continued to pray to God for redemption.*

*The reward soon came, when Marian, the third brother who stayed behind, emigrated also and joined his brothers on ice. It was such a happy family reunion.*

*And the result of freedom? Peter Stastny became the second highest scoring hockey player of the 1980s, after Canadian icon and legend Wayne Gretzky. At the end of his career, Stastny was introduced into the Hockey Hall of Fame and named one of the 100 Greatest NHL Players in history. Peter also raised two successful ice hockey players to continue the family legacy.*

*Even more remarkably, Peter returned to Slovakia when his sports career ended, and entered the turbulent world of Slovak politics.*

*Disturbed at the direction the country was headed and worried by the influence the authoritarian leadership that took over after the collapse of the regime, he decided to do something about it. In 2004, Slovakia became a member of the European Union and NATO. Peter Stastny went on to represent the country as a European Member of Parliament. His successful 10-year career in Brussels continued his childhood dream of putting Slovakia on the map.*

476

# from SOVIET-CAGE
## to AMERICAN DREAM

*Dr Jan and Marica Vilcek achieved the American Dream and so much more, when they fled from Czechoslovakia a few years before the Soviet invasion and landed in New York City. During a taxi ride from the airport, the couple immediately fell in love with the Manhattan skyline. This was home. The desire to integrate into US society inspired them to perfect their English and quickly begin their new chapter.*

*Jan and Marica made a radical decision. They chose to never look back. It did not take long for them to start successful careers in their areas of expertise. At New York University, Jan's research began to gain recognition and he eventually patented a product in America and beyond that went on to become one of the most used drugs for the treatment of autoimmune diseases. Meanwhile, wife Marica used her Czechoslovak university education in art history to acquire a prestigious curator position at the Metropolitan Museum of Art, where she held a flourishing career for several decades.*

*Through dedication, hard work and a stroke of luck, the penniless refugees soon became rich beyond their imagination. Although they are surrounded by wealth, status and influence, the Vilceks remain humble. They are also celebrated in America for their generous philanthropy. The couple donated over 100 million US dollars to New York University, and they operate a foundation that celebrates the contributions of immigrants to the United States. None of that would have been possible had they stayed behind the Iron Curtain.*

Today, many might have forgotten about the impenetrable wall that once divided Czechoslovakia from the West, especially a younger generation that has never experienced the regime firsthand. The youth, accustomed to freedom of movement, dismiss the weight of the cage their parents and grandparents lived with.

Animals prove to be much more sensitive to all that is going on around them and they seem to have a better memory of these brutal, past divisions too. A research study revealed a surprising behavior pattern in deer, on the exact periphery where the Iron Curtain once stood.

Three decades after the barbed wire barriers were dismantled on the Czech and German border, clusters of deer continue to remain uneasy about crossing the invisible border. Most do not dare to cross.

# PART
# FIVE

DOWN COME the WALLS

"FOR US IN RUSSIA, COMMUNISM IS A DEAD DOG, WHILE, FOR MANY PEOPLE IN THE WEST, IT IS STILL A LIVING LION."

*ALEXANDER SOLZHENITSYN*

Towards the end of the 20th century, the USSR was rotting from within. Drained by the arms race with America and the war in Afghanistan, it had stretched itself too far. Although its ambitions were great and grand, reality proved different.

The planned economy was suffering from its own lack of flexibility, and the Red Empire was in need of a capital injection. The self-imposed embargo, alongside a general atmosphere of isolation, did nothing to help.

The USSR and the entire Eastern Bloc was resource rich, but cash poor. There was no money to pay for the military or the KGB and bastions of administrative workers that were making the bureaucracy and surveillance apparatus tick. Morale was waning not just in Russia, but also in Czechoslovakia. Frustration was giving way to anger.

In summary, after the first few years of post-War excitement and boom, the communist regime started to lose steam. What followed were a series of peaks and falls in the ensuing decades. When the economy faltered, the ideology inspired, and this went on for some time.

However, the 20 years of normalization saw little innovation happen, and necessary changes were not made. By the 1980s the economy was weak, social frustration was rife and public dissent growing. The rumbling was not just in Czechoslovakia.

The regime that once ruled over a third of the planet was coming to a halt.

> *The economy began to really stagnate again in the 1970s. It was the effect of centralization, but also a lack of competent people in key positions. For too long, Party loyalty carried more weight than merit. An unsustainable practice, it was only a matter of time before things started to fall to pieces.*

*Eventually, there was no more money available to pay for the government services that proved critical to the public. The state was providing consumer goods to the people, but to continue distracting them with color TVs, the Party had to borrow money.*

*They couldn't borrow money from the Eastern Bloc brotherhood, however, as the same economic slowdown affected them there as well. This time, the government had to reach out to the capitalist West. An agreement was nevertheless met.*

## MISSING GOLD

*Some of the strategies utilized by the regime were flat-out ridiculous. In 1961, the Republic's jewelers and dentists became the targets of a new Czechoslovak witch hunt. The Party was desperate for cash which it equated with gold. In a country that mined away most of its precious metals centuries ago, this posed a problem. Taking gold from small service men appeared to be the only solution.*

*One by one, dentists and jewelers were brought in for interrogation, under the pretence of cracking down on parasites hoarding excessive resources. When only a tiny amount of gold was extracted, the Party was not ready to accept that it might have miscalculated. The only other plausible explanation was that the dentists and the jewelers were lying. They must have been hiding the gold somewhere.*

*Most had no additional precious metals. Sadly, some never emerged from their interrogations.*

In the USSR, the spiraling economic downturn was not just a matter of reduced comfort. It came with the very real threat of nationwide famine. To avert a disaster, the Soviet leadership had to finally face what they tried so hard to deny and ignore. It was a time for a radical change.

As staunch communism gave way to a more liberal regime, Mikhail Gorbachev stepped into power in 1985 and unpacked a series of reforms. Their ripple effect was felt across the Eastern Bloc immediately.

Gorbachev's enlightened political management gave rise to two simultaneous movements. *Glasnost* referred to a general opening of the system, the discussion of problems and their solutions. *Perestroika* referred to a decentralization and reform movement that swept the Soviet Union.

However, not everyone bought into the trend. Some were skeptical and viewed Gorbachev's enthusiasm as naïve, or worse, an instrument of the West. To the Party hardliners, he was a man wearing pink glasses, falling prey to Western machinations.

Although Gorbachev was a communist and a Soviet, he was revered by Czechoslovaks. He was a progressive advocate for change, unlike any of the men that came before him. Desperate times lead to desperate measures, and a new type of leader had finally materialized in the Soviet Union.

Thanks to his openness, the mainstream public started to talk about key social issues, including the obvious deficiencies of the regime, and the need for a change. When Gorbachev visited Czechoslovakia in 1987, he was greeted by a crowd of thousands cheering: *"We want Misa!"*. That was a true hallmark to the impact of his persona. He riled up people, even in a country where apathy took the best of what they had decades ago.

The winds of change had come, and the time was ripe for a spectacular revolution.

*There was a film festival in Bratislava in 1988. This one was different from all the others. Instead of the standard propaganda, the movies presented to the audience also included those that came from a forbidden America!*

*What is more, unusual pins were handed out to the curious attendees - American and Soviet flags crossed in a friendly union.*

*Was this a fluke, a joke? Perhaps it was a premonition of what was to come one year later. In hindsight, locals wondered whether a secret deal had been struck by the global superpowers.*

*Some skeptics continue to argue that the collapse of communism was preordained. The freedom loving revolutions that swept through Eastern Europe, and ultimately led to the dissolution of the Iron Curtain, were allowed to flourish only because of this covert gentlemen's agreement, they say.*

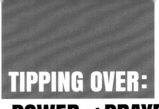

# TIPPING OVER:
## The POWER of PRAYER

It was the Slovaks who first sparked the flames of revolution in Czechoslovakia, via a mass protest that eventually burnt the impenetrable Iron Curtain.

Just 20 years after the Prague Spring, a remarkable event happened in Bratislava's Hviezdoslav Square. A large group of Slovaks gathered to pray the rosary in a symbolic act of peaceful resistance, on March 25th 1988. Their public gathering, an act of treason according to the status quo, was inspired and fed by their faith.

The election of the first Slavic pope in the Vatican proved a powerful catalyst and a symbol of hope for millions of Eastern Europeans.

The demonstration was supported by the Catholic Church. News of the event was announced in churches and travelled further by word of mouth. Organizers expected a handful of attendees, but on the day around 10,000 people turned up, an unheard-of gathering at that time. Moreover, these were not just the usual suspects. A wide profile of people joined, from far and wide, including elderly women and villagers that travelled to the capital on buses.

*Ironically, the regime itself informed the public about the protest. The state announced it on radios and televisions to 'advise' people against attending. Schools and universities in Bratislava sent students home early. They were also informed that if they were caught at the demonstration, they would be expelled immediately. True to their diversion tactics, the Party mobilized the national media. An impromptu broadcast of the Angelique film series was arranged to incentivize women to stay at home.*

The protesters stood side by side in solemn silence, on that dark, cold and rainy spring day. Together with lit candles in hand, they protested against religious un-freedom. Slowly, the chant of religious songs filled the air. But, by then, the police had already moved in. They blocked off all the escape routes and encircled the people like a flock of sheep.

As the sinister sound of sirens came closer and closer, the crowd stood defiantly, refusing to blow out their candles. Their bravery angered the police even more. The cops decided to drive their cars into the public. Yet, the people refused to move. This was a direct face-off between the them and the authorities.

Seeing the determination of the protesters, the next line of attack was brought in. The police rolled in water cannons and blasted them on the unarmed public. Many fell to the ground drenched and wounded. It was at this point, that the people started running away. Once the crowd shrunk to a manageable size, the police moved in and started the arrest ritual.

Seemingly, the demonstration achieved nothing. Indeed, the government acted as if nothing had happened after-wards. However, it was a monumental event and a crucially important civic gesture. It was also noticed abroad and for the first time, it was Bratislava and not Prague, that made inter-national headlines. The Slovaks had made their demand for freedom known.

Yet, no radical change followed. For the most part, life returned to normal. Could it be that the regime had won again?

# The VELVET FORCE of 1989

Ignoring the 1988 Candle Demonstration was the calm before the storm. What Dubcek and the Czechoslovaks had demanded some 20 years prior was becoming reality.

People think that the Eastern European revolutions all began in Germany, with the fall of the Berlin Wall on November 9th 1989. However, it was in Hungary that the Iron Curtain was first pierced.

The Hungarians cut through the fence between Hungary and Austria in May 1989, months before Germans dismantled their wall. Remarkably, there was no reprisal from Moscow. Could it be that keeping people artificially contained behind a wall was no longer productive?

Once the Berliners started to take the Berlin Wall apart, it was official. The division that was once believed to be impenetrable, and unchangeable, was crumbling. The city was once again united, and news of the miraculous event travelled the world. Then it also reached the ears of Eastern Europeans.

> The western side of the Wall was covered with colorful graffiti, anti-communist statements, poems, odes and murals to freedom. For the first time, the Eastern Germans could read them, and see with their own eyes what the world had thought of the regime they had lived in. They were shocked, and others were moved to tears to realize that the world had not forgotten about them.

> The entrepreneurial West Germans also took advantage of the opportunity. They quickly set up make-shift stands and embarked on selling fragments of the wall to tourists and curiosity seekers.

Hope gave way to more hope, and a wave of bottom-up revolutions echoed throughout the Eastern Bloc. The once feared regime was collapsing like a house of cards. And the Czechoslovaks could smell that change was in the air.

First, the Czechoslovak communists tried to contain the news from Berlin and deny that the whole thing had even happened. When that failed short of delivering the desired effect, the Party twisted the narrative to convince Czechoslovaks that 'Berlin' would never happen in their country. They did not count on the many adventurous youth who wanted to experience the atmosphere in East Germany for themselves.

Unable to suppress the rising power of the people, and fearing their backlash, the Party knew it had to tread carefully. Travel permits were produced quickly, and buses full of mostly young people were dispatched to East Berlin. They swarmed the Wall and put their home tools and hammers into action. They wanted to bring back a piece of the wall home with them. It was so much more than a token of an era.

Seeing the collapse of the seemingly impossible, and bringing a piece of it home for their families and friends, made the fall of the regime that much more plausible. It was absolutely within reach. And just like that, a paradigm shift happened.

The call for freedom was unleased. One million people tired of living in fear took to the streets of Prague. The movement was led by students, the literal future of Czechoslovakia, who decided to take matters into their own hands on that momentous November 17th.

Some 20 years after the generation that couldn't (1968), the generation that could (1989) stepped up. Unlike their predecessors, they didn't want a reform. They wanted total change.

*The 17th of November plays an important role in Czechoslovak history and psyche. On that day in 1939, Czech students stood up against the Nazi regime that was occupying the Czech lands.*

*Armed to their teeth, the elite SS commandoes lashed out on the protesters. Two people were killed, hundreds of others were hurt and arrested, but the reprisals did not end there. Eight students and one professor were executed. On that same day, 1,200 others were deported to concentration camps.*

*The bloody event and the sacrifice of the students were never forgotten. The 17th of November was declared International Student's Day in other nations, as early as 1941, to commemorate the student lives lost in German-occupied Czechia.*

*Remarkably on the very same day, 50 years later, Czechoslovak students rose again. But, this time it was against another totalitarian government, the Soviets.*

However, the Communist Party of Czechoslovakia would not go down without a fight. The daring demands of the Czech students were met by a cordon of riot police. The protesters were attacked, beaten and handcuffed.

But nothing could put out the fire. Not this time.

Prague was aflame with emotion. The state's unrelenting brutality against the idealistic students had unintentionally opened the floodgates of the Velvet Revolution. The social momentum was so strong that radio air wave controls were partially lifted to update the people on the situation. The forbidden Western radio stations, like Radio Free Europe and Voice of America, also used their platforms to quickly circulate news of the violence.

Few know that one day earlier, on the other side of the Republic, nothing suggested a storm was about to sweep in.

In the Slovak capital of Bratislava, students too went out into the streets. They wanted to voice their demands, but their requests were different from their Czech counterparts. Although they too were asking for freedom and an end of censorship, Slovak were more concerned about better university living quarters and a higher quality of education.

The Slovak officials had also learned from their earlier mistake, the crushing the Candle Demonstration one year ago. This time the state did not react, nor did it respond with violence. The protest was allowed to continue – uninterrupted. There were no batons, police cars or water cannons, waiting to confront the mass. And so, 200 young people marched straight towards the Ministry of Education.

At the gates, they demanded to speak with the Minister. He did not show up, but the students were invited to discuss their needs with an appointed official. An hour into the meeting, it was agreed that the two parties would seek comprise, and the session was dismissed.

However, the events that followed 24 hours later, in Prague, left no one in doubt. It was no longer possible to reform the regime from within. Police savagery had cast the dice. There was no going back now.

*Who knows, had it not been for the brutal suppression of the public protests in Prague, we might be living in a very different world. Although speculators do not deny that global change was eminent, they argue that the complete destruction of the old in favor of the radically different new was not the only possibility in Czechoslovakia. Had the revolution not come, a modern form of communism might have emerged from within the Republic.*

*A system similar in values, but different in orientation. The new communism was to be more liberal, more entrepreneurial, yet still communism. We just have to look at China to see what could have perhaps happened.*

# The 240 HOURS 41 YEARS that Brought Down of communism

The story of Friday, November 17th, was spreading fast. Very soon, theatres, actors and artists joined the Czech and Slovak students in their protest. Their combined allegiance sent ripples throughout the entire collective. Just imagine the entire cultural scene frozen, as the performers refused to put on their evening shows.

# TRUTH
# HAS
# PREVAILED

On Sunday, November 19th, some 500 people gathered in a Bratislava theatre to discuss 'the next step forward'. Actors, some of the most famous faces of the era, sat on the stage engaged in an active political dialogue with the public.

Instead of passively watching a performance, the audience was encouraged to share their thoughts and opinions an unprecedented freedom. That evening a manifesto was drawn up, setting 12 very clear demands.

First of all, the beating of the Czechoslovak students was to be properly investigated. Then, more freedom in all spheres of life was to be granted to people.

On Monday, November 20th, an agreement of cooperation between dissidents and students instigating the revolution was established. As the two sides got together, an alchemy between wisdom and youth unfolded. Together, they created a movement that became known as the Civic Forum in the Czech part of the republic, and 'People Against Violence' in Slovakia. They would go on to play a central role in transforming Czechoslovakia in the years to come.

By this time, university common rooms were filled with sleeping bags, flyers and posters. Students lived and breathed the revolution. Very quickly, their labor of love started to bring some much-deserved fruit. More and more support began to flood in, ranging from funding to air time on media platforms.

Ironically, some of these young people were the children of high-ranking government officials. That is part of the reason why the state, at least in Slovakia, was reluctant to crack down on them again. Meanwhile, the movement was growing in strength and spreading from universities to the rest of society. More demonstrations were organized, and more and more people joined them.

In Bratislava, the protests peaked at 100,000 participants. This was an astonishing number. The same people who had lived in fear of opening their mouths on everything from the quality of meat to the leadership of the country were coming out in the thousands to show what they really thought of the system. Millions watched the dramatic developments escalate on TVs, across Czechoslovakia, the Eastern Bloc and even the world.

# OPEN UP
## TO THE WORLD!

Parents joined their children. The students who initiated the revolution were the progeny of those who were forced to quietly submit to normalization, after the invasion of 1968. The system had exploited their paternal and maternal instincts. Instead of revolt, they kept their heads down to protect their offspring.

When this generation grew up, and demanded freedom 20 years later, the government broke its tacit agreement with their parents by beating, harming ad mistreating their children. Overnight, obedient citizens turned into active dissidents. In addition, the bitterness of the 1968 betrayal had never subsided. It had only festered and fermented under the surface. November 1989 was an opportunity to unleash it.

When push came to shove, or quite literally when the police pushed and shoved their children, the passive citizenry awoke. This is how parents and children came together and unleashed an explosive force that shook up the world. Dreams can be suppressed, but they can never be denied.

> *The event referred to as the 'Velvet' revolution both in Czech and in English was given a different name in Slovakia. The peaceful nation that outlived oppressions at the hands of many was never keen on spilling blood. Slovaks call themselves the 'dove nation' to seal their love of peace in words. The Velvet Revolution could not be called anything else than the 'Gentle Revolution'.*

The Party was panicking. The domestic and international pressure was immense.

On November 24th, the entire presidium of the Communist Party resigned. A few days later, the totalitarian state surrendered its power in full. Euphoria enveloped the country. Only 20 days after the first stone block was taken out of the Berlin Wall, communist rule in Czechoslovakia officially ended.

Some 150,000 Bratislavans celebrated this monumental victory on December 10th, also known as International Human Rights Day, by walking across the border to Hainburg, Austria. It was a gateway to freedom once denied. For the first time, in a very long time the people could look at their city from the other side of the river, the former Iron Curtain divide.

As they cut through the barbed wire that once was their cage, they sang songs of freedom with tears in their eyes. At last, freedom had come and the door to the world had opened in - their lifetime.

INTERNATIONAL

# HUMAN RIGHTS DAY

On the same day, December 10th, the first not purely communist government was sworn in and Gustav Husak abdicated. Such a diversity had not existed since the coup of 1948. In a political finale, Alexander Dubcek, the leader of the Prague Spring, was named the speaker of the federal parliament. Vaclav Havel, a dissident playwright and the face of the underground movement, was elected Czechoslovakia's President on December 29th 1989.

> *'Little fires', as locals called them, were lit in fields shortly after the Velvet Revolution. When fire brigades turned up to put them out, they were surprised to find folders and documents clustered in files and set ablaze. It was the Secret Police busily destroying evidence of their activities. Not all material was lost. What remains is stored by institutions like The National Memory Institute in Slovakia and the Institute for the Study of Totalitarian Regimes in the Czech Republic.*

In a restless 20th century Europe, the Velvet Revolution set a new precedent. It marked a peaceful, non-violent, parting with a regime.

What happened next?

Caught in a craze of undoing what had been done, Czechoslovaks wanted to erase the past and start again with a clean slate. One by one, the gigantic statues of Lenin, Stalin and the other great men of the failed ideology disappeared. Next, public streets changed their names, and monuments and squares were re-branded.

People also attacked the visual embodiments of the regime in an outburst of their long-suppressed anger. The spontaneous actions of a few individuals soon gave way to the systematic removal of such icons. Some were destroyed, but a great many were simply removed and hidden away from sight, in dark museum vaults. It is symbolic of the Czechoslovak attitude to the era.

> *When the Iron Curtain and communism collapsed, the moral fabric of society crumbled too.*
>
> *The cultural shift resulted in a wild-West form of capitalism, while self-interest replaced the collectivist standards once so upheld. People no longer 'had to' consider the needs of others, their fellow citizens and their neighbors. And it showed.*
>
> *All of a sudden, radio, TV and newspapers were filled with violence and sex. The world seemed freer, but also a lot harsher. Social values and moral codes seemed to have flipped on their head. The new-found freedom was often taken to an extreme. An overcorrection of the pendulum, perhaps?*

With freedom returned, the country committed itself to a new future. At a dizzying speed, Czechoslovakia embarked on a radical wave of transformation. Overnight, the country turned from totalitarianism to democracy, and from a planned to a free-enterprise economy. The transition was not without pain and struggle.

A decade of darkness befell the people, once the Velvet jubilation subsided. The silent Czechoslovak Velvet divorce made room for another authoritarian figure to rise to power in Slovakia. Kidnappings, murders, mafia entanglements and wide scale cronyism plundered the country until dawn finally came, via the arrival of the new millennium.

But that is another story ....

527

KLEME

GOTTWALD

On Christmas Day 1991, Mikhail Gorbachev stepped down as the president of the USSR and one of the most powerful empires of the world dissolved. The ten-minute televised speech officially brought the Cold War to an end, along with the Soviet Union.

# WE'RE NOW LIVING IN A NEW WORLD. AN END HAS BEEN PUT TO THE COLD WAR AND TO THE ARMS RACE, AS WELL AS TO THE MAD MILITARIZATION OF THE COUNTRY, WHICH HAS CRIPPLED OUR ECONOMY, PUBLIC ATTITUDES AND MORALS. THE THREAT OF NUCLEAR WAR HAS BEEN REMOVED."

MIKHAIL GORBACHEV
Moscow
1991

*ALTHOUGH THE REGIME CAME DOWN IN 1989, IT TOOK UNTIL 1991 FOR ALL THE SOVIET BASES IN CZECHOSLOVAKIA TO BE CLOSED DOWN AND FOR THE TROOPS TO BE SENT HOME. ONCE THE AGREEMENT BETWEEN CZECHOSLOVAKIA AND THE USSR WAS STRUCK, TRAIN-AFTER-TRAIN OF MILITARY MEN WERE SEEN LEAVING THE NO LONGER OCCUPIED COUNTRY. TOGETHER WITH THE MEN WENT THEIR FAMILIES, AS WELL AS 1,218 WEAPONS, 1,220 TANKS, 2,505 COMBAT VEHICLES AND 76 MILITARY PLANES. A TOTAL OF 73,500 SOLDIERS LEFT CZECHOSLOVAKIA. THE FORMER SOVIET BASES HAVE BEEN ABANDONED EVER SINCE.*

# Goodbye,
# CZECHOSLOVAKIA!

# THE PEOPLE -
## A LIVING LEGACY OF COMMUNISM

## "TWO NEW GENERATIONS WILL HAVE TO GROW UP TO WASH AWAY THE FOOTPRINTS OF COMMUNISM."

VACLAV HAVEL

Apart from the communist monuments and architecture that can still be experienced in the Czech and Slovak republics, the former regime also left an imprint on the heart, mind and soul of the people. Far less visible, even intangible, it has shaped who the Czechs and Slovaks are today.

For better and for worse, the legacy of the ideology is still alive today in the way they think, feel and behave. It is no surprise. Communism was the greatest ideological experiment of the 20th century, and its manifestation had a very real consequence on the economy, the institutions and the psychology of the countries it enveloped.

The ideology penetrated deeply into professional and personal lives of Czechs and Slovaks. When the Iron Curtain came down, the ways of thinking and behaving that had circulated in society for decades could not change overnight. This is why social scientists and military experts alike say that it takes two generations to heal the gap.

Communism brought forth many good things. The basic premise of equality and sameness really did increase the quality of life and dismantled age-old class divides, especially in Slovakia. The ideology levelled society, and few would argue that it was a bad thing!

Under the old regime, you would always have a roof over your head, food in your belly, a guaranteed pension for when you grew old and frail, and healthcare if you fell ill. That is an achievement that people in some parts of the developed world still have to fight for. These are the perks of collectivist societies, where no one is left alone to their own devices. The collective always takes care of its members.

But every coin has two sides. A collectivist approach to governance also sowed the seeds of extreme insecurity among the people. The state suppressed the individual, squandered human emotionality, underdeveloped soft skills and hampered the ability of people to express themselves and have trust in one another.

In the end, communism was a utopia that didn't live up to its promise once translated into reality.

Communism was built around the idea of sameness. In order for everyone to be equal and equally looked after, the system tried to make everyone the same. That way the state could cater to all. Being different from the norm destabilized the fragile equilibrium. It was a threat to the very idea of equality, as understood by the communists.

Diverging from the mainstream standard was punished, ridiculed or humiliated, and not always just by the authorities but by the ordinary people themselves. To justify and explain their place in the world and to appease the Party, they were quick to chastise anyone who dared to think, act or respond out of the bland norm. Over time, the people forgot how to be themselves, how to have an opinion and know how to express it.

Deep down, the fear of expressing oneself still makes people's throats dry and their minds blank. The terror is particularly strong in Slovakia, where people are still scared to say the wrong thing. Being different is still not entirely OK, especially outside of the capital. Many Slovaks still prefer to play it safe and to do as everyone else is doing to avoid being criticized, punished or even ostracized.

'What would people think' runs though many a mind when deciding whether to do something out of the usual. Being gossiped about or openly criticized is still enough to persuade people to hide who they are - even today. On a basic level, this means that there is little diversity in terms of how people look, think and speak. This also directly contributes to a lack of innovativeness in the society.

In a world where there was only one truth, total knowledge was absolute and pluralism was a non-concept. For decades, people were told what to think and how to act. The purpose of education was to cultivate human capital that was capable of following orders. Hard skills and quantitative sciences were favored as these were deemed to be devoid of ideology and therefore politically safe.

Critical thinking was not encouraged. In fact, it was dis-couraged so that people could not see behind the Party's disinformation campaigns and propaganda. To think inde-pendently means to be able to absorb knowledge, but to also question it. Although the 'who', 'what', and 'where' of knowledge are important, they only comprise descriptive information. Asking 'why' is far more important.

In present-day Slovakia, students are still used to memorizing facts, rather than interpreting the information for meaning. Without critical thinking in place, it is that much harder to harness creativity.

Although Slovak engineers and IT whizzes are world-renowned, the country's soft skills base remains depleted. Social sciences are still suffering from being left behind in the Soviet era. But everything from entrepreneurialism, to marketing and even politics requires soft skills.

The lack of exposure to pluralism also results in a dualist inter-pretation of global matters. In Slovakia, the people struggle distinguishing between conspiracy theories and genuine information. It is not easy for them to integrate complex information and form their own opinion in the process.

Czechoslovak socialism did not really allow people to have their opinions, self-responsibility or to develop their own way of doing things. The system wanted to prevent people from using their mental capacity to think about things they were not supposed to think about. It overwhelmed the population with details, so that they would remain too busy to raise their heads. Burdensome bureaucratic processes also suitably occupied their time.

You might still notice Slovaks overcomplicate simple acts, and have a hard time making decisions. In post-communist Slovakia, many continue to focus on the tiniest details of one's daily routines - cleaning one's house, doing one's chores or worrying about a potential mistake on the recently completed tax form. Indeed, it sometimes appears that Slovaks cannot see the forest for the trees and keep missing the bigger picture.

Totalitarianism lasted for over four decades thanks to a surveillance society. Reporting on one another was a normal part of life and kept everyone in check. The surface of Czechoslovakia's waters were long kept calm due to it. Of course, gossiping about others is an age-old vice. The communists just systematized this practice, and some people welcomed the opportunity to worry and report on their neighbors, to distract themselves from their own dull lives.

Today, everybody's business continues to be everybody else's business, especially away from the greater anonymity of cities. In the provinces, the people still like to keep a close eye on their neighbors. Their dedication also produces some novel intel, including intimate details of their acquaintance's son's marriage, who is visiting whom from abroad, and what wife does not clean her windows every other week.

In the past, the state treated citizens as clueless children and the Communist Party put itself in the role of a stern father who knows best. It rewarded obedience and reprimanded anything else. Slovaks were certainly not fully-fledged responsible citizens, encouraged to take action and have a say over public matters. So, they got used to shrugging their shoulders and sort of getting on with it.

This is the real reason behind the lack of public engagement in Slovakia today, and the country's weak civil society. People are simply not used to governing themselves. For too long it was done for them. It is only in the 21st century, they are learning how to fight for what they believe is right, and to find ways of having their opinion heard and needs met.

The centralized economy made private enterprise obsolete. It also guaranteed jobs for everyone. As a result, Slovaks forgot how to do business, how to take risks, how to sell products and, ultimately, how to compete and take charge of their lives.

The daily psychological terror made life painful for everyone. Pragmatisms replaced emotions, and functionalism did way with a need to have genuine and intimate connection with others. Physical needs were the only needs that were recognized. One of the ways the people coped was to escape into their inner world. In doing so, they further isolated themselves from everything and everyone.

To this day, Slovaks might appear closed off and inaccessible, taking a long time to trust someone and to relax in their company. Stripping off one's public façade is still challenging for many. Role play feels that much more comfortable.

Getting to truly know Slovaks may take a long time. Having wholesome relationships where all is open for a discussion and one is safe to be oneself with a lover, a friend or a mother and father, is rare. Taking care of material needs and securing one's physical survival is still a primary concern. Emotional wellbeing, self-care and nourishment are left behind. Still, the Czech Republic is a positive inspiration.

Nonetheless, Slovakia is also a place of a great many contrasts. While people fear creating genuine and deep bonds with one another, there is also incredible devotion to family, hospitality and endless support, whether you need to fix a leaking tap or build a home. This is a country where families are close-knit, and people are always prepared to lend a hand.

Their tenacity and resistance to ideological rhetoric is partially made possible by their attention to life's rudimentary basics. This dynamic has produced a tranquil pace of life, and that is calming in the whirlwind of the trends and disruptions of the 21st century. Visiting a Slovak family, you will certainly not go hungry and once you make a friend in Slovakia, he or she will probably remain one for your entire lifetime.

Although reminders of the previous era are found everywhere, tides are changing. Teenage Slovakia, that has not officially experienced communism, is nevertheless recovering from past abuse and terror.

Change comes in little and big ways. It seeps into families, businesses, the public sector and public spaces. From arts to sciences and from family living rooms to parliamentary politics, Slovaks are waking up from their apathy. In doing so, they are reclaiming their power and with it, their self-responsibility. In 21st century Slovakia, the people are learning how to take care of themselves, their communities and their country.

Yet, one question remains to be answered. Did communism do any good in the greater global perspective?

Some experts suggest that communism kept capitalism in check. If capitalism went too far, communism would act as its conscience. After the Second World War, Western governments knew that they had to keep their citizens happy, to prevent them from turning red.

This kept the elites engaged. The political, economic and social decision makers knew that they had to pay attention to the needs and interest of society, and not just of those with the deepest pockets. During the Cold War, inequality in the West also decreased.

Today, such moral restraints on the free market no longer exist. If the rise and fall of communism taught us something, then it is the importance of finding a way to balance the individual and the collective, the private and the public. Favoring one or the other can lead to oppression.

# Afterword

## by
## PETER STASTNY

When the authors of this book reached out to me and proposed that I write an afterword for it, I instinctively knew that I had to contribute. After all, my very successful and very blessed life is intimately connected to Czechoslovakia behind the Iron Curtain.

I would like to take this opportunity to remind the young generation of a thing or two.

I was born in the 1950s, in the era of the worst and the cruelest crimes sanctioned by the communist regime. This is when communism was securing its power through murders, executions, long-term prison sentences and other means of persecution. This is when the foundations of the regime built on fear, distrust and corruption, were laid.

They say that power corrupts, and absolute power corrupts absolutely. This certainly applied to the communists and their feared and savage secret police. They brought about devastation and moral disintegration of the individual and society.

I do not remember the 50s, of course. But I do recall the 60s and the 70s - first as a young curious boy and later as an adult man, with a strong belief in justice and a passion for history.

My father loved history, it was a part of everyday family conversations. Our family has always been devoutly Christian, and the love and belief in God has been passed down through the generations like the most precious of gifts. This awareness of the past, alongside my strong Christian values, set me firmly against the regime.

I became an enemy of the state.

In those curious times, I managed to build a fairytale career in the most popular Czechoslovak sport – ice hockey. I had already acquired two World Championship titles, and three titles of Junior Czechoslovak champion. By the age of 23, I soon collected even more international and domestic successes, including that of becoming the first Slovak to be voted 'hockey player of the year' in Czechoslovakia.

However, the communist imperative *with us or against us* made it very hard for decent people to lead normal lives. Fear, mistrust and schizophrenia were everywhere. People behaved differently in public and in private. On the one hand, I was basking in fame; on the other, I knew that a lot of people were suffering because of their views and values, that I too shared.

It was only a matter of time before I got into conflict with the regime. I had refused three offers to join the Communist Party on principle. I was not scared, but I was not naïve either.

I knew firsthand about the disgusting things that the regime was capable of. My coach Gusto Bubnik told me an incredible story of what happened to the Czechoslovak world hockey champions during the 1950s. Back then, the news was censored. But, Gusto was part of a team that was imprisoned and charged with the crime of treason. They were sentenced to jail for decades because of it. Three members of the team even received the death penalty, which was later revoked to three life sentences. Coach Bubnik was released on amnesty, but only after spending many years in prison.

Although the practices of the regime softened somewhat as time went by, its goals remained unchanged. To remove ideological enemies was their daily agenda. Eventually, the unavoidable conflict came. When the state threatened me with a ban to represent Czechoslovakia in ice-hockey, it was the last straw. It felt like a stab in the heart.

It is also why we decided to emigrate.

I had just gotten married and my wife and I were expecting our first baby. Freedom was important to me, as was the future and freedom of my children. I did not want to raise them in hypocrisy. All I wished for my offspring was for them to be able to make free choices and fully actuate their talent and potential. This was only possible in a free country.

The decision to leave was the toughest one I have ever made in my entire life. It was also the best decision I have ever made. The lives of my children and grandchildren are a proof of the resolution I took in 1980.

I am happy and grateful that the times of insecurity, totalitarianism and the dictate of one party are over. Today's young generation has the right to make choices. Their destiny is in their own hands. It is up to them, how they use the privilege of having so many opportunities.

As for me, I had another 25 successful years in Canada and the United States. I had access to uncensored information, that was not available back home. I met with people, I read a lot and I heard so many authentic stories about people who became victims of the communist regime. They shaped me and inspired me to fight against totalitarian communism, that my idol, Ronald Reagan, once labeled the 'Evil Empire'.

I became a member of the Slovak World Congress, thanks to Stefan Roman who unified Slovaks in exile. The organization had a clear goal. To see the rise of a free, sovereign and democratic Slovakia, equal to all advanced nations of the world.

Thank God, all those goals were fulfilled and even surpassed. It was like a dream when Slovakia joined the EU and NATO in 2004, firmly anchoring itself in the democratic family. Slovakia is proof of how a small and young nation can secure freedom, security and prosperity.

I sacrificed a lot to make this dream happen, and I will be forever grateful to Mikulas Dzurinda, an iconic leader and

Prime Minister, for instigating the change. He first beat dictatorial Vladimir Meciar, and then led Slovakia into the EU and NATO. I owe him a lot, for persuading me to become a leader in the 2004 European Parliament elections.

Together we won, and I, now as a member of the European Parliament, had the opportunity to involve myself in the effort of integrating Slovakia into European structures and institutions. This was both meaningful and fulfilling work. It allowed me to witness and contribute to the process of Slovakia rising to the level of the most advanced countries in the world.

The monumental dream of our ancestors, as well as the ambitions of the Slovak World Congress, finally became a reality.

I offer my sincere congratulations to the authors of this unique book, Zuzana and Gabriela. It will become a precious contribution to our literature and our history.

The communists manipulated the past and there are people who are trying to do the same today. This is why the approach of the authors, who narrate authentic stories and accounts of historical events, is key to passing the lessons of the era to subsequent generations – in the noble and important fight against evil. Truth and justice and, above all, freedom is worth any sacrifice.

History teaches us that truth always prevails!

## Peter 'The Great' Stastny

*Top 100 Greatest NHL Hockey Player in 100 years*
*Member of the European Parliament, 2004-2014*

# A PERSPECTIVE OF THE NEW GENERATION

"A NATION WHICH DOES NOT REMEMBER WHAT IT WAS YESTERDAY, DOES NOT KNOW WHAT IT IS TODAY, NOR WHAT IT IS TRYING TO DO. WE ARE TRYING TO DO A FUTILE THING IF WE DO NOT KNOW WHERE WE CAME FROM OR WHAT WE HAVE BEEN ABOUT."

WOODROW WILSON

Human thinking is constantly evolving and creating new ideas about what a stable, well-functioning society should look like. The book you are holding is a window into the past and an opportunity to get to know the story of two brethren nations that remain forever close.

However, the bond between Czechs and Slovaks is akin to that of the closest relatives. This bond also has its dark side. The two global wars and the ideology of communism deeply hurt the people of this region. They left behind wounds that have affected entire generations of Czechs and Slovaks.

So often we run away from our past, forgetting that whether we like it or not, the past stays with us. It shapes our perspective and the decisions we make.

At first the idea of socialism looked attractive in our part of Europe. The ideology offered hope to ordinary people, along with a promise that the quality of their lives could and would increase with time. And they became part of a prosperous society - built on the ideals of collectivism.

From the hindsight of a few decades, we can now say that communism in Czechoslovakia was a risky social and ideological experiment. One that cost the people of this country the most precious thing any human being has – their freedom and individuality.

It is understandable why communism became so popular among all classes of society. After all, this was post-WWII, an era when the days were filled with grave fear over the future. There followed an even greater feeling of powerlessness, steaming from the wide-spread poverty affecting society. There was a lack of any well-thought out political and economic solutions, to bring real resolution to the situation at hand.

The populists of the day offered a society destroyed by war the sweet promise of safety. This predictability stood in stark contrast to the unpredictability of having to fight for survival day by day.

As many psychological studies show, people who live in fear and scarcity are prone to manipulation. Those who vowed to create a classless society and shower endless benefits upon the poor workers used this dire situation to their advantage.

Communism offered the people some basic standards of living, in exchange for denouncing private property, independence and freedom to self-realize. The new regime needed people who were easy to manipulate and dependent on the state for meeting their basic needs. In return for being taken care of, they had to obey the Party.

On the surface, Czechoslovakia looked like a functioning country – the state was meeting people's primary needs via the socialist apparatus. However, the regime did not offer any solutions for repairing and nurturing the inner world of the Czechoslovak population.

Communism created an atmosphere of fear and tension, were people distrusted each other and the masses were tricked over and over again. If anyone dared to diverge from the norms dictated by the regime, he or she was punished in cold blood. The communists in power were acutely aware that the illusion would only last as long as they were capable of controlling people's minds, and so the people were forced to fit the blueprint that was created for them.

The life energy that fuels creativity was suppressed in this fear-provoking and emotionally hostile environment. Emotions were silenced, as were any attempt at expressing them. Apathy and futility became the dominant feelings that mirrored the unmet emotional needs of society. Individuals restrained organic feelings of empathy for others because of the culture of social distrust. In this climate, everyone was driven to solely rely on themselves, even when they were physically surrounded by friends, colleagues and family.

Communism compromised the very hearts and minds of the Czechs and Slovaks. The people were forced to suppress their basic human instincts, their innate need for closeness, intimacy and emotional connection with other human beings. People coped by becoming more egotistical and defensive. The Iron Curtain, which saw Europe divided in half, also manifested in the inner lives of people. It separated the mask that Czechoslovaks presented in public, from their real needs and thoughts, which had to remain hidden deep within.

It is important to note that life in a strictly controlled society also suited many. Freedom comes with an element of insecurity. It makes us take responsibility over our lives. This is not easy and therefore many opted to sacrifice their freedom in return for the comforts of a state deciding matters for them. In every society, there will always be those who will prefer to be looked after.

I was born after the Velvet Revolution and therefore have not experienced communism in my own skin. However, the consequences of the regime can still be seen everywhere and in everyone in the Czech Republic and Slovakia of the 21st century.

The previous totalitarian regime created a deep longing for freedom in the subsequent generations of Czechs and Slovaks. It is only natural given that the desire was suppressed in the previous century. It was done so, to turn people into an easily managed and manipulated homogenic-mass.

However, freedom should not be confused with indifference and absolute independence. Rather, freedom is an invitation to explore one's own individuality, to explore the potential hidden in each individual. There is potential that is awaiting to be discovered, and acted upon, for the benefit of all.

The experienced authors Zuzana Palovic and Gabriela Bereghazyova take you through a history that helps you to understand modern-day Czechs and Slovaks. This understanding will help us to co-create a future that will bring forward real solutions to contemporary challenges. This book will also bring people together.

Freedom means nothing until we use it by fully claiming our power back from those who care more about their own interests than the wellbeing of all. Let's prove that we are deserving of this freedom. The choice to act is ours.

**Tomas Miklosko**
*born in 1991*

**Russia issued two formal apologies for the 1968 invasion and occupation of Czechoslovakia. The first was delivered by Boris Yeltsin in the 1990s and the second one by Vladimir Putin a decade and a half later.**

When President Yeltsin visited the Czech Republic in 1993 he was not speaking just for himself, he was speaking for the Russian Federation and for the Russian people. Today, not only do we respect all agreements signed previously - we also share all the evaluations that were made at the beginning of the 1990s ...
I must tell you with absolute frankness - we do not, of course, bear any legal responsibility. But the moral responsibility is there, of course.

VLADIMIR PUTIN
Prague
2006

# A GLOSSARY
## OF COMMUNISM

### BERLIN WALL

The Berlin Wall was a guarded concrete barrier that physically and ideologically divided Berlin from 1961 to 1989.

### BOURGEOISIE

In Marxism-Leninism, the bourgeoisie are an 'exploiting class' that came to own the means of production during modern industrialization. Their core values are that of property ownership and the preservation of capital. Their prime concern is the perpetuation of their own economic supremacy in society.

### CADRE

Cadre was a nation-wide network of individuals who were the decision-makers of the Communist Party. They formed the political leadership tasked with consolidation of power in the country.

### CHARTER 77

Charter 77 is a Czechoslovak informal civic initiative named after the document Charter 77 from January 1977. It was a petition written by writers and intellectuals that demanded that the communist government recognize basic human rights.

### CLASS STRUGGLE

In Marxist terms, every nonsocialist society has been characterized by a struggle pitching the workers against the property-owning oppressive ruling class.

### COLLECTIVIZATION

Stalin's policy of confiscating privately owned agricultural lands and facilities and consolidating them into large collective farms. The policy was adopted in Czechoslovakia and implemented in the 1950s.

## COMECON

A Council for Mutual-Economic Assistance was a partnership between socialist states set up by Joseph Stalin in 1949. Equivalent to the West's OECD, its purpose was to help unify the countries of the Soviet Bloc by creating an economically self-sufficient and politically unified space.

## COMRADE

The term was initially used to refer to a communist or a communist party member. Later, it became a rudimentary part of both formal and informal greetings and addresses. The titles Mr./Mrs/Miss were replaced by 'comrade' in official communication. In day to day life, children would address their teacher as a 'comrade teacher' and workers would greet their superior with a 'comrade director'.

## COMMUNISM/COMMUNIST

A doctrine based on Marxism-Leninism and the official ideology of the Soviet Union and the Eastern Bloc. It was based on a system of authoritarian government in which the communist party alone controlled state-owned means of production. It sought to establish a classless societal organisation based upon common ownership of the means of production and equitable distribution of goods.

## COMMUNIST PARTY OF CZECHOSLOVAKIA

The Communist Party of Czechoslovakia was a Marxist–Leninist political party that existed between 1921 and 1992. After its election victory in 1946 it seized power in the 1948 coup d'état and established a one-party state allied with the Soviet Union.

## COMMUNIST PARTY OF THE SOVIET UNION

The Communist Party of the Soviet Union was the founding and ruling political party of the Soviet Union established in 1912. It was the sole governing party of the Soviet Union until 1990.

## COMMUNIST PROPAGANDA

This term refers to the scientific, artistic, political and social propagation of communism. It presents facts selectively, uses loaded language to produce emotional response, tarnishes the Western world and promotes the achievement of communism. The term 'propaganda' itself broadly refers to information that is not objective and is used to influence an audience and further an agenda.

## DE-STALINISATION

This refers to a series of political reforms in the Soviet Union after the death of Joseph Stalin in 1953, and the ascension of Nikita Khrushchev to power. Khrushchev exposed some of the worst crimes against humanity committed by Stalin, including the gulag concentration camps and show trials, and saw the end of Stalin's cult of personality. Though a brief thaw ensued, the USSR remained a totalitarian society and ensured that its satellite states remained in the Soviet Bloc.

## DICTATORSHIP OF THE PROLETARIAT

According to Marxism-Leninism, this is the early stage of societal organization under socialism after the overthrow of capitalism. It means the workers' dominance in suppressing the counter-revolutionary resistance of the bourgeois 'exploiting classes'.

## DISSIDENT

Broadly speaking, a dissident is a person who actively challenges an established doctrine, policy, or institution. The word has been used in a political sense since 1940 and the rise of totalitarianism in the USSR and the Eastern Bloc. Dissidents were individuals who demonstrated counter-revolutionary tendencies. Most were artists, academics, actors and authors.

## DISINFORMATION

Disinformation refers to false information spread with an intention to deceive others. The English word 'disinformation' is borrowed from the Russian word 'dezinformatsiya'. This is derived from the name of a KGB black propaganda department.

## FIVE-YEAR PLAN

A comprehensive, centralized plan in which the Communist Party set economic goals for a five-year period. All levels of the Czechoslovak economy were obligated to meet these targets.

## GENERAL SECRETARY

General Secretary or First Secretary was the official title of the leader of the Communist Party of Czechoslovakia. The General Secretary was the country's de facto leader.

## GLASNOST

The term signifies a public discussion of issues and accessibility of information so that the public can become familiar with it and discuss it. It refers to Gorbachev's 1980s policy of using the media to make information available to the population to provoke public discussion.

## IDEOLOGY

Ideology is a belief system through which people find their identity and social orientation.

## INTELLIGENTSIA

Intellectuals are individuals who constituted the cultural, academic, social, and political elite of Czechoslovakia.

## IRON CURTAIN

The Iron Curtain was the political, military, and ideological barrier erected by the Soviet Union after WWII to seal off itself and its allies from open contact with the West. Later, it took on the form of a physical barrier, made of several layers of barbed wire fences. The total length of the barrier in Europe was 6,800 km. Its construction began as early as the 1950s, although Churchill reffered to its falling down as early as 1946.

## KGB (KOMITET GOSUDARSTVENNOI BEZOPASNOSTI)

The KGB, the Committee of State Security, was the main security agency for the Soviet Union from 1954 until 1991.

## KULAK

Kulak referred to a successful, independent farmer of the period before collectivization. The term eventually was applied to farmers and farm hands who opposed collectivization.

## MARSHALL PLAN

The Marshall Plan was a program for the reconstruction of

Europe after WWII announced in 1947 by United States Secretary of State George C. Marshall. The US sought to invest a considerable amount of resources to rebuild Western Europe. The Soviet Union refused the offer of aid and forbade the East European countries it dominated from taking part in the Marshall Plan. Czechoslovakia declined the assistance in 1947, even though it had originally showed interest in participating in the program.

## MARXISM-LENINISM

Marxism-Leninism was the ideology of communism developed by Karl Marx and refined by Lenin. Stalin and subsequent leaders contributed their own interpretations of the ideology.

## PERESTROIKA (RESTRUCTURING)

Gorbachev's campaign to revitalize the party, economy, and society by adjusting economic, political, and social mechanisms was announced in August 1986.

## PIONEER

A pioneer was a member of the All-Union Pioneer Organization. Founded in 1922, and open to children ages ten to fifteen, the main purpose of the organization was to introduce the youth of the Eastern Bloc to the rudimentary basics of communism.

## PRAGUE SPRING

The Prague Spring was a period of political liberalization and mass protest against communism in Czechoslovakia in the late 1960s.

## PROLETARIAT

Proletariat is the class of wage-earners in an economic society. Their only possession of material value is their labour-power.

## RED ARMY

The name for the Soviet army from 1918 until 1946

## SECRET CHURCH

The Secret Church was an underground network of groups and individuals, including priests, bishops, monks, nuns and regular church-goers who kept practising Christianity in hiding. Doing so openly resulted in harsh reprisals of the state.

## SHOW TRIAL

The term relates to a series of fabricated court trials in the Soviet Union in the second half of the 1930s. It was a part of Stalin's strategy of removing competitors from positions of influence. The blue print of show trials was replicated in Czechoslovakia after the 1948 coup d'état. Show trials of the 1950s targeted oppositional political and high-ranking Party officials. Among the biggest show trials were the prosecutions of Milada Horakova and Rudolf Slansky. Czechoslovakia witnessed more than 200 judicial executions during this era.

## SOCIALISM

In Marxist theory, socialism refers to a specific historical phase of economic development. It is an evolutionary stage of communism when individuals own personal property, but all industrial and production capacity is communally owned and managed. It is commonly accepted that Czechoslovakia never experienced true communism, only socialism. This book uses the two terms interchangeably.

## STB (STATNA BEZPECNOST)

The STB, the State Security Agency, was the state security agency of Czechoslovakia.

## VELVET REVOLUTION, OR GENTLE REVOLUTION

The Velvet Revolution was a non-violent protest against communism and transition of power in Czechoslovakia, occurring from 17 November to 29 December, 1989.

## WARSAW PACT

The organisation was a military union between the socialist states, equivalent to the West's NATO.

## YALTA CONFERENCE

A meeting of Stalin, Winston Churchill, and Franklin D. Roosevelt in February 1945 that redrew post-WWII national borders and established spheres of influence in Europe.

# AN EXTENDED TIMELINE
## OF COMMUNISM IN CZECHOSLOVAKIA

**1917**

Communism was born in the minds of German thinkers Karl Marx and Friedrich Engels in the 19th century. It was first applied in Russia nearly 100 years later, in one of the most explosive political events of the 20th century.

In 1917, Russia was teetering on the edge of a political abyss. Having suffered heavy losses in the First World War, the people were losing faith in their ruler. Tsar Nicholas II had a reputation of being a weak man. He was considered an aristocrat who could barely control his family and the influence of the infamous Rasputin, let alone keep together a vast empire.

A confrontation between the deluded elites driven by expired imperial dreams and an awakening lower class of millions of people living in dire poverty proved inevitable.

In March 1917, a huge crowd of factory workers demanding bread clashed with police on the streets of St Petersburg, resulting in open fire. Under the growing unresolved pressure of the protesters, the tsar abdicated, and a provisional government was formed with the Bolsheviks as the integral part of it.

Later that year, the Bolsheviks brought their plan to completion by overthrowing the government in a coup. They made an irresistible siren call – they were going to put power in the hands of the proletariat, the workers and the peasants, for the first time ever in history. This would to end centuries of inequality and oppression of the working class by the ruling elite. It worked like magic.

Russia became the Soviet Union and Lenin the leader of the first communist state on Earth. Yet, the communists still had to prove themselves as fit to rule. A a civil war between the allies of the tsar and old world order on one side and the Bolsheviks on the other raged until 1923. Eventually, Vladimir Ilyich Lenin claimed the ultimate victory and the new socialist universe was established.

## 1918

Czechoslovakia was proclaimed a country on the 28th October 1918. It grew from the ashes of the First World War and the fallen Austro-Hungarian Empire. Czechoslovakia went on to become the 10th strongest economy in the world and one of the most industrially advanced countries on the planet.

## 1938

A decade and half after the elapse of the First World War, Hitler rose to power in Germany, setting his sight on neighbouring Czechoslovakia. He needed to gain control over the country and its advanced industry if he was to succeed in his plan for global domination.

In September 1938, Germany, Italy, Great Britain and France signed the infamous *Munich Agreement* deciding the fate of Czechoslovakia in the absence of any Czechoslovak leadership. The treaty ordered Czechoslovakia to hand a great chunk of its territory inhabited by Czech Germans to Hitler. The country's pleas fell on the deaf ears of the West.

## MARCH 1939

Czechoslovakia disintegrated when Hitler invaded the Czech lands and proclaimed the Protectorate of Bohemia and Moravia. The Slovak portion of the republic became an independent Slovak state under German protection. In reality, it was a satellite of Germany.

## 1939 - 1945

As the Second World War commenced, Czechoslovak leadership fled to London and its communist faction to Moscow, thereby establishing governments in exile. Public resistance against Nazis grew particularly among the Czechs. It later spilled over into the Slovak state.

Klement Gottwald became the head of the Czechoslovak government in exile in Moscow.

Stalin, who in 1924 had replaced Lenin as the head of the USSR, personally groomed Gottwald to become his right-hand in post-war Czechoslovakia.

At the Yalta Conference held in February 1945, the Allies decided what would become the liberation line of Europe. Czechoslovakia fell into the Soviet zone. It would be liberated by the USSR. The foundations for Soviet expansion into the very heart of Europe were laid.

## 1944

The Slovak National Uprising broke out as partisans, democrats, and Soviet-backed communists rebelled against the Nazis and its allied Slovak State under President Jozef Tiso. The rebellion enabled the Slovaks to show that they had also backed the Allied cause. The communists would use the event to highlight their contributions to liberating Slovakia and restoring the Czechoslovak Republic.

## 1945

The most destructive war in global history finished and Czechoslovakia started recovering. Amidst the loss, poverty and rubble, the leadership returned from exile. The war survivors were desperate not to repeat the grave mistakes of the past.

The Czechoslovak middle class was disillusioned with capitalism, as was the working class. The country started to look for an alternative. Wasting no time, the Communist Party of Czechoslovakia, which had the largest following outside of Russia, positioned itself as the solution.

## 1946

In the first post-war election, the Communist Party of Czechoslovakia gained the most votes and became a part of a coalition government. Stalin's investment in Gottwald was beginning to pay off.

The Party gained 39% of votes and Klement Gottwald, the Party leader, became the prime minister and composed a new government.  Being a part of the government was not enough for Stalin or Gottwald. Preparations began for the eventual communist take-over of the entire Czechoslovak government.

The Communist Party gained control of the key Ministry of the Interior and almost immediately began to implement a series of smear campaigns against politicians from other coalition parties, particularly against the democrats, to weaken opponents and democracy.

The Ministry of Interior also prepared for a scenario of civil war and started to covertly arm civilians with artillery and guns to create people's militias.

## 21ST - 25TH FEBRUARY 1948

Communists organized a wave of mass protests and strikes, leading to a government crisis. Events came to head in the winter of 1948, when 12 ministers stepped down in protest of the unethical practices of the Communist Party. The President signed the resignations, although he was expected to refuse to do that in an act of support of the democratic wing of the government.

A plan orchestrated in Moscow and implemented in Czecho-slovakia saw the Communist Party take power in the country in a bloodless coup. The event went into the annals of history as 'Victorious February'.

Days before the coup, the communists began to shut the borders in preparation for a complete isolation from the West. Strict censorship of all media was implemented immediately after the coup.

## 1948 - 1953

The period of a systemic, rapid and often brutal social, political and economic transformation following the blueprint of Soviet totalitarianism was underway. It was not just a theoretical shift of ideology, but a profound change in the way of being for all.

Purges were brought in to remove all those who covertly or overtly disagreed with the new regime. Staged show trials, imprisonments on fabricated charges of treason and based on false testimonies, life sentences, forced labor camps and even executions and death sentences were weaponized to scare the population into submission in Czechoslovakia or the Soviet Union.

The remainder of the population was routinely harassed by street checks, house searches, and pervasive surveillance that unleashed psychological terror on the masses.

By the early 1950s, 422 labor camps and prisons were built in

Czechoslovakia that housed over 15,000 political prisoners. By 1960, 248 people had been sentenced to death for political crimes, with 4,500 dying during interrogations and in prisons.

## 1949

The USSR developed an atomic bomb, ending the American monopoly and escalating the Cold War.

## 1948 - 1959

Private property was abolished. Mass nationalisation of private ventures began with large enterprises in key industrial sectors and proceeded with small and medium-sized enterprises, as well as micro businesses. Eventually, all private enterprises were confiscated, and all facets of economy were centrally planned. Nationalisation of agriculture, so called collectivization, forms a special chapter. It sought to modernise and unify fragmented and archaic agricultural production by merging small plots of land into large collective coops. It affected millions of lives and the traditional lifestyle.

Farmers had to hand over their land, equipment and farm animals, the source of livelihood of their families for centuries, and employ themselves in the now state-owned collectives. Where farmers did not consent willingly, they were forced, imprisoned or even killed for resisting the policy.

## 1950 - 1954

The regime disapproved of religion, particularly the strong, influential, wealthy and highly organized Catholic Church allied with the Vatican. It was a threat to the ultimate power that the Communist Party strived to attain.

To eliminate the threat, Christians, priests, monks and nuns were prosecuted, monasteries and convents were shut down and Christians were punished for attending religious services. The communist forced the Greek Catholic Church out of existence, imprisoned its bishops, and replaced it with the Orthodox Church. The oppression against the Church created Christian martyrs.

## 1961

The construction work on a physical wall dividing Berlin into

East and West, the most famous part of the Iron Curtain, began.

## 1950s - 1970s

Slovakia was still predominantly rural when communism came to power. Then a systematic and thorough industrialisation and modernisation of the country started.

The Party believed that progress was dependent on modernisation and, therefore, it was a part of its manifesto to bring progress to people. Furthermore, in order to meet national economic targets, Slovakia's infrastructure needed to be developed.

The industrial boom altered the traditional rural way of life ingrained into the face and soul of the country through the millennia. It was accompanied by a construction fever that changed the Slovak landscape.

Towns expanded and new ones were founded; a great migration wave from the countryside to cities took place as people moved from, rural areas to find employment mostly in the industrial sector.

Over 170 new factories were opened, and the town and cities of Slovakia received a makeover in the style of architectural brutalism.

## 1953

Stalin's death was followed by the death of Klement Gottwald. The passing of the Soviet Tsar began a period of slow gradual relaxation of the communist regimes in the entire Eastern Bloc.

## 1961

The USSR sent the first man to outer space.

## 1968

The political and social thawing of Czechoslovakia culminated in the Prague Spring. Alexander Dubcek, a Slovak by birth, became the new General Secretary of the Communist Party and set out to change the regime in the spirit of 'socialism with a human face'.

Greater travel and press freedoms gave way to ever more

ambitious calls for social and political transformation and desire to get closer with the West. The USSR was not prepared to compromise its power in the region and the potential loss of one of its most industrialized and socially advanced countries.

On August 21st, 1968, a Soviet led Warsaw-Pact army invaded Czechoslovakia with over 500,000 soldiers. 137 people are killed, another 500 injured and all reforms were revoked. Dubcek was replaced by Gustav Husak, another Slovak, but this time a communist hardliner loyal to the Kremlin.

## 1978

The first and only Czechoslovak flew to space.

## 1968 - 1989

The invasion kick-started a period known as normalization - the restoration of order and the return to Soviet-style totalitarianism. Another wave of social and political purification of political, public and cultural life took place. All untrustworthy individuals were removed from Party ranks and greater or smaller positions of power. All key decisions had to be consulted with Moscow. Institutionalized terror of the population was renewed, this time taking the form of administrative oppression of civilians.

## 1985

Mikhail Gorbachev was elected to the position of the General Secretary of the Communist Party of the Soviet Union and thus the leader of the Eastern Bloc. It was a response to a long period of economic stagnation and social fatigue. The entire Eastern Bloc was facing a grave crisis, and to prevent a turn for the worst, Moscow decided to reform the ideology.

Gorbachev introduced a series of deep and far-reaching reforms known as perestroika. The sole purpose of the movement was to liberalise politics and the economy enough to survive, but not completely.

## 25TH MARCH 1988

Weakening totalitarian was also felt in Czechoslovakia. Long before the fall of the Berlin Wall, Slovaks sensed and used the opportunity to renew their call for freedom. Thousands of Christians gathered in Bratislava. Standing in unison and holding candles, this was a silent demand for freedom to believe in God.

The protest was brutally suppressed, but it proved that the regime was no longer almighty. It was the first important step to dismantling the totalitarian rule of the single party in the country.

## 9TH NOVEMBER 1989

The Berlin Wall fell, sending a clear message to all that communism was on its way out. Czechoslovaks took up the baton instantaneously.

## 17TH NOVEMBER 1989

A massive student-led demonstration rocked at first Prague, and then the rest of the republic. It started a 10-day nationwide protest, when students were joined first by artists, then parents and workers. Vaclav Havel stood at the head of the movement.

Together, Czechoslovaks eventually brought down the regime that ruled for over 40 years. A rapid transformation to democracy and free market commenced almost instantaneously.

## 24TH NOVEMBER 1989

Gustav Husak and the entire presidium of the Communist Party of Czechoslovakia resigned.

## 29TH DECEMBER 1989

Vaclav Havel became the new president of a once again democratic Czechoslovakia.

## 1ST JANUARY 1993

Czechs and Slovaks parted ways as a Velvet Divorce was enacted. After nearly seven decades, the Czechoslovak union was over and independent Czech and Slovak Republics appeared on the map of Europe.

# WHO WAS WHO
## IN CZECHOSLOVAK COMMUNISM

### KARL MARX (1818 - 1883)

Marx was a German philosopher, economist, historian, sociologist, political theorist, journalist, socialist revolutionary and a philosophical father of communism. For his radical opinions, he was expelled from Germany. In 1848, Marx and a fellow German thinker, Engels, published the Communist Manifesto introducing their version of socialism as the solution to the ailments of capitalism. He developed the theory further in his philosophical text, The Capital, giving birth to a new ideology – communism.

### VLADIMIR LENIN (1870 - 1924)

Vladimir Ilyich Ulyanov, known as Lenin, was a Russian revolutionary, politician, and political theorist. He founded the Russian Communist Party, led the Bolshevik Revolution and became the founding father of the Soviet Union. He served as the head of government of Russia from 1917 to 1922, and of the Soviet Union from 1922 to 1924. Lenin died of incurable disease amid a political and personal battle with Stalin, the rising star of the Communist Party, over the future of the Soviet Union.

### JOSEPH VISSARIONOVICH STALIN (1878 - 1953)

Stalin was a Soviet revolutionary and politician who led the Soviet Union from the mid–1920s until 1953 as a de facto dictator. He was the chief architect of Soviet totalitarianism and responsible for the death of millions, but also the engine of mass industrialisation and modernisation of the USSR on an unprecedented scale. One of the victors of WWII, Stalin presided over Czechoslovakia's inclusion into the Eastern Bloc, as a part of his foreign expansionist policy.

### EDVARD BENES (1884 - 1948)

A politician and statesman, Benes was one of the founding

fathers of Czechoslovakia. He was the President from 1935 to 1938 after which he led the Czechoslovak government in exile in London during WWII. He became the president again from 1945 to 1948. He accepted the resignation of 12 ministers, thereby unwittingly catalysing the communist coup d'état in February 1948. He resigned as President in June the same year and died several months later.

## KLEMENT GOTTWALD (1896 - 1953)

Gottwald, a sports instructor and journalist by training, became the General Secretary of the Communist Party of Czechoslovakia from 1923 to 1953 and simultaneously the first Communist President from 1948 to 1953. Prior to the eruption of WWII, Gottwald escaped from Czechoslovakia to avoid being prosecuted by the Nazi regime. He set up a government while in exile in Moscow and became Stalin's emissary for Czechoslovak matters. After the war, the Communist Party won the election and Gottwald became the prime minister. Under his leadership the Party took power in the subsequent coup d'état and unleashed harsh transition policies.

## HELIODOR PIKA (1987 - 1949)

General Heliodor Pika was one of Czechoslovakia's most highly decorated officers who served as the Moscow attaché through WWII. He grew suspicious of the Soviet plans for post-war Europe and Czechoslovakia. Being so close to the nucleus of communist power, Heliodor had to be removed. He was arrested immediately in the aftermath of the coup. Tried for treason and sentenced to death, he was hung, and his body was never found.  He was the first victim of orchestrated show trials.

## MILADA HORAKOVA (1901 - 1950)

Milada Horakova was a Czech politician, a fighter against fascism and communism.  She was hanged by the Communist Party on false charges of conspiracy and treason, the only woman to be executed. The verdict of her trial was annulled in 1968 and her name was fully rehabilitated in the 1990s.

## JAN MASARYK (1886 - 1948)

A son of Tomas Garrigue Masaryk, the founder of Czecho-slovakia and her first president, he was a diplomat and politi-cian. He was a part of the Czechoslovak government in exile during WWII in London. After the war, he returned from London and was actively engaged in domestic politics as the Minister of Foreign Affairs. He disapproved of Czechoslova-kia's foreign policies shaped by the Communist Party, and the country's subsequent orientation towards Moscow. Jan Masaryk was found dead underneath his bathroom window within weeks after the coup. His death remains unexplained.

## RUDOLF SLANSKY

Rudolf Slansky was a leading Czech communist politician who served as the general secretary after WWII. He was one of the brains behind the coup of 1948. When Tito, the leader of Yugoslavia, split from Stalin, the Kremlin unleashed a series of purges across the Eastern Bloc to remove all untrust-worthy individuals and prevent further fragmentation. Rudolf Slansky was one of 14 communist leaders arrested in 1951 and put on show trial before the public. He was charged for high treason and sentenced to death.

## ANTONIN ZAPOTOCKY (1884 - 1957)

Zapotocky, a survivor of a Nazi concentration camp, was the communist prime minister of Czechoslovakia from 1948 to 1953. Next he was president of Czechoslovakia from 1953 to 1957, taking up the role after the death of Klement Gottwald. Zapotocky favoured a more human way of governing. Among his most controversial policies was the drastic Monetary Reform of 1953, which significantly devalued local currency and stripped people of their savings.

## NIKITA SERGEYEVICH KHRUSHCHEV (1894 - 1971)

Khrushchev was a Soviet statesman who led the Soviet Union during the height of the Cold War, serving as the General Secretary of the Communist Party of the Soviet Union from 1953 to 1964. He tended to pursue a policy of peaceful coexistence with the West and initiated a process of "de-Stalinization" that made Soviet society less repressive. This was an era of political relaxation in the entire Eastern Bloc, which eventually lead to the Prague Spring. Yet Khrushchev was also an authoritarian. He crushed a revolt in Hungary, approved the construction of the Berlin Wall and instigated the Cuban Missile Crisis. Yet, his policies were viewed with increasing suspicion as too liberal, thereby destabilising the Eastern Bloc. Eventually, he was removed from power.

## ANTONIN JOSEF NOVOTNY (1904 - 1975)

Novotny, originally a mechanic and a survivor of a concentration camp, became the General Secretary of the Communist Party of Czechoslovakia in 1953 and remained in the position until 1968. He also held the post of president of Czechoslovakia from 1957 to 1968. Novotny was a communist hardliner who rose to the prominence in the era of show trials; he also disdained the Slovaks, and his condescending attitude would eventually help accelerate his demise. He took to power amidst declining economic performance, and as pressure mounted, Novotny lost the capacity to handle the tasks at hand. With the Prague Spring underway, he was forced to abdicate from his post in 1968.

## LEONID ILYICH BREZHNEV (1906 - 1982)

Brezhnev was a Soviet politician who became the General Secretary of Communist Party of the Soviet Union after Khrushchev was removed from power. He served in the position from 1964 until his death in 1982. The Brezhnev rule could be described as that of a bland hard-liner. He crushed the Prague Spring of 1968 and conducted harsh repressive policies in the name of the stabilisation of the regime, following the previous era of relaxation.

## ALEXANDER DUBCEK (1921 - 1992)

Dubcek was a Slovak politician and the force of inspiration behind the Prague Spring. He was born in Slovakia, but his parents moved to Kirgizstan to help build socialism in the USSR when he was three. The family returned when WWII erupted. Dubcek participated in the Slovak National Uprising, during which he lost his brother. After the war, Dubcek steadily rose in the Party ranks, until he was chosen to replace Novotny as the General Secretary of the Communist Party of Czechoslovakia in 1968. He attempted to reform the communist government during the Prague Spring. In 1969, he was forced to resign following the Warsaw Pact invasion. After the 1989 Revolution, Dubcek served as chairman of the former Czechoslovak Parliament and prided himself as a reformist socialist and a source of moral authority. He died in a tragic car accident in November 1992, shortly before Slovakia became an independent state.

## GUSTAV HUSAK (1913- 1991)

Husak was a Slovak politician and lawyer. He joined the Communist Party early on. When WWII broke out, Husak was arrested by the Slovak state for communist activities. Upon release, he continued to organize a communist resistance and became one of leaders of the Slovak National Uprising. When the war was over, he started a career as a government official, but he became a victim of the purges in the 1950s and was sentenced to life in prison. Husak was pardoned during the de-Stalinisation era and started to climb the Party ranks again. In 1969, Gustav Husak replaced Dubcek as the First Secretary and he remained in the role until 1987. In 1975, he took up the role of president, from which he resigned in 1989. The period of his rule was known for normalisation and also its pro-Slovak policies.

## VASIL BILAK (1917 - 2014)

Vasil Bilak was a Slovak communist and one of the signatories of the invitation letter to the armies of the Warsaw Pact countries that served as a pretext for the 1968 invasion of Czechoslovakia. Bilak was a Party hardliner and a proponent of neo-Stalinism, with significant ideological influence during the normalisation era.

## MIKHAIL SERGEYEVICH GORBACHEV (1931)

Gorbachev is a Russian and formerly Soviet politician; he was also the last leader of the Soviet Union. He served as the General Secretary of the Communist Party from 1985 until 1991. His efforts to democratize communism, decentralize the regime and the economy led to the fall of the regime in 1989, and the breakup of the Soviet Union in 1991. He is the author of a sequence of deep reforms known as perestroika.

## VACLAV HAVEL (1936 - 2011)

Vaclav Havel was a Czech statesman, playwright, poet and former dissident. He was born to the family of a wealthy restaurateur, whose business was confiscated by the state. Havel was denied access to education and became a stagehand. During the period of political relaxation of the 1960s, he actively participated in the Prague Spring. After the invasion in 1968, he was repeatedly arrested by the regime. He became the leading figure of the coalition against communism and co-authored Charter 77. Upon the fall of the regime, Vaclav Havel served as the last president of Czechoslovakia from 1989 until the dissolution of the country in 1992. He then became the first president of the Czech Republic from 1993 through 2003.

AUTHOR

DR ZUZANA PALOVIC

Born during the final years of the Iron Curtain, Dr Palovic's family fled the communist regime as political refugees, finally becoming naturalized citizens in Canada. Dr Palovic went on to study at institutions in the United States, the Netherlands and the United Kingdom, completing her PhD in Eastern European migration at the University of Surrey.

A child of communism that was raised in freedom, Zuzana implicitly understands and embodies the perspectives of both worlds. Her know-how has been further enriched by her international experience, having lived in ten countries across four continents.

Dr Palovic's work delves deeply into the Central and Eastern European context, examining the critical cultural, emotional, mental and spiritual structures for a full and holistic analysis of her subject. She argues that 'mental revolution' constitutes the 'final frontier of transition' and, like President Tomas Garrigue Masaryk, the visionary founding father of Czecho-slovakia, Dr Palovic advocates that societal change comes with a shift in individual consciousness. If there is no 'freeing of minds', then the newly freed societies at Europe's Eastern border will remain 'democracies without democrats'.

Dr Palovic actively shares her rich experience and intimate knowledge, working closely with key contacts in Eastern European governments, institutions and businesses. She is the founder of the non-governmental organization, Global Slovakia.

Amongst her many presentations, she has spoken at the Slovak Institute in Moscow, the Slovak Embassy in London, Oxford University, New York's Bohemian National Hall, as well as the Slovak Embassy in Washington DC, the Library of Moscow's Institute of Slavic Cultures, Chicago's Benedic-tine University and the Slovak Institute in Prague.

In 2018, Dr Palovic travelled at the invitation of the Slovak President on a government delegation to New York and Chica-go, where she presented her second book 'The Great Return' in the presence of President Andrej Kiska, the Slovak Am-bassador to Washington, members of the diplomatic corps and distinguished individuals from the Czech and Slovak cultural and business community of the United States.

# AUTHOR

DR GABRIELA BEREGHAZYOVA

Gabriela was born in socialist Czechoslovakia and grew up in the transitional Slovakia amid the political, social, cultural and psychological remnants of the communist regime.

Fascination with the marks that the ideology left on the minds of people brought her to the United Kingdom to study Slovak mentality at world-leading universities. This is where she completed her doctorate.

A scholar in corruption, Dr Bereghazyova's work masterfully captures the challenges, falls and successes of a metamorphosing Eastern Europe. These are presented against the historic backdrop of the complicated region. All in all, Gabriela pieces together an intricate puzzle by relating the present with the all too often unacknowledged past. Her work deepens our understanding of the challenges faced by societies in transition.

Dr Bereghazyova Gabriela actively employs her expert know-how and six years of post-graduate research in her consultancy and global bridge-building efforts. She has presented the insights of her academic and literary work at prestigious platforms, including Sandhurst College in the United Kingdom, the Bohemian National Hall in New York, the Library of Foreign Literature in Moscow and the Slovak Institute in Prague.

# MORE PRAISE
## FOR ZUZANA PALOVIC AND GABRIELA BEREGHAZYOVA'S
## CZECHOSLOVAKIA: BEHIND THE IRON CURTAIN

*"This year both our nations celebrate the 30th anniversary of the Velvet Revolution, after which a dawn of hope and freedom for upcoming generations broke across the grey November sky and drove the clouds of four decades of the totalitarian regime away. Young people today see those events as one of many chapters from their history books, simply too long ago to have any connection to their lives. Today we feel we have the whole world at our fingertips: we can travel, we can consume, we have free will, and opportunities to express our opinions at any time are automatic and natural. But this is not necessarily so. It must be our daily duty to protect the liberties we achieved thirty years ago, and we should never forget that triumph. People´s minds can be merciful and retain only pleasant memories, while bad memories are banished. Therefore, I highly recommend this book, and the form and the passion with which it has been prepared. It is an important memento, a kind of excursion into those dark times, when emptiness, lies, hatred and fear polluted the air. The book guides us through various aspects of life under the hammer and sickle and also reminds us of the glorious moments of the revolution. It is perfectly designed for both Czech and Slovak, as well as for international, readers who are keen to know more about the past of this pair of amazing countries in the very heart of Europe."*

Martin Nekola, Ph.D. (Czech Republic)
Historian, political scientist,
project manager of ''Czechoslovak Talks'

*"Two Slovak authors have crafted an important, ground-breaking work that depicts the intrinsic evil of Communist socialism and its true corrupt, inhuman face. With poignant personal anecdotes, detailed historical context and brilliant*

*use of illustrations, it is a book that is also a timely warning for a new generation of Americans now bombarded by utopian political promises."*

**Mark Dillon** (USA)
1st Vice President, Czechoslovak Genealogical Society International

*"For the majority of the world, communism is something in the past which many people, especially our youth, know little about. This book aims to remedy that gap in a readable narrative. The tone is informal, stimulating and entertaining, yet at the same time, retains a seriousness of purpose. It explains how communism emerged in Czechoslovakia and succeeded in maintaining its rule for so long.*

*In addition to drawing from published works and archives, the authors interviewed hundreds of people from a variety of social strata. The result is a balanced account of how communism was put into practice, with specific examples from real life stories and everyday situations. This work is also richly decorated with attractive illustrations and poignant photos by prominent photographers. This book teaches some valuable lessons about the danger of totalitarianism, and alerts us as to how fragile democracy can be, how precious are the freedoms we have, and why they must be guarded."*

**Michael J. Kopanic, Jr.** (USA)
Historian and Adjunct Professor,
The University of Maryland Global Campus

*"The Dynamic Duo of Zuzana Palovic and Gabriela Bereghazyova have now completed their third collaborative work about Slovakia and Czechoslovakia. These two young ladies provide a unique perspective about their homeland, where they were born still under communist rule and grew up, or spent a large chunk of their lives in the West. They are also accomplished*

*academicians, as they are both Ph.D.s. This book is filled with vignettes about Czechoslovakia's history, but also about the politics, society, culture, and economy of the country. The target audience is for both the general public, to whom much of the information may be a novelty, as well as the specialists who may know the general contours of the region, but who also help the reader to add context to the narrative. For example, the hard currency stores called Tuzex in Czechoslovakia, which were typical in all communist countries, provided a window to the West for those lucky enough to have access to those goods. The authors deal in depth with the terrible price paid for the communist "experiment" in terms of executions, imprisonment, and loss of livelihood. Moreover, the price was severe in forcing conformity. Indeed, when I was trying to do some research in Prague in 1973 for my Ph.D. I was a bit too open in my remarks and one "snitch" promptly reported me. People who grew up under a democracy can find it difficult to understand what their forbears had to endure. But we should also remember that there were different currents in Czechoslovakia, and from the 1960's a slow thaw began, culminating in the events of 1968, where bold and creative writers tried to make space for independent thinking."*

**Paul Hacker** (USA)
Author, 'Slovakia on the Road to Independence:
An American Diplomat's Eyewitness Account'

*"For more than forty years, Czechs and Slovaks had to live behind the so-called 'Iron Curtain' and experience the tragic communist experiment in their own skin. Throughout the (almost) entire 20th century, democracy evaded Central and Eastern Europe. Freedom should not be taken for granted, not even in the 21st century. That´s why it is so important to recall the stories of those who lived behind the 'Iron Curtain' and spread them to the general public. The several years of work behind this book have been rewarded — the authors*

*Dr Zuzana Palovic and Dr Gabriela Bereghazyova have written a really vivid publication that brings these memories to life."*

**Filip Pavcik Ph.D.** (Slovakia)
Historian, specialist on communist regime in Czechoslovakia,
Project 'Memory of Nations'
Post-Bellum NGO

*"This is an inspiring book. The authors brilliantly capture moments in history that anyone can benefit from knowing."*

**Dr Clint G Rogers** (USA)
TEDx speaker, university researcher,
Author of 'Ancient Secrets of a Master Healer'

*"This is a book written by the younger generation for the younger generation. Czechoslovakia: Behind the Iron Curtain does not aspire to be a learned history with references to primary documents. Although it does reflect a major research effort, the methods are nearer to oral history, and communism in Czechoslovakia is presented in a series of vignettes that can all be read individually. The aim is to portray everyday life, and the pictures tell us as much as words. Great care has been taken with presentation to make the book accessible to as wide an audience as possible, and its fresh approach to a difficult topic definitely fills a gap in the existing literature on communism."*

**Kenneth Janda, Professor** (USA)
Professor Emeritus of Political Science,
Northwestern University,
Author of 'The Emperor and the Peasant:
Two Men at the Start of the Great War and
the End of the Habsburg Empire'

"In the contemporary world, where emotions and stories are accentuated, it is difficult to draw the younger generation´s attention - the millennials and generation Z - who mostly know the era of communism only from narratives from their surroundings and from public discourse, to contemporary materials or detailed calendars and facts about the totalitarian regime and the Velvet Revolution. The authors in the case of the book 'Czechoslovakia: Behind the Iron Curtain' chose a different language of the work. Although they do not provide direct testimonies, in an effort to convey information to the widest public possible about the time that has intensively shaped our collective memory, they weave the small histories of people living during the communist era into the bigger picture - the history of the country. Short and interesting chapters, the use of photographs and illustrations, as well as the use of comprehensible language, predestines it also as a useful material for educational purposes, especially in the year of celebration of 30 years after the fall of the Iron Curtain."

Nina Galanska, PhD. (Slovakia)
Director of Milan Simecka Foundation NGO


"Hats off to the authors. This is one of the most complex works on this theme that I have ever seen. Moreover, it is not exactly a light topic to discuss, as it often is the case with recent history. The books masterfully married factual precision with the perspective of ordinary people. Thanks to vivid illustrations and photography, this book is far from boring - unlike many other publications on this topic. As someone who spent his childhood behind the Iron Curtain, I experienced everything from feeling light nostalgia to goosebumps and terror while reading this book. It is also perfect for those who never experienced communism. Perhaps it is especially them who should read it. Some experiences are really not worth repeating."

Martin Lank (Czech Republic)
Politician, Consultant, Journalist

*"This is the history of my home country at its most immediate and moving with many unforgettable testimonials of human resilience. The authors paint the vivid and human portrait of forty years of dictatorship in Czechoslovakia. The true-life stories provide a window into the minds and hearts behind the Iron Curtain. The happy ending in the year 1989 changed Central and Eastern Europe for good. The book comes at exactly the right moment, when democracies around the globe are in danger again and many states are on the road to authoritarianism. This is an essential guide to see what happens when tyrants rule."*

**Michal Hvorecky** (Slovakia)
Author, writer and translator

# CZECHOSLOVAKIA: BEHIND THE IRON CURTAIN'S PATRON

Jan Telensky is the generous patron behind 'Czechoslovakia: Behind the Iron Curtain', as well as Global Slovakia's two previous publications: 'Slovakia: The Legend of the Linden' and 'The Great Return'.

His name is associated with many social initiatives, especially those committed to empowering the region and raising its profile internationally. But few known about the long journey behind his success.

Born in communist Czechoslovakia, he was banned from practicing his religion and was told, at the age of six years, to "forget about school". He was to concentrate on becoming a miner or bricklayer.

But the young Jan did not satisfy himself with the narrow life the regime had laid out for him.

# DESCRIPTION OF PHOTOGRAPHS AND ILLUSTRATIONS
## (in order of appearance)

# RECOMMENDED LITERATURE

Applebaum, Anne (1994) Between East and West: Across the Borderlands of Europe

Applebaum, Anne (2012) Iron Curtain: The Crushing of Eastern Europe, 1944-1956

Brzezinski, Zbigniew (1990) Grand Failure: The Birth and Death of Communism in the Twentieth Century

Bulgakov, Mikhail (1967) The Master and Margarita

Carradice, Phil (2019) Prague Spring: Warsaw Pact Invasion 1968

Communist Party of the USSR (1961) Program of the Communist Party of the Soviet Union

Douzinas, Costas and Zizek, Slavoj (2010) The Idea of Communism

Figes, Orlando (2007) The Whisperers: Private Life in Stalin's Russia

Fowkes, Ben (1995) Rise and Fall of Communism in Eastern Europe

Gellately, Robert (2013) Stalin's Curse: Battling for Communism in War and Cold War

Golding, William (1954) Lord of the Flies

Havel, Vaclav (1979) The Power of the Powerless

Havel, Vaclav (1991) Open Letters: Selected Writings, 1965-1990

HMSO Civil Defense (1963) Handbook No 10: Advising the Householder on Protection Against Nuclear Attack

Hrabal, Bohumil (1983) I Served the King of England

Kaplan, Karel (1987) The Short March: The Communist Takeover of Czechoslovakia, 1945-1948

Kotkin, Stephen (2015) Stalin: Paradoxes of Power, 1878-1928

Kristufek, Peter (2014) The House of the Deaf Man

Kristufek, Peter (2018) Atlas of Forgetting

Kundera, Milan (1984) The Unbearable Lightness of Being

Le Carre, John (1963) The spy who came in from the cold

Lenin, Vladimir (1964) Essential Works of Lenin: "What Is to Be Done?" and Other Writings

Lewis, Ben (2008) Hammer and Tickle: A History of Communism Told Through Communist Jokes

Marx, Karl and Engels, Friedrich (1848) Communist Manifesto

Mollow, Peter (2009) The Lost World of Communism: An Oral History of Daily Life Behind the Iron Curtain

Montefiore, Simon Sebag (2003) Stalin: The Court of the Red Tsar

Muravchik, Joshua (2019) Heaven on Earth: The Rise, Fall, and Afterlife of Socialism

Nguyen, Viet Thanh (2015) The Sympathizer

Orwell, George (1945) Animal Farm

Orwell, George (1949) 1984

Priestland, David (2010) The Red Flag: A History of Communism

Radzinsky, Edvard (2008) Stalin: The First In-depth Biography

Simecka, Milan (1979) The Restoration of Order: Normalization in Czechoslovakia

Simecka, Milan (1999) Letters from Prison

Simecka, Martin (1992) The Year of the Frog

Sis, Peter (2007) The Wall: Growing Up Behind the Iron Curtain

Smith, SA (2016) Russia in Revolution: An Empire in Crisis

Snyder, Timothy (2010) Bloodlands: Europe Between Hitler and Stalin

Solzhenitsyn, Alexandr (1962) One Day in the Life of Ivan Denisovich

Solzhenitsyn, Alexandr (1973) The Gulag Archipelago

Staar, Richard (1974) Communist Regimes in Eastern Europe

Tatarka, Dominik (1963) The Demon of Conformism

Trotsky, Leon (1937) The Revolution Betrayed by

Von Bremzen, Anya (2013) Mastering the Art of Soviet Cooking: A Memoir of Food, Family and Longing

# RECOMMENDED FILMS

...a bude hur / It is Gonna Get Worse (2007)

Andel na horach / Angel in the Mountains (1955)

Bajecna leta pod psa / Those Wonderful Years that Sucked (1997)

Cerni Baroni / The Black Barons (1992)

Cervanová case / Normalization (2013)

Chernobyl (2019)

Dubcek (2018)

Ecce homo Homolka / Behold Homolka (1969)

Estebak / The Confidant (2012)

Fair Play (2014)

Hori, ma panenko / The Firemen's Ball (1967)

Hořící keř / Burning Bush (2013)

I served the King of England (2006)

Ja / I, Olga Hepnarová (2016)

Jan Palach (2018)

Kladivo na čarodějnice / Witchhammer (1970)

Kolja / Kolya (1996)

Listopad: A Memory of the Velvet Revolution (2014)

Masaryk / A prominent Patient (2016)

Milada (2017)

Na samote u lesa / Secluded, Near Woods (1976)

O slavnosti a hostech / A report on the Party and the Guests (1966)

Obcansky preukaz / Identity Card (2010)

Odcházení / Leaving (2013)

Okupace 1968 / Occupation 1968 (2018)

Oratorio for Prague (1968)

Pelíšky / Cosy Dens (1999)

Príbehy obycejného šílenství / Wrong Side Up (2005)

Pupendo (2003)

Rebelove / Rebels (2001)

Sedím na konári a je mi dobre / Sitting on a Branch, Enjoying Myself (1989)

Sedmikrásky / Daisies (1966)

Skrivánci na niti / Larks on a String (1990)

Slunce, seno, jahody / Sun, hay, strawberries (1984)

Tankový prapor / The Tank Battalion (1991)

The Unbearable Lightness of Being (1988)

Toman (2018)

Ucho / The Ear (1970)

Ucitelka / Teacher (2016)

Vesnicko ma strediskova / My Sweet Little Village (1985)

Vsichni dobri rodaci / All My Compatriots (1969)

Žert / The Joke  (1969)

# 'CZECHOSLOVAKIA: BEHIND THE IRON CURTAIN'
# WALL OF GRATITUDE

In deep gratitude, we offer a big THANK YOU to the organizations and individuals who financially contributed to the project and helped to make this book a reality.

A big thank you goes to John Palka, our patron, advisor, friend and wise man who has been supporting our mission not just financially, but also with words of encouragement when they were most needed.

We also extend our thankfulness to Pavol Vesely, Peter Stastny, Boris Fugger, Michal Repcak (Vila Zvonica/ Raimund Guesthouse&Restaurant), Tania Snabl, Oto Racek, Joseph Seliga, Clint G. Rogers, Paul Krejci and the Czech Slovak Genealogy Society International.

# 'CZECHOSLOVAKIA: BEHIND THE IRON CURTAIN' PARTNERS

The Slovak-American Cultural Center (SACC) was founded in 1967 in New York City as a not-for-profit organization by Slovak immigrants who came to the United State to escape political persecution after WWII. They immediately set out on a rich program of lectures, seminars, concerts and other cultural events.

The mission of SACC is to preserve Slovak heritage in the United States and to promote Slovak cultural, scientific, and athletic activities at home and abroad. It also seeks to familiarize the American public with Slovak culture and history and to promote the achievements of Slovak-Americans in the United States.

For over 50 years, SACC has offered Slovaks in the States the opportunity to socialize and to study, enjoy, preserve, and further develop their rich cultural heritage.

SACC is proud to advocate the work of Global Slovakia and financially supports the release of 'Czechoslovakia: Behind the Iron Curtain'. We congratulate the two passionate, dedicated and brave young women who worked tirelessly to document, share and ensure that the stories of Slovaks are preserved for future generations. Congratulations!

The Czechoslovak Talks project was created in 2016 by the Dotek Endowment Fund. Since then, we have met great Czechoslovaks living around the world, who shared their amazing stories with us. We want to ensure that these will not be forgotten. They are published on our website in Czech and English. We have also created comics books with selected stories. We believe the rich heritage of Czechoslovaks abroad needs to be preserved. Please get in touch with us if you know any Czechs or Slovaks in your family or neighborhood.

Visit us at www.czechoslovaktalks.com/en

The law firm H&P Law was founded in 2013 by JUDr. Jaroslav Horky, due to increasing demand for legal representation. We are a dynamic and fast-growing law firm based in Prague providing complex law services in all areas of Czech, European and international law. Our service is personal, flexible and discreet. We work closely with experts from forensic science, accounting, finance and real estate among others to ensure maximum satisfaction of every client. In addition, we have a diverse international portfolio as we collaborate with law firms in the USA, Israel, Germany, the UK, Austria, Poland, Slovakia and many other countries.

The First Catholic Slovak Union of The United States of America and Canada (FCSU) is a non-profit fraternal organization head-quartered in Independence, OH, USA. Founded in Cleveland in 1890 by 11 Slovak immigrants with the guidance of the Slovak immigrant priest the Rev. Štefan Furdek, the FCSU is also often called "Jednota" which in Slovak means "Union." This is the same name as its bilingual newspaper that has been published virtually throughout its history until today. During the communist era, the Jednota Press was one of the few places in the world that printed Slovak Catholic literature. The FCSU's original purpose was to help to immi-grant Slovaks deepen their religious faith, protect their language and heritage, and provide an insurance fund for those working in and near Cleveland's dangerous factories. Today the FCSU offers very competitive annuities, wealth transfer, and life insurance products and services to 50,000+ members in communities throughout North America, and continues to support fraternal activities and events that preserve shared values of faith, family and heritage. More complete information can be found at www.fcsu.com.

# *Tatraship*

Tatraship is a fully certified US company located in Chicago, Il. Established in 2008, we have more than 10 years of experience. With our boundless transportation capacity, we offer all kinds of ocean freight, air freight and related services:

- Ocean/ Air Freight
- International moving
- Special cargo
- Export vehicles
- Parcel services

We are the only company with Slovak roots in the United States that is OFF certified (Ocean Freight Forwarder) by the Federal Maritime Commission (FMC) agency.

Tatraship is very excited and pleased to help support the release of this book. Specifically, we will be providing international shipping of 'Czechoslovakia: Behind the Iron Curtain'. We would like to congratulate and thank the authors for writing this book as its message is very dear to our hearts. We wish them luck in the future.

## SLOVAKIA: THE LEGEND OF THE LINDEN

This book takes you on an emotional journey deep into the Slovak and Slavic inner world. Follow the trail that opens your eyes to the magical realm guarded by the Linden tree and its sacred heart-shaped leaf. It is a code that carries the story of the people born at the crossroads of worlds.

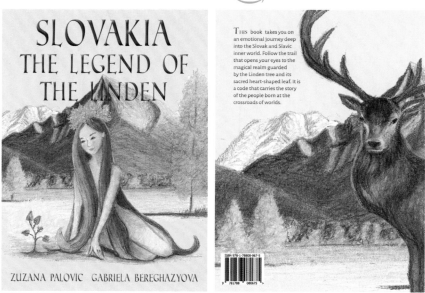

www.legendofthelinden.com

# SLOVENSKO: LEGENDA LIPY

Táto kniha pozýva na sentimentálnu cestu do hĺbky slovenskej a slovanskej duše. Otvára chodníček do čarovného sveta, ktorého vstup chráni lipa. Jej posvätný srdcovitý list je šifrou nesúcou príbeh ľudí, ktorí sa zrodili na križovatke svetov.

www.legendalipy.sk

# THE GREAT RETURN

In the beginning of the 21st century, Europe opened its borders to the countries from behind the Iron Curtain. Since then, over 100 million citizens, including Slovaks gained the freedom to move West without a visa. Now, a decade after the East-West exodus, our pioneers are returning home.

Telling the stories of international Slovaks who left, learned and returned, 58 voices including government, business and society share their views on the transformation of a nation. The 59th voice is that of the author, who reveals a personal tale of loss, lessons and reconnection through a rite of passage shared by millions of people across the planet.

Time-travellers to culture-shifters, Slovakia's lost daughters and sons come home, proving that return is not just a possibility, but an opportunity.

Available on **amazon**

www.thegreatreturn.eu

# VEĽKÝ NÁVRAT

Na začiatku 21. storočia otvorila Európa svoje hranice krajinám spoza bývalej železnej opony. Víza na západ sa stali minulosťou a viac ako 100 miliónov občanov vrátane Slovákov získalo slobodu pohybu. Po viac ako dekáde hromadných odchodov sa mnoho priekopníkov vracia zo západu domov.

Táto kniha prináša 58 hlasov z politiky, biznisu a spoločenských organizácií. Medzinárodní Slováci, ktorí odišli, spoznali a prišli späť, sa delia o svoje pohľady na prerod svojho národa. Päťdesiaty deviaty hlas patrí samotnej autorke. Odhaľuje podmanivý osobný príbeh straty, uvedomenia a znovu nájdenia.

Dnes sa stratené dcéry a synovia Slovenska vracajú domov. Sú cestovateľmi v čase a nositeľmi zmien. Dokazujú, že návrat nie je len možnosťou, ale i nesmiernou príležitosťou.

www.thegreatreturn.eu

# ČESKOSLOVENSKO ZA ŽELEZNOU OPONOU

Preneste sa na pomedzie Červenej ríše v čase ideologickej vojny, ktorá rozštiepila svet vo dvoje. Odvážte sa vstúpiť na pôdu socialistického Československa. Práve tu sa komunistický Východ a slobodný Západ ocitli nebezpečne blízko seba. Toto je príbeh obyčajných ľudí, ktorí sa zachytili do siete najväčšieho politického experimentu 20-teho storočia. To, o čom píše táto kniha si mohli len šepkať. Nahliadnite do denno-dennej reality tých, ktorých svet sa točil okolo nekompromisnej vlády kladiva a kosáka.

www.communistczechoslovakia.com

# Truth and love must prevail over lies and hatred

*Vaclav Havel*

# CZECHOSLOVAKIA:
## BEHIND THE IRON CURTAIN

*A History of Communism*

*www.communistczechoslovakia.com*